FINAL SCORE!

DAN FARR

FINAL SCORE!

SPORTS DEVOTIONS
VOLUME II

TATE PUBLISHING
AND ENTERPRISES, LLC

Published by Tate Publishing & Enterprises, LLC
127 E. Trade Center Terrace | Mustang, Oklahoma 73064 USA
1.888.361.9473 | www.tatepublishing.com

Tate Publishing is committed to excellence in the publishing industry. The company reflects the philosophy established by the founders, based on Psalm 68:11,
"The Lord gave the word and great was the company of those who published it."

Book design copyright © 2011 by Tate Publishing, LLC. All rights reserved.
Cover design by Kate Stearman
Interior design by Sarah Kirchen

Published in the United States of America

ISBN: 978-1-61346-795-4
1. Sports & Recreation / General
2. Religion / Christian Life / Devotional
11.11.23

ACKNOWLEDGMENTS

This book is dedicated to my wonderful wife, Becca, and our beautiful daughters, Allison and Jillian, and to my greatest teachers, coaches, and role models; in honor of my father, Lester Farr Sr., and in memory of my mother, Allene Farr, my father-in-law, Damon Ray, and Pete Maravich, whose testimony God used to change my life for eternity.

TESTIMONY

I am honored and privileged to share my testimony with you. On a Sunday morning in the late 1960s in a small Methodist church in Middle Georgia, I could have received Christ. I was drawn by the Holy Spirit during a message by a lay speaker, but I was afraid of what people would say if I went to the altar. I escaped into the warm sunshine and convinced myself that I would have enough nerve to accept Christ the following Sunday. But I went back into the wilderness for thirty-five years. I did not attend church when I moved to Atlanta, but I met my future wife, Becca, through the sports ministry at Peachtree Presbyterian Church. We married the following year and were later blessed with two beautiful daughters, Allison and Jillian. We visited Mt. Zion UMC in East Cobb, which had a new gym. Two years later, I started a basketball program and poured my energy into it for the next twelve years. It was great seeing the program grow and packing the sanctuary on basketball Sunday. But my focus was too much about personal achievement and not enough about helping young people know Christ.

I continued to live a self-centered life and could go for days without communicating with God. But in 2001, I watched the ESPN Classic special about basketball star Pete Maravich, my idol throughout high school, college, and adulthood. My vintage Maravich jersey hung in my closet for twenty-five years. I bought throwback jerseys, books, and videos on eBay. One VHS tape was Pete's testimony that I watched one Sunday night out of boredom and curiosity. That video was a divine appointment. At the time, I was drifting away from the basketball program and was very unhappy with myself. I was so far from God after many years of living without him. Jesus on the cross? It was just a story until I heard Pete tell how Christ transformed him. I always wanted to be like Pete, but I realized I wasn't because Jesus Christ knew Pete Maravich, and Jesus didn't know me. Occasionally, I wondered during sermons, *Am I going to heaven?* Then I would fool myself by falling back on my good works. But I knew that if I died that evening, I would never see Jesus face to face. I cried out in my heart that I wanted my life to change. As my former pastor, Steve Lyle, often said, "It's not the words you pray as much as the attitude of your heart."

God has blessed me with many opportunities to share my testimony. At first, I was sure I had it all figured out, but instead, there was so much to learn. God led me to turn that basketball program into our Christ-centered Hoops2Heaven ministry. I eventually allowed him to change me in the workplace when I went through trying times after a merger. An opportunity came to teach high school Sunday school and lead the basketball ministry again, which led to the start of a year-round youth sports ministry at Mt. Zion. Sports ministry. Can you see a pattern? Youth sports ministry is my fishing hole. I continue to pray that I can get it right for Christ for our families at Mt. Zion and in our community. God loved me unconditionally, wooed me, and showed me mercy time after time until I repented, trusted, and obeyed. Repent, trust, and obey. There is no other way. I'm far from perfect, but God thinks I'm worth it. I was lost and then found and forgiven.

TABLE OF CONTENTS

FOOTBALL

BASKETBALL

BASEBALL

GOLF

SPORTS

FOOTBALL

FB33:
BUYIN' OR SELLIN'?
NEED ONE!

Matthew 7:13

Heaven can only be entered through the narrow gate!

I have found tickets for a World Series game in Kansas City, the Georgia-Florida game, the football national championship game in New Orleans, and the basketball Final Four in Atlanta. My keys are to arrive several hours in advance, find a high-traffic area away from the stadium, dress well, be polite, put two fingers in the air, and have my cash ready. Eventually, a non-scalper will offer to sell you tickets. Finding one ticket is easier than finding two and much easier than finding four.

If you're really desperate, have your daughter stand on the street with the 'Need Masters Badges' sign she made and say, "Look as pitiful as possible." On Sunday afternoon of the 2001 Masters, a man in a car pulled over and said, "Is that your daughter (Allison) down there with the sign? She sure looks sad. I have a couple of badges I'm willing to sell you." My daughters Allison (Georgia-Auburn 2002) and Jillian (Georgia-Florida 2007) have learned to fend for themselves. I tease them that Becca taught them most things they need to know, but Dad taught them how to buy tickets.

In the upcoming anecdote, I want to be perfectly clear that I do not condone my behavior and actions. The only reason I got away with it is that security was pretty lax in 1982. I could have been arrested and fined several hundred dollars for improper possession of a football ticket and resisting arrest by running, which would have been quite embarrassing for me and my wife.

One time I didn't follow my keys. In 1982, number-one-ranked Georgia played at Auburn. Becca and I drove down with Joel and Marlene. But we got there later than intended. There was no TV and perfect weather, which made tickets really scarce. A friend sold us two tickets at face, but at game time, we were still two short. We weren't prepared for this scenario, so the ladies chilled, and Joel and I kept looking. Midway through the first quarter, an Auburn student inside the stadium slipped me an Auburn faculty pass through the chain-link fence for $20. I went through the pass gate with no problem, handed the faculty pass to Joel through the fence, and he got in. Yes! We celebrated with a leaping high five, and security saw us. I was empty-handed, so I took off running. I finally reunited with Becca before halftime in the Georgia section. The game was almost an afterthought. Georgia won 19-14 to qualify for the Sugar Bowl after Auburn tight end Ed West tripped over the Georgia 20-yard line, and Georgia hunkered down for a last-minute stand. Georgia announcer Larry Munson yelled, "Oh, look at the sugar falling from the sky!" and an Auburn fan threw a drink in his face.

Obviously we took quite a risk going to the game with no tickets. We worked very hard to get inside. Since it was a faculty pass, only through the pass gate could I enter. If the ticket taker had denied me, two of us would have never seen the game.

Please realize that I broke the Ten Commandments by lying, coveting, and stealing. You should never try what I did.

One-Way Complimentary Ticket
Site: Heaven
Gate: Pearly
Price: Paid in Full by Christ

Make sure you have secured your ticket to heaven. You are at risk if you haven't done it. You can work hard, but you cannot earn one. No matter how rich you are, there won't be any tickets for buyin' and sellin' outside heaven's gate because Jesus purchased all tickets at the cross. There is only one gate, the pearly gates, where you can enter. To secure your ticket to enter heaven, you need to repent, which means to turn away from your sinful life, ask for forgiveness, and place your trust in Christ. Then you'll see the greatest game ever.

Prayer: Most holy and gracious Father God, thank you for the excitement and pleasure that I get from attending sporting events. May I always keep these contests in perspective and thank you for forgiving me when I lose it. Thank you for purchasing my ticket to heaven. In Jesus's name, amen.

FB34:
EVER FEEL LIKE VANDY?

Romans 8:18

What we suffer now is nothing compared to the glory we
will receive later.

(TLB, paraphrased)

Vanderbilt University is one of the elite academic institutions in
America, but Vandy has traditionally been the football doormat
of the SEC. Since the creation of the Southeastern Conference in
1933, Vandy is the only charter member still in the conference that
has never won or even shared the SEC football title. The odds that
Vandy will win the SEC next season are probably 500 to 1. The
school eliminated its athletic director in 2003 and placed the athletic
department under the vice chancellor of the Department of Student
Life and University Affairs. Vandy's stadium is rarely full and is half
the capacity of seven of the schools in the conference, so Vandy will
never truly have a home field advantage. Due to its higher academic
standards, Vandy will never get the same athletes as most of the
schools in the SEC, especially the half-dozen elite programs. A
great season at Vandy is getting to any bowl game. A great record at
Vandy could get you fired at an elite SEC school. Vandy went to its
first bowl game in twenty-five years in 2008. That's a tremendous
year at Vandy. The odds are simply stacked against the 'Dores being

a consistent winner. The occasional upset that Vandy achieves makes it worthwhile to keep playing in the league.

Does your life ever feel like you're trying to compete against a stacked deck like Vandy? Maybe it's because your job isn't going well and you're the lowest person in your team's ratings. Perhaps you're struggling to make your grades as a student. It could be an uphill battle trying to make the varsity team or saving to pay for a car while your friend gets a new one. Maybe it's failing health or the health of a loved one that has you on the treadmill that never seems to stop.

Whatever your challenge, relish in the fact that you've made it this far. Relish in the fact that God wants to help you through any situation that you encounter. God gives us today, and God never takes a day off. Occasionally, I say a short prayer as I approach the revolving glass doors of my office building. It goes like this: "God, give me the strength to make it through today." Nine hours later, I walk through those same doors and don't remember what I was so concerned about. God always delivers. His mercy is great, and his grace is even greater. Remember to celebrate the blessings and victories that you and God have achieved together, and know that your rewards for perseverance, loyalty, and simply having the courage to show up each day and battle will be great in heaven.

Prayer: Most gracious Lord, you have come through for me so many times when the deck seems stacked against me. I appreciate you always being there and never leaving nor forsaking me. In Jesus's holy and precious name, amen.

FB35:
TAKE A KNEE

Philippians 2:8-11

Every knee will bow, and every tongue will confess that
Jesus Christ is Lord...

Philippians 2:10

One of the most joyous moments for a football fan is when your
team's defense has prevented a last-gasp scoring drive and your
offense takes over on downs. Your team has a four-point lead, there
are forty-five seconds remaining, and the opposing defense has no
time-outs. You shout, "There's no way we can lose!" Many years ago,
the quarterback would hand off to the running back to plunge into
the line. But the New York Giants changed that approach in 1978
by losing a game to the Philadelphia Eagles in the last thirty seconds. Quarterback Joe Pisarcik (Giants fans just groaned at the sight
of that name) fumbled an exchange to fullback Larry Csonka, and
defensive back Herm Edwards picked up the loose ball and rambled
twenty-five yards for a touchdown. That was a big ouch.

Ever since that play, teams take absolutely no chances. Before
the ball is snapped, the entire offensive team forms a shell around
the quarterback to protect him even further. The quarterback takes
a direct snap from center and kneels immediately. By taking a knee,
the quarterback stops the play and cannot be tackled. The quarter-

back might take a knee two or three times to run out the clock. After the last knee is taken and the play clock has more seconds than the game clock, it's time for the coach's Gatorade bath as players pour onto the field to shake hands.

The Bible makes it clear that all will honor Christ when he comes back on a white horse to establish his rule on this earth as prophesied in the book of Revelation. Philippians tells us that one day everyone in heaven, on earth, and under the earth will take a knee when Christ returns. Every knee will bow, and every tongue will proclaim that Jesus Christ is Lord. His second coming and the symbolic taking of the knee will signify that the New Ruler of the earth, Jesus Christ, has won the eternal victory over Satan. When you take a knee, give thanks to God for the prophecy and his perfect plan to return Christ to the site of his victory over death.

Prayer: Dear Father, when I take a knee tonight before I go to bed, I will thank you for Jesus and his impending victory over Satan's forces here on earth. In Jesus's holy name, amen.

FB36:
THE GATORADE BATH

Luke 3:21-22, Ephesians 4:30

And the Holy Spirit descended bodily upon Jesus like
a dove …

Luke 3:22

Invariably, the winning head football coach receives the traditional
Gatorade bath at the end of the game. According to the Atlanta
Journal-Constitution, the Gatorade bath originated when New York
Giants OG Jim Burt doused Head Coach Bill Parcells after a game.
Apparently, Burt teased Parcells all week at practice that he would soak
him if the Giants won. Now, I'm a cold-natured person, and I don't
like cold showers at all. I won't take a cold shower unless there is no
alternative. My first thank-you of the day to God is sometime in the
first five seconds of that soothing hot water hitting my back. So when
I see two burly linemen carrying the bucket of ice-laden colored liquid
to dump it on an unsuspecting coach, I cringe, especially when the temperature on the field is colder than the water. Dumping an icy torrent
of Gatorade seems appropriate for a young coach on an eighty-degree
day, but when you dump it on an old coach on a cold day, that's insane.
The winning coach gets the icy bath. Why not dump the Gatorade
bucket on the loser? It's also dangerous. My wife, Becca, recalled that
Long Beach State Head Coach George Allen, seventy-two, formerly of
the Washington Redskins, received an ice-cold water dousing in 1990

from his overzealous Long Beach State football team. Unfortunately Coach Allen came down with pneumonia and died six weeks later, and the dousing may have been a contributing factor to his decline. Maybe Gatorade baths are one reason that head coaches make the big bucks.

So we see these coaches being baptized with Gatorade. The effect on their nervous systems must literally take their breath away. The Holy Spirit comes upon you in a different way when you receive Christ. The same Holy Spirit that you and I received also descended bodily upon Jesus just after he was baptized in the River Jordan. I wonder how cold that water was. You are changed forever when you are bathed in the Holy Spirit. It doesn't feel like the Gatorade bath, thank goodness. When you are bathed in the Holy Spirit, you are sealed for eternity. What is God going to do if you sin, because you will still sin? He's not going to reach down and yank the Holy Spirit out of your body like you've got on a cheap shirt because you have been sealed for eternity with the Holy Spirit. God says to Satan, "This one is mine! You can never take this one away from me." Soon, you will observe that the worldly things that drove you to distraction no longer have the same hold on you because that is Living Water flowing through your body.

Envision the Gatorade bath after an upset of your archrival washing away the frustration of a losing season. In a similar fashion, the baptism of the Holy Spirit washes away the frustrations of trying do it all by yourself your whole life. Now you will learn to allow God to lead you and direct your life. Being cleansed by the blood of Jesus Christ is imperative for salvation, and the Holy Spirit is God's way of putting the icing on the cake. It's a gift that only God can pour on you and into you.

Prayer: Most gracious and loving God, please pour out your mercies, blessings, and grace upon me. I am grateful for every single gift you give me. And I'm especially appreciative of the Holy Spirit, the gift that seals me for eternity in you and with you. In Jesus's name, amen.

FB37:
IS GOD NUMBER ONE
THIS WEEK IN YOUR POLL?

Isaiah 42:8; 44:6, 8; 45:5, 22

I am the Lord Your God. There are no gods besides me.

Isaiah 45:5

Alabama was crowned 2009 national champs by virtue of their 37-21 BCS Championship Game win over Texas. For all of the passionate Alabama and Texas fans who returned from Pasadena, their re-entry into the real world in the middle of January must have been difficult, especially for the Texas fans.

Certainly you must appreciate the fans who avidly support their teams. However, passion overdone can leave a person in a deep funk, even withdrawal, when his or her team loses. Fandom that becomes idol worship is something each sports fan must guard against or else God will be displaced from his number-one ranking.

Speaking of number one, if you were to rank your passions from week to week, how many weeks would God occupy the top spot in your life? There are your favorite teams, your favorite athletes, blogs, Internet, TV, selfish pursuits, work, and school. All of these god-isms vie for top spot in your life. Think about the number of hours you spent on each activity when you don't consciously include God. It's easy to give God the top spot each Sunday morning, but by Sunday evening, has he slipped in your poll? How about Thursday night after you've slogged through a difficult week as the world has tried to drag you through the mire with work and school challenges and family problems? How about any strongholds that Satan has used to separate you from God and shove him further down your poll?

If you asked your closest friends, family members, and coworkers to vote and be perfectly truthful, how many first-place votes would God really get compared to first-place votes for the I team (me, myself, and I)? God can easily be knocked off the top rung if you allow yourself to lose focus on him. It has happened to me with Georgia football, Kentucky basketball, golf, and too much TV and Internet. Once God drops to number two behind your self-interests and idolatry, your kingdom work ceases.

Beware of Satan's toehold because the toehold can become a foothold, which can become a stronghold, which can become an entire possession. Daily perspective gained through prayer and reading the Bible, which helps us be more obedient to God, is essential to keep God number one in our weekly poll. Otherwise, we unconsciously give Satan the top spot, which is like your team's bitter rival pulling an upset. If we realize it is Satan we've allowed to climb to the top, we'll fight harder to defeat the stronghold and put God back in his proper position.

Prayer: Father God, help me take a daily checkpoint and realize when I'm focused on something that has taken your place. Please, Lord, help me to always keep you at the top. In Jesus's name, amen.

FB38:
COLT MCCOY EXHIBITS
GOD'S GRACE IN DEFEAT

Job 1:13–2:10

Shall we receive good at the hand of God, and not receive evil?

Job 2:10

Alabama defeated Texas 37-21 for the 2009 BCS football national championship. Colt McCoy, Texas's Heisman candidate and quarterback, was knocked out on the sixth play from scrimmage on a hit he had taken many times before. Though Texas fought bravely, Bama's running game and ball-hawking defense proved to be too much to overcome.

After the game, Colt McCoy was interviewed by Lisa Salters, the ABC sideline reporter. She immediately asked him a point-blank question about how it felt to get hurt and miss winning the national championship. Colt took five to ten seconds to collect himself emotionally, and his answer was replete with humility, grace, and gratitude. For a young man who saw his dreams of winning a national championship taken away when he was forced to the sidelines, it was a demonstration of tremendous character. First, he made sure that he gave Alabama credit and congratulated them on a great game. Second, despite the outcome, Colt said, "I always give God the glory. I'd never question why things happen the way they do. God is in control…I know I'm standing on the Rock." It reminded me so much of Job when Job's wife told him that he should curse God and die after the calamities struck. But Job's response was that he gave God the glory when things were going great, and he was going to give God the glory now when things were going bad. Colt said that he would still exalt God in his disappointment and sadness. Third, he told the national TV audience that he had a dead arm from the hit. Here was a young man with a chance to be drafted in the first or second round telling the NFL scouts the truth about exactly what happened.

I was totally moved by the grace that Colt demonstrated. Without the injury, Colt might not have had the platform to make such a moving statement, and he took full advantage of it for the kingdom. Hallelujah and to God be the glory, honor, and praise.

Prayer: Father God, thank you for the Christian example of Colt McCoy and so many young athletes who recognize their opportunities to give you the glory and to honor you with praise. May I take advantage of the chances that I have to share my faith eloquently and passionately. In Jesus's holy name, amen.

FB39:
THE RIGHT PLAY AT
THE RIGHT TIME

Zephaniah 3:17, 1 Corinthians 9:22, John 3:30

I am made all things to all men, that I might by all means
save some.

1 Corinthians 9:22

College football is no longer "three yards and a cloud of dust." The
athletes are too fast and too strong, and the coaching is too sophis-
ticated. Plus, football tickets need to be sold to pay the bills for all
of the interscholastic sports. There are hundreds of possible offensive plays and defensive formations. Intense film study into the wee
hours pays off when a play is discovered that will score against a
particular defense on a particular down and yardage situation.

I Googled the scoring drive with the most plays in history.
Against New Mexico in the 2004 Emerald Bowl, Navy reeled off
an incredible twenty-six-play, ninety-four-yard scoring drive that
lasted almost fifteen minutes. Consider there are at least twenty-six
different ways to score TDs: QB sneak, bomb, corner, post, post corner, hook and ladder, sprint draw, down and out, QB draw, wildcat,
off tackle, sweep, tunnel screen, screen pass, fumblerooski, slant, end
around, reverse, double reverse, tackle eligible, tailback hurdles the

line, flea flicker, Statue of Liberty, fade, running back pass, and buttonhook. Most football fans would agree that each of these twenty-six plays has produced many touchdowns. The key is to call the right play at the right time.

God has an infinite number of plays in his playbook that he can call to score for his kingdom. Here are twenty-six different ways God uses to bring people to Christ: sermons, the Word, intercessory prayer, spiritual pamphlets, mission trips, devotions, VBS, Young Life, evangelists, revivals, Kairos prison ministry, parents, grandparents, confirmation class, FCA, sports ministries, Christian music, personal testimonies, Christian movies, Sunday school, relationship building, Gideon Bibles, youth retreats, youth group, lay speakers, family reunions, and last but not least, good deeds in the name of Christ. Oops. That's twenty-seven. Most Christians would agree that God has used each method to produce many scores (conversions or new believers).

One key is to follow God's guidance and employ an appropriate method that is consistent with God's timing. God always "gives the increase" (John 3:30), which means that only God brings people into his kingdom, but we are his hands, feet, and spokespersons. My good friend, Dr. George Morris, Senior Professor of World Evangelism of the World Methodist Council, shared the following quote by William Barclay: "God has his own secret stairway into every heart." A person can have significant spiritual experiences and influences over a lifetime. Then comes the game-breaking special occasion in a person's life that breaks the bondage of sin for eternity through Jesus Christ.

As Christians, it is our duty to sow seeds and shine our light in prayerful expectation that many will receive Christ as Savior and Lord. Sometimes our faith sharing is the first play in a person's fifteen-play faith drive. It could be the fourth play or the eighth play. Occasionally, we experience the thrill of the last play that catapults a person into Christ's end zone. All of the plays contribute, but it's the final seed sown at the right time that pays off.

I believe that as Christians, we must be open to various approaches. To say, "That way doesn't work. You must use this way," puts God in a box. As the heavens are higher than the earth, his ways are greater than our ways (Isaiah 55:9). Only God knows how many hearts are changed using a particular approach. When Paul taught us to reach people by all means, I believe that he meant use every good and holy way at our disposal. Discernment means understanding which approach to use, how to use it, and when to use it. God has incomparably great power, and God is mighty to save. Yet he chose flawed human beings to spread the good news. Unfortunately, we sometimes stumble when we try to tell people what Jesus means to us, but it still pleases God when we make the attempt. I read that an evangelist once said that he would always choose sharing the gospel imperfectly over someone else not trying. God uses his children's efforts every day to push people over heaven's goal line.

Prayer: Most wonderful and creative God of the universe, open my eyes wide that I may see there is more than one way to "skin a cat." Thank you for the incredible variety of ways that you have given us to share the gospel. In Jesus's name, amen.

FB40:
COMING OFF THE BENCH

Matthew 11:28, 27:32

And they compelled one Simeon, a Cyrenean who passed by, coming out of the country, the father of Alexander and Rufus, to bear his cross.

Matthew 27:32

Certainly, there are times when athletes unexpectedly enter important contests. Garrett Gilbert, a freshman quarterback at the University of Texas, was thrust into the glare of the national spotlight in the 2009 BCS Championship Game. He had only appeared in mop-up roles behind Colt McCoy, Heisman Trophy finalist and the winner of more FBS games than any quarterback ever. But suddenly, Colt went down with a shoulder injury, the first significant setback of his career, in his final game. Fortunately, Garrett performed admirably. After a rough first half against the nation's top defense that included a pick six on the final play, Garrett settled down and threw two touchdown passes and kept Texas in the game until the final few minutes. He had a chance to lead his team to victory before a blindside sack ended the Longhorns' hopes.

Almost two thousand years before, a man named Simeon and his two sons had no idea what they were in for when they awoke one morning. Amid the hustle and bustle of Jerusalem packed with people for holy week, Simeon wondered, *What's all the shouting about, and what's with this cadre of Roman centurions?* One of the centurions pulled Simeon from the crowd into the Via Dolorosa and ordered him to carry a cross. Simeon thought, *Who is this man, savagely beaten, bleeding profusely, bruised, gasping for air, in excruciating pain, yet no complaints come from his lips?*

You want me do what? Simeon surely thought. *And what about my sons?*

The Roman guard yelled, "Do as you're told, and don't ask questions! Help him carry this cross! Just do it!"

The man was Simeon of Cyrene, and he certainly never expected to become a part of the story. He was a bit player in the midst of the most important event in history. Simeon did as he was instructed and helped Jesus drag that cross up a hill named Golgotha, where Jesus would be nailed to the cross while carrying our past, present, and future sin with him.

You and I can suddenly be thrust into the spotlight and have no choice but to play an unexpected role in the game of life. A family member could become ill, and you might need to take a part-time job to help out financially. This additional responsibility could place stress on you as you try to keep up your grades. A knee injury could derail your dreams of a college scholarship. Your friends could drop you because you chose to take a stand for Christ. But through a close relationship with God, you can rely on him to see you through any difficulty that you may encounter.

As Simeon helped Jesus shoulder his cross, God will help you shoulder your daily trials. His yoke is easy. Give him your burdens and cares. God will help you dig deep and find the faith to keep from losing it. No matter what life might throw at you, God is there to give you strength, perseverance, grit, and hope to help you handle stress and strain like a saint. Now is the time to build your reserves through daily walks with God that include gratitude, Bible study, and prayer. Without the daily walks, we are ill-prepared when trials come.

Prayer: Father God, you are so merciful and gracious to me. Help me realize that every day you want to sit with me and talk with me and walk with me. When those stormy days happen and I really need you, I will come to you out of habit developed by love, not out of desperation. In Jesus's holy name, amen.

FB41:
THE ICING ON THE CAKE

Matthew 6:33

Seek first the Kingdom of God and his righteousness, and
all these things shall be added to you.

UGA's Drew Butler is the son of Kevin Butler, the former Georgia
All-American and College Hall of Fame place kicker. Drew was
signed as a punter and place kicker, but he didn't resemble a chip off
the old block during his first two seasons on campus. He was the
backup punter as a redshirt freshman and was no threat to erase his
dad's kicking records. "He got a scholarship because of his daddy!"
some cried. But when the punting job opened up the following season, Butler was ready. Man, was he ready. He consistently boomed
high punts and placed them beautifully, especially against Arkansas
when his seventy-five-yard kick from scrimmage sealed the victory.
For the season, Drew averaged an astounding forty-nine yards per
punt, which was four yards more than a trio of kickers who were distant in the rearview mirror. Four yards might not sound like much,
but that margin on the PGA Tour would be like driving the ball
twenty-five yards farther than your closest competitors. His father,
Kevin, commented that his consistently good punts were his outstanding accomplishment.

Through excellent technique, thorough mental preparation, and through a newfound passion for punting, Drew achieved great success. The post-season awards rolled in by the bushel basket. There was the Walter Camp Award, the Ray Guy Award, and numerous first-team all-American honors. But the awards were not what Drew set out to achieve. His singular focus was to become the best punter he could be and win the starting position at UGA. As a result of his hard work and excellence, the post-season accolades were the icing on the cake.

Jesus taught us in the book of Matthew that you and I are to put first things first. Seek first God's kingdom and his righteousness by being a daily disciple devoted to right living with fervent focus on prayer, Bible study, love for God, and obedience. A self-righteous person will perform good works and say as the Pharisees said, "Look at me! Look what I've done!" That selfish attitude won't get you special blessings from God. But a person who receives God's special favors is the one who gives God the glory no matter what comes out of situations. That's when God pours out the whipped cream and the cherry on top. Those blessings can be unexpected, wonderful compliments from a Christian brother or sister or special opportunities that God grants you. It could be a kind word when you need it most from a friend who saw your light shine for Christ. First things first. Jesus, then others, then yourself spells J-O-Y, joy.

Prayer: Father God, help me to work hard not simply for the pats on the back, which are cool, but because I have a mindset and a heart set on serving you. Not because of what I've done, but because of what you've done for me. Not because of who I am, but because of who you are. In Jesus's name, amen.

FB42:
SOLD OUT!

2 Corinthians 11:23-28;
Philippians 1:20-21, 3:8; James 1:2-4

For to me to live is Christ, and to die is gain.

Philippians 1:21

A sellout means all tickets have been sold and none remain. A sellout crowd adds another level of excitement to a sports contest when you look around and realize that there are virtually no empty seats. The only thing better than a sellout is SRO, standing room only, which is beyond capacity. Nothing pleases a team's marketing director like a sellout. The Masters wouldn't be the same if you could walk up and buy badges the day of the tournament. Successful teams that routinely sell out publish the same attendance figure. Sanford Stadium's published capacity is 92,746. Nebraska has sold out 190 consecutive games dating back to the 1970s, when coaches Bob Devaney and Tom Osborne put the Huskers on the national map. A sellout can make finding tickets a real adventure.

God loves sellouts too. He can't get enough of them. But a sellout to God is when a person consistently gives God 100 percent in each facet of their lives. Too many Christians settle for partial sellouts, which aren't nearly as exciting. A partial sellout is when a person holds back certain parts of their lives. That's no sellout at all.

God wants complete surrender to maximize a person's value to his kingdom. When you sell out to God, he will maximize his blessings to you. That doesn't mean you'll get rich monetarily or never have problems, but you will have a special coping strength that others do not have.

A person who is sold out to God doesn't take days off. A person who is sold out to God thinks about eternity virtually every day. He or she goes out the door in the morning expecting to see opportunities to share God's love and to expand the kingdom. A person who is sold out to God will find where God is working and join him there. A person who is sold out to God doesn't need to be reminded that there is kingdom work to be done. A person who is sold out to God illumines the Holy Spirit. Know any sellouts?

When newspapers and websites publish box scores, the attendance figures are shared, and the capacity of the stadium is shown in parentheses. For example, 15,370 (20,468) indicates that there were over five thousand empty seats for the contest. How would your actual contributions compare to your capacity to contribute if God were to reveal it? Would it be 25 percent or 100 percent most days? Which is closer to your true measure?

Certainly Paul was sold out to God. He counted everything that he had experienced or possessed to be dung or manure when compared to knowing Christ. Only a sellout could have endured so many mental and physical hardships and stayed steadfast in promoting the good news of the resurrection and the love of Jesus Christ. Paul sold out to Christ because Christ first sold out for Paul on the cross. We love because Christ first loved us.

Would you love to have joy even in the darkest tribulation? James 1:2 says "...count it all joy when you fall into various trials." I can't tell you that I understand it, but I've seen it. I saw it when my friend, Melinda, told the estimated eight hundred people at her daughter's funeral that if any of them didn't know Jesus Christ, she wanted to talk to them after the service. Surrendering and selling out to Christ is the only way to true joy. Otherwise, you are settling for second best. Selling out to God adds excitement to your life. What a difference it will make if you approach each day with an eternal focus.

Prayer: Lord Jesus, thank you for selling out for me on the cross. I can never repay you, but I can think about you each day and try to live my life as a disciple of Christ should live. May you help me in that endeavor each day with the strength and courage that I need to succeed not as the world sees success but as you see it. In Jesus's name, amen.

FB43: PROPHETIC PROGNOSTICATIONS

Daniel 9:24-27, Revelation 20:11-21:5

And I saw a great white throne, and Him that sat on it ...

Revelation 20:11

Think of all the talking TV suits, the panel of so-called sports experts who spend hour upon hour on pre-game shows, picking the winners of games. I saw seven ESPN experts pick the NFC and AFC championship games. They were a combined one game above 50 percent picking winners in the previous NFL playoff games. That percentage is the same as flipping a coin.

Consider your emotional reaction when an expert picks your favorite team to win. It gives you a false sense of confidence that is shaken thirty seconds later when another prognosticator picks your archrival to win. You seethe a little at that guy and say he is biased. And, of course, he doesn't know what he's talking about, does he?

The spectacle of game predictions and expert advice can be pretty comical. I heard one basketball pundit, an ex-college and pro player, say before the Kentucky-Florida basketball game that "Florida needs to employ their running game to beat Kentucky." When Florida was down twelve at the half, the same guy says, "Florida can't afford to get into a running game." I couldn't make those two statements up, the second of which was a correction of his misinformed assertion one hour before. Then there are the talking heads on ESPN who always pick opposite each other.

At one time in my young Christian life, I disrespected the teachings of the Old Testament by thinking that the New Testament was all that was needed since we are saved by faith through Jesus Christ. What does it really matter what happened before Christ was born as long as we have Christ? But as I delved into the Old Testament, I became enamored with the prophecies, particularly those that predicted the birth, life, death, and resurrection of Jesus. The odds that so many prophecies would come true are staggering, approaching 10 to the 132 power according to Lee Strobel, who authored *The Case for Christ*. Those are incomprehensibly huge odds, because 10 to the 9th power is a billion to one!

God bats 100 percent in his predictions, unlike the flip-a-coin prognosticators. Not only that, but God's timing is perfect. Consider the prophecy of Daniel (9:24-27) that predicted almost five hundred years earlier the exact day that Jesus would humbly and triumphantly enter Jerusalem on a colt as the crowds cheered, "Hosanna in the highest!"

Unlike other religions, such as Islam, Hinduism, Jehovah's Witnesses, Buddhism, and Mormonism, Christianity is the only religion with the element of proven prophecies, hundreds of them, and the only religion that worships a risen savior. All others trace their roots back to people who were of this earth. Jesus came from beyond this earth to be born to a virgin. The sheer amount of evidence of proven prophecies ought to be enough to silence the greatest naysayers.

There are some big prophecies remaining in the book of Revelation. These predictions will come true in God's timing. As revealed to the writer John as he was exiled on the isle of Patmos, the Great White Throne Judgment, the lake of fire, and the second coming of Jesus will occur. I would never pick against God, and neither should you.

He is the incomparably great and mighty Most Holy God that we serve. If it's between God and Satan for the second coming, I'm taking God, who will be the favorite to win every time. You and I must have unshakable faith that God will do what he said he would do.

Prayer: Most Holy and magnificent Father, you are perfect, and your Word is perfect. I believe that what you say has happened and will happen even though I don't understand all of the events. May I live my life like Jesus will be on my doorstep later today. In Jesus's holy and precious name, amen.

FB44:
STAY UNTIL THE END

Matthew 27:38-43

And they that passed by reviled him, wagging their heads.

Matthew 27:39

Let's admit it. Many of us take great pleasure in seeing our archrivals lose to us. In the SEC, if you are a visiting fan, be prepared to take some ribbing. Unfortunately, the ribbing can become taunting and meanness from some unruly fans. It's enough to make you want to leave the stadium early. Oftentimes that's exactly what happens. You're on the road, and things turn against your team from the start. Then you're down three touchdowns and the opponent punches in one more just for good measure. As soon as the official lifts his hands to signal touchdown, it starts. "I've seen enough. Let's go." "Let's beat the traffic." "He [the coach] has gotta go." "I can't believe I wasted my money to come here." Before the extra point sails through the goal posts, the visiting section of the stands is empty. "Hey, hey, good-bye!" is one of the milder chants that goes up. "See you! Wouldn't wanna be you!" Your only goal is to get to your car in the parking lot, load up, beat the traffic, and set sail for home because visions of an undefeated season have gone up in smoke. And it's only October.

Imagine how your team feels when their fans abandon them after they have played their hearts out. They can't help but see it, especially if it's the home crowd that leaves in droves. Then the visiting fans take great delight when the vast majority of the stadium exits.

These circumstances have an interesting parallel to what Jesus experienced in the final hours on the cross. Many of the chief priests, scribes, and elders and the Roman soldiers took great pleasure in seeing Jesus "get his." After all, Jesus had been a major thorn in their sides for three years. The air at Golgotha was filled with taunting and meanness. "If you're the Son of God, save yourself! Come down from the cross!" they cried with glee. It was enough to make the disciples of Jesus flee the scene early. Things had suddenly turned against them, and they ran like scared rabbits. Even Peter, who had vowed hours before that he would be faithful to the end, denied Jesus three times just as Jesus had predicted, and the cock crowed. The only followers of Jesus left were the Apostle John, his mother, Mary, another Mary, and Salome. Jesus had virtually no other followers in the stands, and he still had several hours remaining in the longest game of his life.

Imagine how Jesus felt when his disciples abandoned him, and their sins had helped put him on the cross. After Jesus turned what was seemingly the worst loss ever into the greatest victory for mankind, these same eleven would become the greatest spokespersons for Christianity after receiving the power of the Holy Spirit. Today, Christians can take great delight in the hope, peace, joy, and eternal life that only Jesus Christ brings.

Prayer: Father God, before I leave the stadium, help me consider how my team feels when I abandon them in their time of need. Jesus, I never want to turn my back on you when the going gets tough because you never turned your back on me. You hung to make me strong, to help me endure and bounce back for another day. In Jesus's name, amen.

FB45:
I'M IN THE BATHROOM
'CAUSE THERE'S NO
PLACE FOR ME TO SIT!

Luke 2:10-16

And they came with haste, and found Mary, and Joseph, and the babe lying in a manger.

Luke 2:16

In 2003, UGA football was coming off its best season in twenty years, having won the SEC in 2002 and having finished in the top five in the nation. Optimism was high; UGA was undefeated and headed for an SEC showdown with LSU in Baton Rouge in late September. I scraped together four single tickets for our family before we left Atlanta. Allison was a second year at UGA, and Jillian was a high school sophomore.

As I read the *Baton Rouge Advocate* on Saturday morning in the hotel lobby while the three ladies got ready, it became obvious that this was not just another game. The sportswriter touted the contest as the biggest in Baton Rouge since 1963. *Man, am I glad that we have tickets, even if they are singles,* I thought and breathed a sigh of relief. *Surely Allison and Jillian can sit together since theirs are on the same row and only four seats apart.*

As we headed for the stadium, there were no tickets anywhere, so the stands would be jam packed. We sorted through our game plan. Becca and I were in the same section about ten rows apart, so we could at least see each other even if we couldn't sit together. I helped Allison and Jillian find their section and encouraged them to ask people to let them sit together. But the people on that row were not very pleasant, so they never sat together. To make matters worse, when Jillian returned to her seat, two large male LSU fans were sitting in their seats and had consumed hers.

I found out her predicament just after kickoff as a hostile Tiger Stadium was in an uproar. I checked my cell phone and read this desperate text from Jillian, "I'm in the bathroom 'cause there's no place for me to sit!" I dashed down the aisle and brought her to my seat on the back row of the lower level. I crouched behind her for three and a half hours, and we watched our Dawgs lose 17-10. The day's events made Jillian pull against LSU forever, and the experience caused her to feel overwhelmed, rejected, alone, and afraid.

When the baby Jesus was born, he didn't exactly have the best seat in the house or even have a seat for that matter. The innkeeper had a sellout that night. Joseph and Mary were told that there was no room in the inn, so they made their way outside the inn (stadium) and found themselves outside in a stable (under the stadium). The humble circumstances of the birth were just the beginning as Jesus found himself shuttled to Egypt to escape Herod's massacre of newborns. Christ would be rejected in his home town of Nazareth. Jesus would even be rejected by his family and constantly faced rejection for the new values that he had brought from the Father. Considering what Jesus went through during his life, certainly Jesus knew exactly how a frightened, lonely teenager felt in the bowels of Tiger Stadium, hiding out in a bathroom with nowhere to go and no place to sit. He knows exactly how you feel when you are in circumstances that threaten to engulf you.

Prayer: Father God, thank you for comforting us when we feel like outcasts with nowhere to turn and no place to sit. You've been through every uncomfortable situation that we can face and help us turn to you when we have nowhere else to go. In Jesus's name, amen.

Note: Before that Georgia-LSU game, I walked around the ancient Cow Palace arena where my idol, Pete Maravich, performed so many times and wondered what it must have been like to watch Pete play in that building. Six weeks after this game, after being disconsolate over Georgia's second loss of the season, on a Sunday night, I was saved for eternity after watching a video of Pete Maravich's testimony in my living room. I never saw my salvation coming.

FB46: JAW-DROPPING ASTONISHMENT

John 14:2-4

In my Father's house are many mansions; if it were not so, I would have told you. I go to prepare a place for you.

John 14:2

Jillian and her friend, Liz, drove to Jacksonville for their first Georgia-Florida game in 2007. They arrived at the game site without tickets early on Saturday morning and were thrilled to find two tickets from two kindly UGA gentlemen who had extras. They were overjoyed just to get into the stadium. If the tickets had been for the worst seats in Alltel Stadium, it wouldn't have mattered. But the biggest thrill came when they went into the stadium. First, they entered through a fancy private suite with all the trappings and comforts and discovered their seats were on the 40, fourth row, behind the Bulldogs' bench.

Jillian called us and screamed, "This is the best game that I've ever been to!"

I replied, "Well, Jillian, that's great, because the game hasn't even started."

To top off the incredible experience, Georgia upset Florida 42-30 in the "Celebration Game" that will forever be remembered fondly by Jillian, Liz, and all UGA fans who were there. It was a day that started with joy and ended with jaw-dropping astonishment.

Following the Last Supper, Jesus shared with his disciples in the upper room that he would go before them and prepare a place for them. That place would be a special mansion/room in heaven with God and Jesus. Imagine what your special room in heaven will look like. It's far nicer than we can possibly fathom! God knows every hair on your head and every innermost thought. God knows exactly what makes you tick. I believe he will prepare us a special place to live with him for eternity that matches us to a T. I can't wait to see mine, and I bet you can't wait either. I believe our home in heaven will be absolutely jaw dropping!

Prayer: Father God, you know exactly what makes us tick and what we enjoy. Thank you that you would prepare a place for us in heaven that we will be thrilled and overjoyed to see! In Jesus's name, amen.

FB47:
YOU ARE A
FIVE-STAR RECRUIT!

Psalm 139:1-14

I am fearfully and wonderfully made ...

Psalm 139:14

National signing day for the 2009 college football season was predictable with a few surprises. Fans gathered in anxious anticipation at major college campuses across America or checked the Internet for the latest signing news throughout the day. There were the usual last-minute defections, and according to Rivals.com, mostly the rich got richer. My head was already spinning from the shakeout of major college football coaches getting dismissed for allegedly mistreating players and bolting for greener pastures. One father said he and his son should have bought into the university instead of the coach before signing. The impact of signing day on the future of many young men was life changing.

The pressure on these teenagers and their parents to make life-altering decisions is enormous. Savvy recruiters have used their polished sales pitches and stretch limos, sat in basketball bleachers to be seen, or attempted to sway the top recruits at their official visits. Each recruiter tried to outwork and outsmart the others to bring home the four-star and five-star recruits that could mean a championship team instead of a runner-up finish.

In a more subtle way, but just as intently and for a much longer period of time, God spends a lifetime recruiting us to join his team. Just like football teams, God replenishes his eternal team each year with new recruits. Just like the coaches who are passionate about their teams and universities, God needs Christians who will recruit for Jesus because they are passionate about God and will share their faith stories. Hear this. Unlike recruiters who line up players that come and go, God never stops working to woo us to his team permanently. God works hard at it because since Adam and Eve suffered the fall from grace in the garden, every boy and girl is born a sinner. We don't become Christians by birthright, or good deeds, or living in a Christian home. Everyone eventually selects a team for eternity. Satan's team looks like a lot of fun in the beginning because there is pleasure in sin. If sin weren't fun, people wouldn't succumb to it. As a young man in my Sunday school class observed, Satan doesn't appear as a red-tailed devil with a pitchfork, but he lurks in familiar scenes around every corner. Satan's team brings us only heartache and bitter pain in the end.

God is longsuffering and wants to see every person come to know Jesus Christ. God woos us and longs for us to join his team, and he creates a unique plan for each of his five-star recruits. Believe it or not, you are a five-star recruit in God's eyes. Coaches have their eyes on five-star football recruits from the time they enter eighth grade. God loves you perfectly and had his eyes on you even before you were born.

Despite any past failings, iniquities, and current strongholds, you're still a hotshot recruit. God thinks you are uniquely the greatest thing to come along because he fearfully and wonderfully made you with special talents and a passion for those talents. So you don't believe all the recruiting hype and promises from the football recruiters? You can believe the promises that God makes and stand on them. You can know full well that whatever he has promised, you will receive because God is a promise keeper.

Prayer: Most Holy Lord God Almighty, it's exciting to know that you see me as a five-star recruit despite the many times that I have failed you and will fail you still. You are so good to me and want to enrich my life and save me if I will only put my trust in Jesus. Help me live up to my end of the recruiting deal. In Jesus's name, amen.

FB48:
AM I WILLING
TO BE RUDY?

Philippians 2:17, 4:12

I've learned by now to be quite content, whatever
my circumstances...

Philippians 4:12

Rudy is one of my favorite sports movies. The movie is about Rudy
Ruettiger, a walk-on at Notre Dame. Rudy is pint sized and athletically
challenged compared to the scholarship football players at Notre Dame,
but he has a heart the size of a mountain. He would do anything that he
possibly can to run through the tunnel at Notre Dame Stadium just one
time. But first he must get into Notre Dame because his academics didn't
qualify him.

After he overcomes that monumental hurdle by the skin of his teeth,
a minor miracle in itself, he makes the scout team by beating out a dozen
other boys for one position. His job on the scout team is to mimic the
opposition's defense against the first-team's offense. Rudy gets pulverized,
battered, and bruised week after week. Each Friday, he looks for his name
on the dress-out list, and it is never there until the last Friday, after all of
his teammates insist to the head coach that he dress in his final game as a
senior. Rudy not only gets the thrill of dressing out and running through

the tunnel, but he gets into the game and makes a sack on the final play of his career.

It's a sappy, tear-jerking storybook ending for a young man who never quit and never gave up. Rudy's ultimate reward of running out of the tunnel was eclipsed by the tackle that got him into the Notre Dame record book. Perhaps Rudy never even imagined playing; he simply wanted to dress so that his father would know that he was on the team.

Indianapolis and New Orleans competed for the 2010 Super Bowl trophy, which was won by New Orleans. The Colts and Saints were led by two outstanding quarterbacks, Peyton Manning and Drew Brees. The problem is that most of us want to be like Peyton and Drew, and we don't want to be Rudy. Peyton and Drew are much more exciting, and Rudy? Well, he's just got too much to overcome, and he will never get the headlines. But God has a plan for each of our lives, and that plan (I am sorry to break this to you) might not call for you to be the Peyton Manning or Drew Brees of your school, your office, your church, or even your family. What the plan calls for is to love God and to be obedient. If you will be faithful and stick it out like Rudy did, your just rewards will come.

There are many different positions to be played on God's team. Some positions are more prestigious than others. Your position might be one of the least attractive. You might just be a tremendous encourager so that when the stars with the big assignments feel down, you share just the right words to lift them up and refocus them on God's work. As believers, we can take a page out of Rudy's work ethic and commit to work day in and day out for God wherever he needs us. No matter how obscure the circumstances, God can and will do great and mighty things through us and for us.

Prayer: Father God, may we learn from the wonderful story of perseverance in this classic movie. Even if I don't get any credit, may I be bursting with joy just from the opportunity to be on your team. When I am obedient, I know that you will give me playing time. May I never grow tired of serving your kingdom. When I stumble and fall and life has me looking out of the ear hole of my helmet, I know that you will pull me out of the mire, straighten my helmet, pat me on my shoulder pads, and get me back into the game of life. In Jesus's name, amen.

FB49:
WINNING WAS A BREES

2 Corinthians 12:6, James 2:17

I don't want anyone to think more highly of me than he should, than what he can actually see in my life and my message.

2 Corinthians 12:6

I watched the 2010 Super Bowl along with a record 106 million viewers. The game featured two of America's favorite athletes: Drew Brees of the New Orleans Saints and Peyton Manning of the Indianapolis Colts. The 31-17 victory meant so very much to the city of New Orleans to have their first world championship in forty-four years of professional sports. How fitting that the Saints parade came during Mardi Gras. The irony was that the man who stood in the way was once a huge Saints fan because his dad played for the Saints. A native of New Orleans, as a child, Peyton Manning and his older brother, Cooper, and younger brother, Eli, spent many Sunday afternoons in the Superdome, watching the Saints lose as Archie would get pummeled by one more defense. As the Saints fans booed Archie one day, Cooper, who was seven, asked his mother, Olivia, "Can we boo too, Mom?"

Super Bowl XLIV had great story lines and was extremely well played with very few penalties. One story line that many people would not recognize is that both starting quarterbacks are believers. In the book *Manning* by John Underwood, Peyton recalled the encounter with God that led him to proclaim Jesus Christ as his Savior. Thirteen-year-old Peyton heard the oft-repeated question from the pulpit of his church in New Orleans one Sunday morning: "If you died today, are you one hundred percent sure that you are going to heaven?" The message spoke to Peyton differently than it did to his brothers, and he felt small in the big church. When the pastor asked who wanted the assurance of eternity in heaven, Peyton raised his hand. He found the courage to come forward and take a stand that day for Jesus Christ. Peyton shared that while he has no problem with players taking more overt stands for Christ, he prefers to let his actions speak. He is aware that Christians make mistakes just like those who do not know Christ and that he is forgiven through Jesus Christ. In my opinion, Peyton has done a marvelous job being a role model in a high-profile, pressure-filled sport. He displayed grace and humility as he answered post-game questions from the Super Bowl media who were making way too much of one ill-advised throw.

The lesser-known quarterback was Drew Brees, who was on the cover of FCA's January/February 2010 *Sharing the Victory* magazine. Brees described the encounter that led him to Christ. When he was seventeen, his Austin, Texas, pastor asked the congregation if there were any who were willing to be one of a "few good men" for Jesus Christ. Drew made his commitment to Jesus Christ that morning. Soon, his high school football career blossomed, and he led Purdue to the Rose Bowl and starred for the San Diego Chargers. But an injury made him a backup, and he was traded to New Orleans in 2005. He came to a team with a tradition of mediocrity and no home games in a city ravaged by Hurricane Katrina. Drew was disconsolate about the trade, his new home, and his career. When he moved to New Orleans, he was immediately befriended by Cooper Manning, Peyton's brother. Drew recovered from his injury and thrived under Coach Sean Payton. He made good on his "few good men" commitment and became a leader on the field, in the locker room, and, most importantly, in the community. Drew and his wife Brittany have helped raise over six million dollars through the Brees Dream Foundation to help the children of New Orleans, San Diego, and West Lafayette, Indiana.

There were two talented quarterbacks who desperately wanted to achieve the pinnacle of their profession. One celebrated the victory, and the other contemplated what might have been. But both understand that greater things await them in God's kingdom now and forever. Through the sacrifice made by God's own Son, may God be glorified in our stadiums and arenas.

Prayer: Father God, thank you for the incredible theatre of sports that reveals character. May you receive all the glory when your children lead their teams and honor you with their efforts. May someone see Jesus Christ in me today. In Jesus's holy and precious name, amen.

FB50:
IF I WERE A
BETTING MAN

John 3:16-17

For God sent His Son into the world not to condemn it,
but to save it.

John 3:17

One of our high school students in Sunday school shared that his
friend's dad placed a $4,000 bet on the Saints-Colts Super Bowl
game. Across the country, billions of dollars were placed on Super
Bowl XLIV in office pools and through bookies in Vegas. The big
winners were the bookies, who cleared hundreds of millions of dollars from this game by controlling the betting line. Their goal was
to get as much money on the game as possible by shifting the point
spread to balance the betting on the two teams and simply take their
10 percent. You could even bet on the first player to score a touchdown, the number of points scored in the game (called the over
under), and any number of statistical aspects of the game. After the
game people brag about their betting wins at the water cooler, and
the ones who lost keep it to themselves.

Disclaimer: I do not condone betting, which can become an idol
in a person's life and an addiction, just as alcoholism and drugs can.

After I became a Christian, I had no desire to wager on sporting events or even friendly golf matches. But I remember my first parlay card in college. What a thrill it was to win $25 on a five-dollar bet. I picked three underdogs to beat the spread as I proved my superior football knowledge. Of course, there are the times that I didn't win that I don't talk about. If only our study of the Bible was as intense as the analysis of Indianapolis defensive end Dwight Freeney's sprained right ankle prior to the 2010 Super Bowl.

Many people will bet big sums in hopes of a quick payoff to balance previous losses or to offset the impact of our struggling economy. Many of the same people are betting their lives last at least one more day before they receive Jesus Christ into their lives. There will come a day for each person that God will call your bluff and ask you to place all of your cards on the table. That day is known as judgment day, and God will be seated on the Great White Throne. If you know Jesus, he will speak for you. If you don't know Jesus, you will be the one answering to God. You will get to explain why you squandered your life on temporary pleasures and selfish pursuits. Each morning, millions of people bet they are going to leave and return home safely in cars, trains, and planes. It's a risk to walk out that door without Jesus Christ. Why would a person ever bet against Christ if they believe there is a God and that our God is a God of justice? One reason is a false sense of security that comes from a hardened heart.

I shudder when I think about how I bet the farm on some risky situations as an unsaved teenager. When I was fifteen, I sat in the backseat of a souped-up Chevy SS 396 as David pushed the speedometer needle to the H going back to school from PE. That was the H as in MPH, which was to the left of 120 at the bottom of the odometer. Was I so insecure and needed attention that badly in order to brag about how fast the car I was riding in was going? There was the night that six of us sped down a dirt road at 100 mph as the car floated like a magic carpet. If either car had wrecked, I would have been history forever where it's jalapeno hot.

As adults, the odds of dying increase each year. But it doesn't shake some of us that we need Christ until we hear the dreaded *c* word, or until we hit rock bottom with addictions, or until we finally hear the gospel presented in a way that shakes our foundations.

You certainly have nothing to lose if you bet that there is a God. If somehow there wasn't a God, you haven't lost anything. But if you bet there isn't a God and there is, you've lost everything. Of course, there is a God, and when you put your faith in him, you've gained everything for eternity in heaven. What will it be?

As the same Sunday school class concluded with prayer requests, one student shared that her math teacher had been brutally murdered only three days before. The teacher was at school on Thursday and gone on Friday; here today, gone tomorrow. Only God knows where that teacher had placed his faith. With whom does your eternal life assurance policy lie? I pray that your policy is based solely on the death and resurrection of Jesus Christ. If it isn't, today is the best day to take out a policy in the Lord that will beat all odds.

Prayer: Dear most gracious and wonderful Father God, thank you for the eternal life assurance policy that I have received when I turned from my sinful life and placed my faith in Jesus Christ. I am so thankful that you redeemed me and that I don't roll the dice for eternity every time I get in a car or a plane. I am at peace because I know my final destination. In the holy name of Jesus and his saving grace, amen.

FB51:
OVERCOMING ADVERSITY

Psalm 18:29, John 16:33

In this world you will have tribulation, but be of good cheer, for I have overcome the world.

John 16:33

It was the final game that I would attend as a student at the University of Georgia as we played our archrival Georgia Tech. Anticipation was high because Georgia had enjoyed a surprisingly good season. The temperature was unseasonably warm for the Saturday after Thanksgiving, in the seventies, and it was a perfect day for college football in Athens before a sellout crowd of sixty thousand fans.

The game started terribly for the Dawgs due to three early turnovers in Georgia territory, and Georgia trailed 20-0 late in the first quarter. But the Dawgs rallied with a couple of touchdowns, and Scott Woerner took a punt sixty-five yards for a touchdown to give the Dawgs a 21-20 lead late in the second half. However, speedster Drew Hill from Georgia Tech took the ensuing kickoff a hundred yards for a touchdown, and the air just seemed to come out of Sanford Stadium as the Tech contingent cheered deliriously in the northwest corner.

On Georgia's final drive with two minutes remaining, freshman Buck Belue rolled right on fourth and two and searched desperately for an open receiver. Amazingly, Amp Arnold had broken clear of the Tech secondary and Buck hit him for a long touchdown. Coach Vince Dooley made the decision to go for two in an attempt to win the game. Buck rolled left and was tackled. Just before his knees hit the turf, he pitched the ball to Arnold, who easily scampered into the end zone for two points, giving the Dawgs a thrilling 29-28 win. The chapel bell on North Campus tolled throughout the night in celebration of the hard-fought win.

Georgia overcame numerous adversities during the game to achieve the victory. Throughout our lives, we will be faced with numerous obstacles, and we can also be triumphant. Psalm 18:29 assures that we can leap over walls because we have the strength of the Lord. We are also assured that Christ has overcome the world, and that God will never leave us nor forsake us. Sometimes the consequences of our actions will result in obstacles, and other times, God will put up walls simply to test our faith. No matter the trials we face, we can always be assured that God is in us, for us, and with us to help us be victorious.

Prayer: Father God, thank you for the assurance that I have through Jesus Christ, who overcame the greatest of all adversities when he beat death by rising from the grave. For that reason and through your promises in the Bible, I can cling to the hope that is available to me and to every person who confesses you as Savior and Lord. In the holy and wonderful name of Jesus Christ, amen.

FB52:
CRUNCH TIME

Psalm 119:100-105

I understand more than the ancients, because I keep your precepts.

Psalm 119:100

NFL and major college football teams have a playbook that is about three inches thick with hundreds of offensive plays. These plays are studied by each player and rehearsed again and again. The pressure is especially on the quarterbacks because as the decision makers, they must know the second and third options in case the first option breaks down. When the pressure is on and the quarterback calls "Z-87 trap swing right overload," each player must know where to run and who to block for the play to work. If the players don't know the plays, it's pretty obvious that the chance to win the game will be slim to none.

There comes a time for all of us when we're faced with pressure-packed situations and dire circumstances. It could be personal illness, the death of loved ones, betrayal by close friends, or job loss. These events can leave us reeling and fill us with the FUD factor: fear, uncertainty, and doubt.

The Bible gives us instruction for everything that Satan and life can throw at us. We must know now that the Word of God is Truth and that the Truth will sustain us when nothing else will. Just like the playbook, the Bible has guidance for any situation that life brings us.

But we can't just open the Bible when we're in dire straits or in the middle of a hotly contested battle with Satan. We must be constantly studying the Bible when things are going well in order to know where to go for the perfect Scripture that will sustain us through tough times. Setbacks in life can take us where we've never been, and we won't know how to respond in faith without the knowledge and instruction from the inspired Word of the living Almighty Creator.

We need to understand it, memorize it, and be able to regurgitate it to sustain ourselves and our loved ones. The Bible is full of promises, but we need to know the promises to be able to stand on them. What are some of the most important promises in the Bible? That Christ died once for all of our sins (John 3:16-17), that God will never leave us nor forsake us (Hebrews 13:5), and that the Holy Spirit will help us with our daily problems (Romans 8:26). There is always hope through Christ Jesus, who experienced all of the pitfalls and emotions that we will ever encounter. With God, we will never walk alone, and Jesus has already walked where we're walking, no matter how dark the path (Psalm 119:105).

Prayer: Father God, help me constantly turn to the Bible and understand your magnificent promises that are available to me even though I am a sinner. Thank you for your forgiveness and the grace through Jesus Christ, which I cannot earn. In the holy name of our precious Lord and Savior, amen.

FB53:
I'M GOING TO
DISNEY WORLD!

Philippians 1:6

He who has begun a good work in you will complete it…

Usually, it takes six to eight years to make a complete quarterback in the NFL. Rookie quarterbacks come into the NFL with the ability to throw the ball hard and throw it a long way. But in the first few years come the inevitable interceptions. What signal caller threw twenty-four interceptions and only six touchdown passes in his first NFL year? It was none other than four-time Super Bowl champion Terry Bradshaw.

There are so many challenges that young quarterbacks must overcome. A young quarterback must learn to put touch on the ball in order to loft it over dropping linebackers. The NFL cornerbacks are so much quicker and more physical than the college corners, and they don't drop balls thrown near them. Consider the vast experience and knowledge that are needed by the NFL quarterbacks to read complex defenses, which are much more complicated than the defenses in the college game. The quarterback must also learn to manage the clock in the last two minutes of the game. Finally, there is the ability to perform in the Super Bowl, the most intense, pressure-packed game that is watched by over 100 million Americans. When all of these facets of the game are mastered, the maturation of the quarterback is complete. As he waves the Super Bowl trophy after conquering that pressure, it's no small wonder he yells, "I'm going to Disney World!"

It takes God an entire lifetime to complete us, and it is never complete until we win our faith "Super Bowl" and leave this earth to be with God in heaven. We mature by diligently studying his Word, by frequent and fervent prayer, and by learning to apply our faith to all facets of our lives. We must learn to trust in God and have faith in him during our toughest times. God uses these situations to sanctify us or make us more holy.

Prayer: Father God, just like the tough times make the NFL quarterbacks better so that they can reach the pinnacle of their game, help me reach your pinnacle. Give me a hunger and a thirst and a desire to be as holy as possible and to give you the glory. Forgive me when I fail to be obedient. In the name of Jesus, amen.

FB54:
TOUCHDOWN MOSES!

Exodus 17:11-14

Aaron and Hur stayed up his hands, the one on the one side, and the other on the other side; and his hands were steady until the going down of the sun.

Exodus 17:12

It is widely known that the six-story-tall mural of Jesus at the University of Notre Dame in South Bend, Indiana, is known as "Touchdown Jesus." In the mural, Jesus has both arms in the air, and it does look like he is signaling touchdown just as a linesman would. The dramatic mural was captured on film in the movie *Rudy*. Surely it is an awe-inspiring scene for the Notre Dame students and faculty to be able to see daily. Touchdown Jesus certainly beats the larger-than-life pictures of athletes that Nike plasters on downtown buildings in Manhattan and Los Angeles.

Moses heeded God's call to lead the Israelites, God's chosen people, out of Egypt, where the Pharaohs had kept them in bondage for 400 years. After they escaped Egypt for the promised land, Israel would battle different sects of people for rule over the land.

One day God's chosen people fought the Amalekites. Moses might have been the first person in the Bible to signal touchdown. Israel was winning so long as Moses held his arms in the air. But when he dropped his arms, Big Mo (Momentum, not Moses) hopped on the Amalekites' bench. Moses held his arms in the air for a long time, and he got very tired. So he called in his brother Aaron and a man named Hur to prop up his arms. The reason is that as long as Moses diligently held up his arms, God gave Israel the power to "score the winning touchdown" and defeat the Amalekites.

Prayer: Father God, thank you for the legacy of Moses and for all of your prophets who spoke your truth. In Jesus's name, amen.

Note: An interesting sidebar is that there is no remnant of the people known as Amalekites. God was true to his promise that they would be removed from the face of the earth (Exodus 17).

FB55:
BREAKING TACKLES

Hebrews 12:1

Therefore, since we are surrounded by such a great cloud
of witnesses, let us throw off everything that so easily
entangles us, and let us run with perseverance the race
marked out for us.

The goal of any running back is to put the football over the goal line
for six points. There have been some great touchdown runs in football history. The greatest run that I ever saw was by a quarterback,
Steve Young, who broke eight tackles on the way to a forty-yard
touchdown. The game was played in San Francisco, and it was third
down and long when he began his scramble. Young swiveled his hips
and shed tackler after tackler. Nothing or nobody was going to slow
him down, and he collapsed from exhaustion after crossing the goal
line for the touchdown.

In 1959, Billy Cannon's eighty-nine-yard punt return on
Halloween night in fog-shrouded Tiger Stadium gave LSU a 7-3
win over Ole Miss that sealed the national championship. Cannon
was "Cannon-ized" as the Heisman Trophy winner and the most
famous football player in LSU lore. He fielded the punt near the
LSU 10 and, through clever moves and tremendous balance, shed
arm tackle after arm tackle by the Ole Miss defenders. He finally
broke clear of the pack at the Ole Miss 30. What's amusing in the

grainy YouTube video is that the official running with him is actually running faster than a very tired Cannon as he crosses the goal line.

The author of Hebrews challenges us to be just as determined to obey God in our daily lives as the great runners in football strive to keep from being tackled. Satan tries to tackle us each day, trip us up from serving the kingdom, and interrupt our obedience to God. If Satan can make us disobedient, he can stop our work for the kingdom. When we are apart from God due to the entanglement of sin in our lives, it's a sure thing that nobody will get saved during our self-centered actions.

When we confess our sins and receive God's forgiveness, God removes the tangles that keep us from scoring touchdowns for the kingdom. God always gives us a way to break through any obstacle that Satan uses to bring us down short of his goal line.

Prayer: Father God, thank you for giving me ways to avoid the entanglement of sin that threatens to bring me down and make me ineffective. You are so good to me all the time, Lord. Thank you. In Jesus's name, amen.

FB56:
GAMEDAY OUTLOOK

Galatians 5:22-23

But the fruit of the Spirit is love, joy, peace, patience, kindness, goodness, gentleness, faithfulness, and self-control ...

When a big college or pro football game occurs, the experts will compare the different facets of the teams and determine which is the stronger in each area. The team with the stronger component is given the X. The team with the most Xs, Texas, will be favored to win this game.

Texas-Nebraska Comparison		
Area	Texas	Nebraska
Quarterback	X	
Running Back	X	
Offensive Line		X
Receivers	X	
Kicking Game		X
Defensive Line	X	
Linebackers	X	
Defensive Backs		X
Intangibles	X	
Coaching	X	

When you compare a believer who is solid in Christ in all phases of his or her life to an unbeliever who does not have the Holy Spirit, the comparison is one sided. It's no contest. The believer who is strong in obedience to Christ will ache for those who are unsaved, find joy in difficult circumstances, and consistently have more peace. The believer should usually have more patience, and kindness and goodness will be demonstrated through good deeds in the name of Jesus Christ. The believer should walk by faith, be gentle to his fellow man, and control his anger. A tall order? Certainly. Infallible? Certainly not. But anything is possible with God. Is the believer better than the unbeliever? Certainly not. But the believer has one distinct advantage. The believer has been washed in the saving blood of Christ and received the seal of the Comforter, the Holy Spirit. Advantage: believer.

Fruit of the Spirit Comparison		
	Believer	Unbeliever
Love	X	
Joy	X	
Peace	X	
Patience	X	
Kindness	X	
Goodness	X	
Faithfulness	X	
Gentleness	X	
Self-Control	X	

Prayer: Father God, may I understand that I do have an advantage over those who are unsaved. Help me be pure so that I can consistently exhibit the fruit of the Spirit and bring honor, glory, and praise to your holy name. In the wonderful name of Jesus Christ, who is our precious Lord and Savior, amen.

FB57:
THE SIZE OF THE
FIGHT IN THE DOG

2 Corinthians 4:18

We look not at what can be seen but at what cannot be seen; for what can be seen is temporary but what cannot be seen is eternal.

When a college team like the University of Georgia signs a recruiting class, fans enjoy reading the statistics and swooning over the size of the players. Fans get excited when the team has signed a behemoth six-foot-six-inch, 325-pound offensive lineman or a six-foot, 215-pound running back with blazing 4.4 speed. The players look very impressive at first sight and on paper, but sadly, some of them will never play a down due to injury, bad grades, or simply not having a strong enough will to compete at the D-1 level. Despite the predictions of the experts, there is really no way to predict how each player will fare.

An old saying is what really counts is not the size of the dog in the fight but the size of the fight in the dog. You can see how big the dog is, but you can't tell what's in the dog's heart. The best coaches are able to identify how to get the most desire out of these players during the next four years.

"We look not at what can be seen, but at what cannot be seen. For what can be seen is temporary, but what cannot be seen is eternal" (2 Corinthians 4:18). The awesome speed and strength of each player is fleeting and temporary. As his speed decreases and strength is diminished, a player will eventually be replaced by a faster, younger, and stronger player. When the player is no longer able to compete and must retire, how will the player adjust to his new life after football?

If the player's faith in Jesus Christ is strong, he will have a much better chance of dealing with retirement from competition. If the player's heart is grounded in Christ, he knows that eternal awards await that are so much greater than the fleeting fame and fortune that he once experienced. A player who knows Jesus Christ personally will be able to find joy more often despite circumstances and become more productive for the kingdom.

Prayer: Father God, may I display a portion of the heart that you displayed when you fought for your life on the cross. Thank you for loving me so much that you would stay on the cross for me. In Jesus's name, amen.

FB58:
TAKE ONE FOR HIS TEAM

John 18:3-11

Jesus answered, "I have told you that I am He: if therefore you seek Me, let these go their way."

John 18:8

An admirable character trait displayed by a coach is when he is willing to give credit to his team for a win and take the blame for a loss. In this day of online blogs, Twitter, websites, and online newspapers all vying for attention, the writers and bloggers and radio hosts come looking for blood when the team loses. But the admirable coach will step up to the microphone and say, "I know you want to know what happened. The players played their hearts out. I didn't prepare us well enough. I didn't anticipate the defense they would use in the second half. I made a decision on fourth and three that I wish I had back. I should have kicked the field goal when we were down nine. It was my fault, and it's my responsibility to have us better prepared."

That coach essentially said, "Leave them [my players] alone. It's me you want." Even though he might have been fearful that admitting fault could cost him his job, those players will play even harder for him the next game.

Jesus took one for his team in the garden of Gethsemane. When Judas brought the Roman soldiers to arrest him with their weapons and torches, they were looking for blood. Jesus protected his disciples by asking, "Who is it you seek?" He asked the soldiers twice and said, "Take me." Jesus protected his disciples even though he knew they would flee at the first sign of danger.

There is no doubt that the disciples deeply appreciated the love that their Savior showed them when they didn't deserve it. Once they received the baptism of the Holy Spirit, they played their hearts out for Christ and changed this world forever.

Prayer: Father God, help me play my heart out for you this day. I could never repay you sufficiently. In Jesus's name, amen.

FB59:
YOUR DADDY
MUST BE CRAZY!

John 3:16-17

For God sent His Son into this world not to condemn it, but to save it.

John 3:17

This story was shared with me and our high school boys at open gym one evening by my brother in Christ, Paul Sligar. In the 1980s, two Class A teams in Mississippi vied for the final playoff spot to advance to the state playoffs. Tishimingo led by two points, 16-14, late in the fourth quarter and had the ball on the opponents' 40-yard line. There was not enough time left for a touchdown drive. The Tishimingo coach called his son, the quarterback, over to the sideline and said, "Son, I know this sounds crazy, but I need you to give the ball to our tailback. Tell him to run sixty yards in the wrong direction."

The QB said, "Dad, are you kidding?"

The coach replied, "Son, just trust me."

The QB relayed the play in the huddle, and the team drew a delay of game penalty because of the confusion. When the QB called the play again, the tailback said, "Your daddy must be crazy!"

But Tishimingo executed the play, and the tailback ran through the back of Tishimingo's end zone for a safety, which tied the game at 16-16. The game went into overtime, and Tishimingo scored a touchdown to win the game 22-16.

It turned out that the head coach had information none of his players had. He knew that his team needed to win the game by four points or more to advance to the state playoffs. Eventually, they placed their trust in his seemingly wacky advice and won the game.

God also has information that none of us have. He knows that we must commit our lives to Christ if we are to experience eternal life now and forever with him in heaven. It sounds wacky to give your life to a man who died on a cross two thousand years ago. But God knows how the game ends, and we must trust his advice. Place your trust in Christ and advance to the eternal playoffs in heaven.

Prayer: Father God, before I was a believer, I thought that the story was a crazy one. But I know it's real, and I can't wait to see how the story ends when I get to see Jesus face to face. In the precious name of my Savior and Lord, amen.

FB60:
RUNNING FIRST STRING
OR THIRD STRING?

Jeremiah 17:5-8, 29:11; John 21:19

Follow me.

John 21:19

A football team builds its offense around key players such as a triple-threat quarterback. If the first-string QB runs a 4.4 40-yard dash and has the arm to gun the ball sixty-five yards in the air, the offensive coordinator will use the full repertoire of plays to take advantage of his skills. However, this player is very difficult to replace when he is injured. If the second string quarterback is also injured and the third-string quarterback has 5.2 speed and can only make the short and medium throws, the coordinator must reduce his play calling to a few basic plays. This severe limitation enables the defense to put eight in the box and play the run much more aggressively, making it very difficult for the offense to score enough points to win the game.

We need to use our entire repertoire of kingdom plays to overcome the defense of the enemy. In his book *This Day with the Master,* Reverend Dennis Kinlaw points out that when we fail to surrender our lives completely to Christ, we force God to shrink the game plan that he has for our lives. God has key plays that he wants us to run, but if sins such as pride, selfishness, worry, and disobedience separate us from him, many kingdom plays must go back on his shelf. When we fail to develop our spiritual lives to the fullest extent, we limit his play calling from those suited for a first stringer to a third stringer.

God is much more concerned about our *availability* than our ability because it is God who empowers us to do things that we never dreamed we were capable of doing. We are all capable of sharing the gospel effectively through his unique plans for us and circumstances that he arranges in our lives.

What is the key to executing God's complete game plan? Jesus put it very simply. He said, "Follow me." Follow Jesus. God alone gives us the strength and power to execute his game plans, but we must do it through him. He must always be part of our plans. Apart from God, we can do nothing (John 15:5).

Prayer: Most holy, gracious, and merciful God, may I realize what an awesome contribution that I could be making to your kingdom. I want to commit myself to your plan for me, not my plan for me. I want to stand before you one day and know that you received my best. In Jesus's holy name, amen.

FB61:
JOE WILLIE'S SCARS

John 20:25-29, 2 Corinthians 5:7

Unless I see in his hands the print of the nails...I will
not believe.

John 20:25

Joe Willie Namath was one of the most popular players in football
during the 1960s and 1970s. "Broadway Joe" was an all-American
quarterback at Alabama and suffered his first knee injury during his
senior season. Namath played for the New York Jets of the upstart
American Football League. The AFL was the little brother to the
established NFL until Joe led the New York Jets to a 16-7 upset victory over the Baltimore Colts in Super Bowl III. Even though the
Jets were seventeen-point underdogs, Joe brashly guaranteed a win
at a poolside interview three days before the game. The incredible
upset helped position the AFL as the equal to the NFL, and the AFL
merged with the NFL two years later. The NFL teams were divided
into the American Conference and the National Conference, which
is how they are still divided.

   After his stunning Super Bowl victory, Joe played nine more seasons and had four serious knee operations. Eventually, Joe would
have both knees replaced long after his playing days were over.

Let's fast forward over twenty-five years after Super Bowl III to a steamy, hot summer night at Disney's Epcot. Becca, Allison, Jillian, and I had just spent a long day at Disney World. After the fireworks show, we boarded a small boat that stops at the various onsite Disney resorts. Nobody was talking. I think everybody was just drained from the heat. At the next stop, a man and his two young daughters boarded. The man and the girls took the seat directly behind us. *There is something vaguely familiar about his silhouette*, I thought. *He might be Broadway Joe! I can know for sure if I get a good look at his knees.* Very slowly, I leaned forward and peeked over my left shoulder. There was the proof: a foot-long, zipperlike scar on the inside of each knee. *I know it's him!* I didn't speak because if the people on the boat knew, he would have been swamped with autograph requests.

Joe and his daughters departed at the very next stop. As they walked toward their resort hotel, I turned to Becca and said in a medium voice, "Becca, you know who that was? Joe Namath."

Immediately, the boat came to life. A woman behind me said, "Joe Namath? Really? I can't believe he was on this boat."

A second woman gushed, "I *loved* Joe Namath." No one questioned me that I had made up the story. They took my word for it. After all, I had seen the scars.

Let's consider the reactions of the disciples when Mary Magdalene and the other Mary breathlessly shared their eyewitness accounts that the tomb was empty and Jesus had risen. The disciples didn't believe the women. They finally believed when Jesus appeared to them in the upper room.

All of them believed except Thomas. Thomas said he would believe only if he saw the scars and felt them. When Thomas saw the nail-scarred hands of Jesus eight days later, he exclaimed, "My Lord and my God!" Jesus replied, "Because you have seen Me, you believe. Those who do not see Me and believe are blessed" (John 20:28-29). Are you blessed? We cannot see his scars that saved us from the grave, but as believers we walk by faith, not by sight (2 Corinthians 5:7).

On that Disney World boat I sat smugly, knowing that I had seen what no one else did. But I was blissfully ignorant that many people on the boat knew what I did not know: that Jesus had taken the nails for each of us. It would be almost ten more years before I came to the heart knowledge of this most important discovery.

Prayer: Father God, thank you for the faith that enables me to believe even when I cannot see. Help me walk by faith, not by sight. I thank you for the scars that saved me for eternity when I finally believed. In Jesus's name, amen.

FB62:
IN SEASON AND OUT

2 Timothy 4:2

Preach the Word of God urgently at all times, whenever you get the chance, in season and out, when it is convenient and when it is not.

Many people believe that the state of Alabama has the most passionate college football fan base in America. There are several reasons, including proud winning traditions at the two major universities, which frankly dislike each other's program, and an absence of professional teams. It has long been said that there are two sports seasons in Alabama, football during football season, and football recruiting when the football season is over.

It appears that in the decade beginning with the year 2000 that there are two sports seasons in the SEC—football and football recruiting—that last twenty-four-seven, three hundred sixty-five days a year. At one time, there was a signing day in February for seniors, and this day was preceded by five or six weekends of college visits. Then juniors began announcing early verbal commitments at various times during the year. Because these announcements can happen at any time the way the current rules stand, you can have football recruiting news on any given day of the year.

Just as football and football recruiting extend the football year to all 365 days, Paul taught us in 2 Timothy that Christians should follow a twenty-four-seven, three hundred sixty-five-days-a-year schedule for sharing the gospel. He declared that there are two times for preaching the gospel urgently. Those times are when we are moved by the Holy Spirit, and on those days when we have the blahs and can't believe our efforts would be fruitful. We are placing way too much importance on ourselves when we believe that we need to be perfect in telling people about Christ. God will use the most feeble and botched attempts to draw people to his Son, Jesus Christ. Looking for opportunities to share the gospel and God's love should be on our minds each day when we leave the house and begin to interact with the public.

Prayer: Father God, help me realize that there are opportunities to share what you have done in my life at times other than Christmas and Easter. May I be obedient and have my eyes to see and ears to hear where you are at work and join you there. In Jesus's name, amen.

FB63:
OUR TWELFTH MAN

Psalm 46:1, Daniel 3:12-25

Then Nebuchadnezzar the king was astonished, and rose up in haste, and spake, and said unto his counsellors, "Did not we cast three men bound into the midst of the fire?" They answered and said unto the king, "True, O king." He answered and said, "Lo, I see four men loose, walking in the midst of the fire, and they have no hurt; and the form of the fourth is like the Son of God."

Daniel 3:24-25

Texas A&M University fans support their football team with great passion. Perhaps their passion is best exemplified by the tradition of the twelfth man. This tradition was recently ranked number three of all college football traditions. Kyle Field earns its nickname, "The Home of the Twelfth Man," from this tradition of the team and the pride of many fans that stand throughout every game. When Coach Dana Bible was shorthanded in a game against Centre College in 1922, he asked former player E. King Gill to be his twelfth man in case his team needed him. Gill did not play in the game but stood on the sidelines throughout the game just in case. The Aggie fans never forgot the extra man who stood ready if needed.

The extra man on the Aggie sideline reminded me of Meshach, Shadrach, and Abednego, the three Hebrew lads in the book of

Daniel. They told King Nebuchadnezzar that they believed that God would save them from harm and, furthermore, that they would never bow down to worship his golden idol. The furious king ordered the furnace to be heated seven times hotter than usual, a fire that was so hot that the men who heated the furnace died. The three lads were bound and cast into the furnace. Yet when the king and his court looked into the furnace, the boys were walking around, unharmed, with not one hair on their heads singed. Furthermore, they also had an extra man walking with them, a man who looked an awful lot like the Son of God. Many theological experts believe that the extra man was Jesus Christ.

When all was said and done, God proved to be stronger than Satan, as he always is. God stands by us and is our "ever present help in time of trouble" (Psalm 46:1). The Holy Spirit will be your extra man if you will allow it. How awesome it is that we can always turn to God when the odds are overwhelmingly against us.

Prayer: Father God, thank you for your presence and for the presence of Jesus Christ, the extra man, in my life. Most of all, thank you for the sacrifice that Jesus made for me on the cross. I give you the honor, the glory, and the praise. In Jesus's name, amen.

FB64:
A STARTER'S ATTITUDE

Philippians 2:17, 4:12

I've learned by now to be quite content, whatever my circumstances...

Philippians 4:12

My friend Kevin told me about his experiences and attitude as a member of the scout team on his high school team in the Canadian province of Prince Edward Island. Kevin's story was very much like Rudy; he never got to play in the games but was dedicated to helping his team win on Friday night. As he described the practices, he said, "I was a starter four days a week," which I thought was a really cool attitude. True, he didn't get the accolades on Friday night as he stood on the sideline with the team, but he had the satisfaction that he had done everything he could to get his teammates ready for the game.

My dad played on the scout team at Hamilton (Alabama) High School in the 1920s. He was smaller than the other players, but he kept using his quickness to break up the offensive team's plays despite wearing makeshift football shoes with metal Coca-Cola bottle caps nailed to the soles for traction. Dad's high school coach, who played some college football, sent word that if Dad kept coming out for football, that he "was going to get killed." Yet Dad tried his hardest although he too would never play a down of varsity football.

Wouldn't it be great to have the same attitude for Christ, doing whatever God puts in front of us without hesitation or complaints and doing it for his glory and not ours?

God has a plan for each of our lives, but that plan might not call for us to be the star players. The plan calls for us to love God and be obedient to him. If we will be faithful and stick it out, our just rewards will come in heaven. As believers, we can take a page out of these scout team experiences and commit to work day in and day out for God wherever he needs us. No matter how obscure the circumstances, God can and will do great and mighty things through us and for us.

Prayer: Father God, even if I get no credit, may I burst with joy from the opportunity just to be on your team. Help me realize that my eternal reward is to join you in heaven. May I never grow tired of serving your kingdom. When I stumble and fall, please pull me back on my feet and get me back in the game of life. In Jesus's name, amen.

BASKETBALL

BK35:
IT'S AMAZING

Luke 7:44-50

You can be forgiven all your sin in half the tick of a clock, and pass from death more swiftly than I can utter the words.

Evangelist Charles Spurgeon

An Aerosmith song from the late 1980s has a special place in my heart. Comedian and author Wayne Federman created an awesome six-minute highlight tape of Pete Maravich's greatest plays set to this song. The lyrics fit Pete's story so well that I thought this secular song was especially written for Wayne's video until one day my friend Neal said, "Oh, that's 'Amazing' by Aerosmith."

"I put the right ones out, and took the wrong ones in." Pastor Michael McQueen reminded our St. James UMC Bible study that bad company corrupts good habits (1 Corinthians 15:33). There is a reason your family wants to know if you are hanging with the wrong crowd.

"Had an angel of mercy to see me through all my sin." Take a moment to reflect on times that God has sent an angel of mercy, an angel of protection, or a guardian angel that took you through dangerous situations. You will never really know how many times until you see the replay in heaven.

"There were times in my life when I was going insane, trying to walk through the pain." We cause ourselves pain by trying to walk through situations and decisions in life without allowing our Father to be in control. If God is in control, he can make those seemingly insane times bearable. Certainly Jesus lived through his share of insane moments with the self-righteous Pharisees, the incredibly painful walk on the pathway to Golgotha, and the hurtful desertion of the disciples during the final hours of his crucifixion.

"In the blink of an eye, you finally see the light." You can walk in darkness for many years until you finally admit it's not about you and what you can do but it's about Christ and what he did for you, how he died for your personal sin. When you admit before your Most High God that Jesus died for your sins on the cross, God will change you in the blink of an eye. You will no longer walk in spiritual darkness, and you will begin to walk in the light. It's amazing what happens when the Holy Spirit comes into you the moment you receive Christ into your cleansed self.

Are you discouraged by a family crisis? Have you been deserted by a friend? Are you struggling in school? You've got nothing to lose and everything to gain. Just let God do what he can do. Let go and let God. Pete Maravich finally let go, and I finally let go, and God changed us for eternity. He changed us, and he can change you. "In the blink of an eye, you finally see the light."

Prayer: Dear Father, thank you for the lyrics that Wayne Federman overlaid on the Maravich video. The video spoke to me, and it can speak to others. Thank you for the lyrics and videos that can help us communicate your transforming power and grace. In Jesus's name, amen.

BK36:
SEE THE FLOOR

Matthew 2:1-12

When they saw the star, they rejoiced with exceeding great joy.

Matthew 2:10

One of the most exciting plays in basketball is the fast break. The purpose of the fast break is to move the ball as quickly as possible down the floor before the defense gets back. A well-timed fast break will result in a lay-up, slam dunk, or three-pointer. A successful fast break energizes the crowd and fills the team with confidence and energy. My father taught his high school teams a great fast break, and several times his teams scored over a hundred points in a regulation game.

When the player in the middle of the break dribbles with his head up, he can see all of the passing and driving options in front of him. Even better is to have a player with excellent peripheral vision to see players with a 180-degree vision. People thought that Pete Maravich must have had eyes in the back of his head the way that he passed the ball to teammates who were trailing him on the break. It's important for young players to learn to dribble with their heads up so that they can see the floor. When your head is down, you can't see where you are going, and you won't see the players who are open on the wing or breaking to the basket.

The three wise men who came from the east had their heads up to see and follow the star. They kept looking up to follow the star until it stopped above the manger. The wise men paid attention to God's calling and the clues about Jesus's birth. They were very brave because they could have been killed by Julius Caesar for finding Jesus and not killing him.

It's important to look to God each day for guidance in living as a Christian. By keeping our heads up spiritually, we can be ready to make the right plays as we live out each day for him. When we allow the world's cares to make us drop our heads in sadness, despair, or frustration, we miss the people to whom God would have us witness and we miss the blessings that God places in our paths. We need the power of God to keep our heads up and eyes alert for chances to serve the kingdom.

Prayer: Father God, thank you for the wise men who followed the star. Help me keep my head up when tough times happen so that I can still see the plays that you would have me make for your kingdom. In Jesus's name, amen.

BK37:
IT'S A SLOW FADE

1 John 3:4

For sin is the transgression of the Law.

I shared a random story at open gym about a highly touted high school prospect from Durham, North Carolina, named John Wall. John was rated the number-one point guard nationally. Apparently, John and his friends entered a vacant home without permission. Fortunately, no one was harmed. John received a misdemeanor and began his college career as planned.

I told the boys that it is important to walk with Christ each day because the further you get separated from God the worse your choices are likely to be. The worse your choices are the worse your consequences will be. The teenagers had no business being in that house. One choice can lead to another choice and then another until one day you find yourself in the wrong place at the wrong time. Casting Crowns offered a stirring song called "Slow Fade" that I played for the boys. "It's a slow fade, when you give yourself away … People never crumble in a day." I shared with the boys that I wanted them to be really careful over the summer and not do stupid stuff. You usually don't just do something really stupid unless you've done some less stupid stuff and gotten away with it. "Thoughts invade,

choices made, a price will be paid when you give yourself away…"
It can happen to anyone when he or she lets his or her guard down.
John Wall was very fortunate. He could have been shot for being
an intruder. His rise to fame made the story much more memorable. Wall signed with the University of Kentucky, arguably the most
storied program in the history of college basketball. Immediately, he
triggered a wave of enthusiasm and optimism in the Big Blue Nation
that had not been seen since the 1997-98 season. A few overzealous Kentucky fans called him Blue Jesus, a takeoff on former New
York Knicks star Earl "The Pearl" Monroe's playground nickname
of Black Jesus. Wall's explosive speed to the basket with the ball is
unparalleled, and he was the number one pick in the 2010 NBA
draft. He led the Wildcats to an SEC championship, an Elite Eight
appearance, and a 35-3 record. During the season, Wall endeared
himself to UK fans by handling himself with poise, humility, and
teamwork and played extremely hard at both ends of the floor.
During the first semester, John had the highest GPA on the team
and made the Freshman Academic All-SEC team during second
semester. But it could have all been for naught if the circumstances
in that house had been different.

Prayer: Lord, thank you for the mercy that you have shown
me many times when I've done stupid stuff and I didn't receive
what I deserved. I thank you for your patience with me and your
guiding hand that gives me a chance to convert for you. In Jesus's
name, amen.

BK38: BEWARE OF TECHNICAL FOULS

John 14:26, Romans 8:26, Ephesians 4:29

Don't use bad language. Say only what is helpful and good to those you are talking to, and what will give them a blessing.

Ephesians 4:29

My father and father-in-law were both high school basketball coaches and principals. My dad, Coach Lester Farr, coached over 1,200 ball games and received only three technical fouls. That's one per decade, which is pretty doggone amazing. Once, he was convinced that the officials were calling too many fouls on his team. Dad called a time-out and told his player in the huddle loud enough for the official to hear, "Virginia, when that girl comes near you, I want you to run up in the stands so that you can't foul her." Whistle, T!

My father-in-law, Damon Ray, also helped the officials from time to time when he was the principal at East Hardin High School in Kentucky. Ray enjoyed roaming the far sideline while the game was in progress to keep an eye on the officials. One official said to him, "Are there twelve of you? You're over here under the basket, you're over there, and then you're under the other basket." Another official came over and tried to put his lanyard and whistle around Ray's neck, indicating, "You're going to help us anyway." When he passed away in 2008, the funeral services were appropriately held in that gymnasium to accommodate the crowd.

A technical foul should be called when an official feels that a player or coach has exceeded the proper decorum via unsportsmanlike conduct such as swearing or arguing too much. A certain amount of tension is expected in hard-fought games, and a well-timed technical foul can diffuse a volatile situation and keep the game under control.

Our conscience combined with the Holy Spirit lets us know immediately when we have overstepped our bounds through anger and improper speech. The moment we snap at someone or are rude to someone, no matter how irritating the person was, our conscience/ Holy Spirit calls a T on us. If it's bad enough, I get that sinking feeling in my stomach and yucky taste in my mouth, and that's the technical foul. It's time for an immediate apology when that situation occurs. Then you're freed up to stay connected with God, or else you'll be riding the pine until you come clean.

Prayer: Most wonderful Father God, thank you for my conscience and the Holy Spirit that whistles those actions that I wish I could take back. Help me have the courage to follow through and apologize when I should and as I should. In Jesus's name, amen.

BK39:
SOMETIMES YOU GOTTA
CUT SOME FOLKS LOOSE!

Proverbs 13:20

He that walks with wise men shall be wise, but a companion of fools shall be destroyed.

I was a starting guard on my high school basketball team as a fifteen-year-old junior at five feet six inches tall and 115 pounds. What a physical specimen. Our new coach, Coach Bowman, put our team through the most grueling conditioning program that any of us had ever experienced. The dividends certainly did not pay off during the first half of the season. In fact, we were 2-9 going into our road game at Adrian High School. At halftime that night, we were down by thirty-one, 62-31, when we hit rock bottom. Our two leading rebounders were giggling when Coach Bowman was talking, and the next thing we knew, they had quit the squad. To say we were discouraged when we left the gym that night would be an understatement.

However, things turned for the better. Coach Bowman revamped our offense and went with three guards to give us more quickness. Our superior conditioning paid off in the second half of games. We reeled off seven wins in our next ten games, including a stunning upset of the state's number-two-ranked team in our classification. There is no question that our team rallied and united to salvage the season after those two players left the team.

Sometimes it is necessary for us to disassociate ourselves from some folks who are dragging us into their sinful lifestyles. We're no better or worse than these folks. As Christians, we are supposed to associate with unbelievers because they need what we have, which is a relationship with Jesus Christ. Jesus said that he came to heal the sick, and he was certainly comfortable in the presence of sinners. However, Jesus never caved into their sinful desires. The line that we are not to cross is when we start committing the same sins as our friends. If we sense that they are dragging us into bad habits, it's time to hang with another crowd.

Paul focused solely on Christ when he preached to the Corinthians about their sinful lifestyles, but Paul never adopted their lurid habits. We get into trouble when we start to imitate lifestyles that are not of Christ. There is only one lifestyle that should be emulated, and that lifestyle is the sinless one exhibited by Jesus Christ. To follow the lifestyle of Christ, we might need to let some folks go who are dragging us through the mud. Sometimes we've just gotta cut some folks loose.

Prayer: Dear Father God, please help me realize right away when I'm being dragged into sinful living by others. Give me the godly confidence that I can hang with them and try to influence them for Christ without slipping myself. In Jesus's name, amen.

BK40:
PULLING ON THE
DOG'S EARS

Proverbs 21:9, 26:17

You get a mad dog by the ears when you butt into a quarrel
that's not of your business.

Proverbs 26:17

My wonderful wife, Becca, is a fervent University of Kentucky basketball fan. She converted me and our girls, Allison and Jillian, to
cheer for the Cats when the girls were very young. After all, it's
pretty easy to cheer for the winningest college basketball program of
all time. The knowledge, dedication, and passion of the UK fans is
second to none, and Becca is no exception.

I bought two center-court seats for a UK-Georgia game in
Athens, and we were the only people for Kentucky in that section.
Early in the game, she clacked her clacker shaker at a Georgia free
throw shooter. *Hmm. She's a little more fired up than usual,* I observed.
Midway through the first half, Georgia's seven-foot, 275-pound
power forward gave UK's 180-pound point guard a shove from
behind on a drive to the basket on a fast break. The UK player flew
through the air like Superman and landed on his chin at the feet of
the Georgia cheerleaders. He lay motionless on the floor and left

the game with a concussion. Becca was infuriated. She leaped out of her seat in a flash and yelled at the official, "Call an intentional foul! That was intentional! C'mon!"

That's when the Georgia fan sitting to her right made his first mistake. He commented loudly and condescendingly, "*That* wasn't intentional."

Becca whirled around and said, "Bull! He shoved him on purpose!"

Trying to diffuse the situation, I told the guy, "Look, she thinks she just lost her point guard for the season. Just let it go."

Ten seconds later, I heard, "Don't you touch me!" He placed his hand on her shoulder to tell her something else, and that was his second mistake. If you are a stranger, you don't touch my wonderful wife when she is emotional about her Wildcats!

I had always wanted to meet former Bulldog Herb White because Herb played against Pete Maravich at LSU and with Pete on the Atlanta Hawks. Herb was sitting below us, but I thought, *That can wait until another day.*

Do you realize that the Bible addresses this type of situation? I never realized it until I read Proverbs 26:17 one day. This gentleman had no business touching Becca, and he didn't have any business commenting on the disagreement between Becca and the referee. The Bible makes it clear in the book of Proverbs that intervening in an argument between two people is as foolish as pulling on a dog's ears. Many people read one Proverbs chapter a day, 31 chapters in a month, for knowledge, wisdom, and discernment. Study Proverbs to expand your knowledge for daily living and stay out of trouble.

Prayer: Dear heavenly Father, thank you so much for the wisdom that can be gleaned from studying the book of Proverbs. Help me to absorb the knowledge that will keep me in step with your intentions for my daily walk. In Jesus's name, amen.

BK41:
IT'S A LONG SEASON

Psalm 119:105, John 14:26, 1 Thessalonians 5:17

Pray without ceasing.

1 Thessalonians 5:17

A top major college basketball team will play between thirty-five and forty games in a five-month season. After two-a-day practices in October, teams will usually open their season against weaker opponents in November before playing tougher games in December. The team plays its conference season in January and February when the really tough games occur. Then comes the conference tournament in March, and if the team has performed well enough, the reward of March Madness awaits. The best teams will reach the pinnacle of the Final Four on the first full weekend in April, and one team will be crowned NCAA champion for the season. Next comes personal training and preparation over the spring and summer.

Before each game the point guard must learn the particular defenses that the opponent will use to thwart the team's offense. The trickier the defenses the more preparation is necessary. The point guard is especially important since he or she initiates the offensive plays. If the point guard simply relied on prior knowledge and failed to practice for the next team's defense, he or she would throw the wrong pass or run the wrong offensive plays, which would create more turnovers than assists and fewer points. If the point guard commits too many turnovers, he or she will end up on the bench and possibly lose a starting position for several games or the entire season.

As a Christian, you can't rely on what you learned in Sunday school or from the sermon and expect that you will get through the week on that practice. There are games to be played every day as Satan throws different wrinkles, situations, temptations, and obstacles at you to trip you up. These obstacles are specifically designed to get you to commit sin (turnovers). That's why you must practice each day, praying with God and reading his Word, to minimize the mistakes (turnovers) and maximize the good deeds (assists) in the name of Christ.

Most medicines for illnesses and maintaining good health are taken daily. You can't take seven pills in one day and optimize your physical health all week. You need a steady dosage. It's that way with prayer and Scripture. A steady daily dose of prayer and Scripture will keep your spiritual health in good order. Refuse to take any days off with God, and you'll see your assist-to-turnover (good deed to sin) ratio improve dramatically. With the Holy Spirit living in you and Jesus living in your heart, you've got plenty of help to make the right plays for God. You'll get through the long season in flying colors for the kingdom.

Prayer: Father God, thank you that I get the chance to practice daily by praying and reading your Word. Help me be consistent so that I'm always ready for the trick defenses that Satan throws my way. May I always honor you in all that I do. In Jesus's name, amen.

BK42:
KAY YOW (1942-2009)

Romans 8:18

Yet what we suffer now is nothing compared to the glory
that we will receive later.

For more than thirty years, women's basketball coaches sought guidance from Kay Yow, the head women's basketball coach at North
Carolina State University. An undeniable legend in the sport, her
bio reads like an excerpt from College Basketball's Most Desirable
Accomplishments. But when thumbing through the pages of that
biography, you'll discover that Yow's fiercest competitor wasn't on
the court.

Four times, Yow was diagnosed with breast cancer, most recently
stage IV in 2008. But like any other rival, she showed up for cancer's
game, determined to fight. In an interview with *Sharing the Victory*,
the magazine of the Fellowship of Christian Athletes, Kay explained
her faith and the source of her strength to fight cancer on four different occasions.

STV: "Have you ever wondered why cancer happened to you?"

KY: "I've never questioned why I have cancer. I have an idea, but
I know that God has a plan for me, and I just try to trust his plan
and what it is that he wants me to do. That is the main thing. I do
know that he loves me and that it is a love that is deep. I know he

wants the best for me. I feel sort of fortunate to even get a little bit of an answer. I wouldn't expect one, but I don't want to miss what he wants me to get out of all of this."

Prayer: Father God, thank you for the inspiring legacy of Kay Yow. May I learn from the trust and faith that she placed in you that I can overcome the obstacles in my life by relying on you to be my strength. In the holy name of Jesus, amen.

BK43:
"PISTOL PETE" MARAVICH
(1947-1988)

Ecclesiastes 2:11

Yet when I surveyed all that my hands had made, and what I had toiled to achieve, everything was meaningless. A chasing after the wind, nothing was gained under the sun.

Pete Maravich is recognized as one of the legends in the game of basketball. "Pistol Pete," who got his nickname from a sportswriter because he shot from the hip in the eighth grade, became the all-time leading scorer ever in college basketball. His popularity reached an all-time high for a college basketball player during his three-year career at Louisiana State University. He averaged just over 44 points a game when freshmen could not play on the varsity, and there was no three-point line!

Despite his success on the court, Pete was miserable off the court. He shared some of the many things he tried to satisfy his soul. At the depth of his despair, Maravich remembered the message of hope that he heard at a Campus Crusade for Christ event in San Bernardino, California in 1966, just before entering LSU.

"At the height of my popularity, I was miserable. I plunged into karate, Hinduism, reincarnation, TM, and UFOs. I became a radical nutritionist and a vegetarian. I took life-extending drugs from Eastern Europe ... Then I began thinking, 'Why am I here? Is this all there is to life?' I had rejected Christ at nineteen and gone back into the wilderness, and I hated it.

"In 1980, I quit basketball out of pride and immaturity. I was so bitter I divorced myself from everything in basketball. I stayed home, changed my phone numbers, and moped for two years. Then one fateful night in November 1982, I could not sleep. All the sins of my youth kept parading through my mind all night. I cried out to God, suddenly remembering the gist of the prayer offered at that Campus Crusade for Christ sixteen years earlier. I asked Jesus to come into my life. Nothing gave me the peace that Jesus gave me that night."

Pete was transformed that evening and dedicated his life to sharing Jesus Christ with as many people as possible through speaking engagements and his basketball camp in Clearwater, Florida. In 1988 he died tragically on a basketball court at the Church of the Nazarene in Pasadena, California, while playing the game he loved with Dr. James Dobson and his friends.

Prayer: Father God, thank you for the lessons that I can learn from Pete's life. No matter how much fame and success that I have as measured by the world's standards, only Jesus Christ can ever satisfy the longing that I have within my soul. In Jesus's name, amen.

BK44:
DAVID ROBINSON

Matthew 5:14

You are the light of the world. A city that is set on a hill cannot be hidden.

If David Robinson had not been a late bloomer, he would have never entered the US Naval Academy. The academy will not allow anyone over 6 feet 6 inches tall to enter Annapolis. That was David's height as a freshman, but he quickly grew five more inches! Nicknamed "The Admiral" while he was at Navy, Robinson became the most celebrated basketball player ever at Navy and enjoyed a stellar career as an Olympian and NBA World Champion with the San Antonio Spurs. David shares his story of receiving his "second birth" when he committed his life to Jesus Christ.

David Robinson has been called the Goliath of giving. For at least ten years beginning in the mid-90s, Robinson has given 10 percent of his substantial income to the David Robinson Foundation and has physically given his time and energy. Matthew 5:14 sets the tone and defines the work of his foundation. Robinson said, "God has given me more than I ever hoped for, so it's my responsibility to give back."

In an interview with Eads Home Ministries, David recalled the circumstances of his second birthday, which was the day that he received Christ as his Savior on June 8, 1991. David explained, "That day, Christ became a real person to me … I felt like a spoiled brat. Everything was about me, me, me. How much money can I make? It was all about David's praise and David's glory. I had never stopped to honor God for all he had done for me. That really hit me. I cried all afternoon. That very day, I was saved."

Prayer: Father God, thank you for David Robinson and the legacy of his foundation in San Antonio that has helped thousands of young people enjoy a better life. May I learn from David's generous giving of both time and money to honor you with gifts of my own. In the name of Jesus, amen.

BK45:
DO YOU WARRANT
A SPECIAL DEFENSE?

Psalm 21:11-13, Ephesians 6:10-18

Be strong in the Lord, and in His great power!

Ephesians 6:10

Suppose that you play on a NCAA Division 1 basketball team. If you are one of the weakest players and your grade point average is higher than your minutes per game or scoring average, you are surely a bench warmer who rarely gets into the game. The opposing team doesn't do any special preparation to stop you since you don't score points. You probably aren't a threat to them defensively either.

But pretend that you are the leading scorer on your team. In fact, you lead the conference in scoring at thirty points per game and ten assists per game. You are a bona fide, prime time superstar. The opposing teams plot late into the night to slow you down and take you out of your game. The opponents will try trick defenses, double teams, and aggressive defenders. The opposing coach will do anything that he can to make you less productive.

Take an unbeliever, a person who does not know Jesus Christ and has not accepted Christ as Savior or a lukewarm Christian who has stopped working for the Lord because of some stronghold that has separated the person from God. Folks who are separated from God are of no threat to Satan. These people have the same abilities and talents as believers do, but they aren't wired to God.

But if you are a believer with a passion for reaching the lost, you had better know that Satan is burning the midnight oil trying to shut you down. Satan is probing every nook and cranny to find the chinks in your armor. It could be lust, or a sports team, or a sport, or money, or positional power, or selfishness that Satan uses to take you out of your game.

Satan doesn't follow the rules and will use any scheme possible to deceive you. The devil will throw up distractions, obstacles, doubts, half-truths, diversions, and selfish desires to derail you. If Satan can derail a pastor or a believer, it could mean hundreds of people will not come to know Christ.

You need God's incomparably mighty power and protection from Satan's schemes more than ever before. Be wary that Satan is out there, waiting to thwart you, just like the teams that go up against the superstars. Know that daily you need God's special power through his Word and frequent prayer to continue to shine his light.

Prayer: Father God, thank you so much for the tools you give me to ward off the evil clutches and ways of the devil. You are so much stronger, and the devil knows it, and I know it. Flee from me, Satan, because I have God's mighty power through Jesus and the Holy Spirit. In Jesus's name, amen.

BK46:
GOT ENOUGH POINTS?

Ephesians 2:9

Not because of works, lest any man should boast.

"Pistol Pete" Maravich was one of the all-time greatest basketball players and is recognized as the most innovative player because he changed the face of basketball with his spectacular Showtime array of passing and dribbling wizardry. Pete became a tremendous evangelist for Christ after his playing days ended and traveled the country and the globe proclaiming the good news through his powerful testimony. God still uses Pete because when the latest hotshot guard comes along, there is a leap back in time to compare the latest phenom to Pistol. That's one way the legend of Pete Maravich is remembered. There are several hundred videos of Pete Maravich on YouTube so young people can marvel at his tremendous skills and hear his testimonies.

Pete shared this story in one of his testimonies to illustrate that you cannot earn your way to heaven no matter what title you hold or how great your accomplishments are. Only by the grace of God are we saved.

A senior pastor approached the pearly gates and was greeted by St. Peter, who told him that he needed a hundred points to get into heaven. The pastor proclaimed that he had been the senior pastor at a five-thousand-member church.

"One point," St. Peter replied.

Somewhat perplexed, the pastor said, "Well, I started four orphanages."

"Two points," came the reply.

"I served dinner to fifteen thousand homeless people every Thanksgiving."

"Three points. What about Jesus? Do you know Jesus?" asked St. Peter.

The pastor said, "Yes, I know Jesus Christ."

"That's worth a hundred points. Come on in," St. Peter said as he welcomed the pastor to heaven.

Certainly "faith without works is dead" (James 2:17). As Christians, we are recognized by the fruit that we bear once we are saved, but good works alone will never get us into heaven. First and foremost, we must know Christ to enter the gates of heaven. How many points do you have?

Prayer: Father God, thank you for your free gift of saving grace that cost Jesus his life. I am so thankful that I don't have to earn my way into heaven because I could never perform enough good works. But I appreciate the opportunity to show people through my works that Christ lives in me. In Jesus's name, amen.

BK47:
YOU CAN GO 1-0!

Psalm 118:24, Matthew 6:25-33, Colossians 3:17

This is the day that the Lord has made, let us rejoice and
be glad in it.

Psalm 118:24

I want to sign Your Name to the end of this day.

Lifesong by Casting Crowns

Kentucky basketball is back thanks to coach John Calipari, who
brought in a slew of hotshot freshmen for the 2009-10 season and
brought back a swagger that the Cats had been missing. In January
UK was 16-0 and ranked second in the country. Coach Cal was
the first to admit that there were several games that UK could have
lost but for the heroics of super frosh John Wall. On the day before
UK played undermanned Hartford, Cal was asked about UK's next
game after Hartford against bitter rival Louisville. Cal insisted that
he had watched no tape of Louisville and would not until after the
Hartford game. Calipari's approach is to take it one game at a time
no matter who the next opponent is and focus intently on the immediate game. By focusing on only one game, he relieves pressure on
the team from rabid fans who believe he can win 'em all.

I received an e-mail from Rick Johnson, the head coach of the
Trinity Lady Crusaders (Dublin, Georgia), who were also unbeaten

midway through the 2009-10 season with a perfect 17-0 record. Coach Johnson acknowledged that the winning streak was exciting, but he said that he controlled the pressure by trying to go 1-0. Each game is a mini-season. You start 0-0. If you win the game, you're 1-0. Then you go back to 0-0 and get ready for the next one.

You and I can choose to go 1-0 or 0-1. God gives us one day at a time, and each day, we decide how we will spend it. We can worry and ignore God and try to do it all ourselves or we can rejoice in the day he gives us and live it for him. Start each morning in the Word and talk to God. This pre-game preparation before we come out of the tunnel (go through the front door) gives us a great chance to live that day for God. With God by our side throughout the day, we've got a great shot at going 1-0 by putting up a W for God and hanging an L on the biggest loser of all time. You could go 0-1 by compartmentalizing God and intentionally not allowing him to come to work or school with you. "Hey, God," and, "Good night, God," with nothing in the middle won't cut it. He is interested in everything we do and yearns to help us if we will only look to him.

Can we possibly go 30-0 for God? It seems impossible, so take it one day at a time and go 1-0 again and again. Going 1-0 doesn't mean without sin, but it does mean obedience. God always gives us sufficient strength for today. Today has plenty of challenges without worrying about tomorrow. Today I had a 1-0 mindset, and it paid positive dividends. I've got a shot at putting together a win streak come tomorrow.

Prayer: Most wonderful and mighty God, help me go 1-0 today as a person, as a friend, as a servant, as a brother or sister in Christ, as a disciple. When my head hits the pillow tonight, I want to know that I put this day in the win column for you. In the name of the One who took my place, amen.

BK48:
HOW WILLING ARE
YOU TO STAND UP FOR ME?

Matthew 10:32-33

Whosoever therefore shall confess me before men, him
will I confess before My Father which is in heaven.

Matthew 10:32

During a testimony in Shreveport, Louisiana, Pete Maravich once
shared this story, which he heard from a man who had been an
interpreter at a Billy Graham crusade in Tokyo, Japan. The story,
which is one of courage in the face of death, occurred during the
sieges by Communist North Korea to stamp out Christianity, which
is booming in South Korea today, perhaps because of many stories
like this one.

"There were these Northern Koreans, about two hundred of
them, who rounded up all the Christians in this little town (in South
Korea). They made them all go inside their little church at the end
of town, and the Northern Koreans said, 'All right. We're going to
line you up single file. You're going to walk by this picture of Jesus
Christ (which they had nailed to the inside of the front door), and
you're going to spit in your Messiah's face. If you don't, you'll be shot
in the head.' The first person was a man, and he walked by and spit

in Jesus's face. The second man walked by and spit in his face. The third man walked by and spit in his face, as did the fourth. The next person in line was a little girl. She walked up to the picture of Christ, took her dress, and wiped the spit away. Then she said, 'Jesus, I love you, and I am willing to die for you.'"

This act of courage completely flabbergasted the Northern Koreans, and they yelled, "Get out! Everybody get out!" Later, they said that the reason they let everybody go was that to be a good Communist, you would need the undeniably strong faith of that young Christian girl. Then they took the four men who spit in Christ's face and shot them dead.

Prayer: Most Holy and powerful God, I will likely never face a situation quite like the one that young girl faced, but I might face opportunities to deny you to the world. May I have just a portion of that young Korean girl's amazing courage to stand up for Jesus Christ. In Jesus's holy and precious name, amen.

BK49:
THE POWER OF THREE

John 14:16-26

And I will pray the Father, and He shall give you another
Comforter, that he may abide with you forever.

John 14:16

I've observed over the years that any basketball team needs three
reliable scorers to be a consistent winner. During the 2009-10 season, Kentucky typically had at least three reliable scorers. However,
when they played at South Carolina, there were only two, and those
two could not score enough to prevent their first loss. A team needs
an inside scorer, a good outside shooter, and a guard who can pen-
etrate the lane and get off his shots. When a team is in trouble,
they're going to need the three-point shooter, the inside force, or
the slashing drive to the basket. That balance makes for an excellent
offensive team.

John 14:16 and John 14:26 refer to all three members of the Holy
Trinity: God, Jesus, and the Holy Spirit, who Jesus sometimes called
the Comforter or Helper. It's very unusual to see a reference to all
three in the same verse. For sure you need the help of all three to
become who you need to be in Christ. First of all, God, Jesus, and
the Holy Spirit existed before the beginning of time because God
invented time and space when he created the world in six days and

rested on the seventh. God created Adam and Eve, who lived in paradise until the fall when they were tricked by the guile of Satan. The world eventually multiplied, and generation after generation tried but failed to keep the Ten Commandments that God gave Moses on Mount Sinai for the people of Israel.

So God sent Jesus who died for our sins and rose from the grave, and Jesus sent the Holy Spirit after his ascension to heaven. God the Father, Jesus, his Son, and the Holy Spirit, the Comforter and Helper. We are Christians, believers, and children of God when we have Jesus in our hearts and have received the Holy Spirit. We need all three members of the Holy Trinity.

Jesus told his disciples, "I will be with you always, even to the end of the world." But we also received a bonus from Jesus. That bonus is the Holy Spirit, a person who dwells in us. Jesus also called the Holy Spirit the Spirit of Truth. Depending upon the situation, you can call upon the One (Jesus) when you need an intercessor, or the One (God) who loves you so much that he sent the One (Jesus) to the cross to die for our sins, or the One (Holy Spirit) who lives inside us as a person who fills in our prayer gaps and helps us with our daily problems. All three will never leave nor forsake you and will be with you always. When you receive Christ, you place yourself into eternity *now* and receive access to the three who have the power to transform the worst of sinners.

Prayer: Dear holy and precious Father, I don't really understand why there are three, but I am grateful for what each of you do in my life. I can never thank you enough, but I will try each day to count my blessings and learn to rely on you throughout all circumstances. In Jesus's holy name, amen.

BK50:
HMM ... I WONDER WHAT
MY NEW NAME WILL BE

Revelation 2:12-17

And I will give him a white stone, and on the stone a
new name written which no one knows except him who
receives it.

Revelation 2:17

At my Friday morning Bible study group, my friend George and
I swapped high school basketball stories from the glory days.
Apparently, he got up the nerve to ask his coach on behalf of his
teammates if the team could have their last names on the backs
of their jerseys. His coach replied, "Son, if you put it in the basket enough times, they will know your name." That was the end of
the discussion. Some teams are adamant about not having players'
names on jerseys. Penn State football, Indiana basketball, and the
New York Yankees come to mind, and those teams have three pretty
good pedigrees over the years.

I have a collection of Pete Maravich throwback jerseys. All but
one, the LSU jersey where Pete saw his most fame, have "Pistol" or
Maravich on the back. In his seventh pro season, Pete switched from
"Pistol" to Maravich after the NBA foolishly outlawed nicknames

at a time that the NBA desperately needed to market its star players. By the way, Pete's senior LSU home jersey was auctioned for $103,500, a record at the time.

When I first refereed college basketball, a veteran official named Robert "Poochie" Hartsfield helped break me into the leagues. As we drove to Columbus or Savannah for games, Poochie, who worked as a pro baseball scout during the spring and summer, regaled me with stories of ACC and SEC games. Poochie once bragged, "Had (Coach Adolph) Rupp for four of his twelve home losses (at Kentucky), he ain't said a word to me yet." A Tulane coach told Poochie that he would never again referee at his gym. Poochie replied, "I've been through five Tulane coaches, and I'll be here when you're gone." The Tulane coach was fired after that season, and sure enough, Poochie sent him a letter.

My favorite Poochie anecdote happened in Baton Rouge where Pete had already reached legendary status reminiscent of another great entertainer: Elvis. Pete was on his way to one of his twenty-eight fifty-point games before a vociferous, overflow crowd at LSU's Cow Palace. But Pete's dad, LSU Coach Press Maravich, was complaining about Poochie's lack of foul calls. Press screamed, "They're killing my son in the lane! Do something about it, Poochie!" At a dead ball in front of the LSU bench, Poochie strolled nonchalantly over to Press, looked at him, and said, "Coach, I'll take care of it. (Pause) What number is he wearing?"

Poochie was making a point to Press that his son and star player would not receive preferential treatment. But Poochie knew who number 23 was, and so did everybody in the arena and in college basketball. Maravich or Pistol wasn't on the back of his jersey, but Pete put it in the basket so many times to the tune of forty-four points per game, that every basketball fan knew his name.

Our sinful human nature cries out that we want everybody to know our names. We yearn for accolades and recognition, and sometimes we forget to give God the glory. For eternity, we will either get a white stone with our new names written on it, or we won't get one. Receiving a white stone with your name on it will be better than getting the number one jersey at the NBA draft, and millions of saints and angels will applaud in heaven.

Prayer: Father God, help me play not for my name on the back of the jersey but for the Eternal Coach I represent. May all the accolades that I receive be funneled directly to you for your glory. In Jesus's name, amen.

BK51:
HE'S ALWAYS
THERE FOR YOU

1 Peter 5:7, Hebrews 13:5

Let Him have all your worries and cares, for He is always thinking about you and watching everything that concerns you.

1 Peter 5:7

On February 10, 2010, my family and I celebrated my dad's ninety-seventh birthday with many former students dropping by to say hello. We ate steak for lunch. Imagine yourself living to be ninety-seven and eating steak. It's a testament to Dad's determination to take good care of himself, including his teeth. As Becca and I drove down that morning, I reflected on numerous good times that we've had together. As we passed my high school, one moment stood out as I recalled how my dad was there for me when I needed help.

I was a senior at West Laurens High School in 1971-72 during the first year that Laurens County's west side schools were consolidated. We had a pretty fair basketball team, and the excitement grew as we prepared to play Dublin High School for the first time. It was the classic "Old McDonald Had a Farm" serenade of the county school team by the Dublin students who must have thought they were some big city school in a town of fifteen thousand. We were 5-2, but Dublin was

8-0 and ranked number 2 in Class AA. An overflow crowd packed the Dublin gym, and the doors were closed thirty minutes before the girls' tipoff. We were down thirteen at the half but rallied in the second half to send the game into overtime. That's when we reeled off the first nine points in the overtime to seal the victory.

In the midst of that 9-0 run, I drew a charge against one of my best friends, who had transferred to Dublin. When Mickey fell on top of me, I caught a cramp in my right calf and screamed. As I writhed on the floor, Coach Wildes came out to see about me, and there was my dad. I don't know where he came from, but he got there as quick as a flash. I stayed in the game and made two free throws followed by an eighteen-foot jumper. My team was ecstatic as the game ended. West Laurens had upset Dublin.

I was unaware of Dad's presence during the game and didn't know where he was sitting. But I know he was thinking about me during the entire game. When I cried out and needed help, he was there in an instant. His love and concern brought him immediately out of the stands to make sure that I was all right. I have always appreciated that support when it appeared that I was injured.

Our relationship with God as believers has similarities. We are often unaware of God's presence during our trials and don't always sense his presence. But the scripture from 1 Peter 5:7 assures me that God is thinking about me and watching over me throughout the day. When I need help, God is there instantly when I reach out to him. God's love and concern for me is so infinite that he sent Jesus to the cross for me. My sin helped put Jesus there, but God's perfect love and grace kept him up there. Let's thank God every day for the unwavering love and support that comes only from God and his Son.

Prayer: Father God, thank you for my parents who were there to patch up my skinned knees, see me through disappointments, and to encourage and support me. May I return the same support for my children and their children and know that everlasting love comes from knowing Christ. Thank you for the Holy Spirit, who teaches me, leads me, and guides me. In the holy and wonderful name of our Savior, Jesus Christ, amen.

BK52:
HEAVEN'S FINAL FOUR

Jeremiah 29:11, Romans 5:8, 1 John 1:9,
John 3:16, Ephesians 2:8

But by grace you have been saved through faith ...

Ephesians 2:8

In October 2009, over three hundred NCAA men's Division 1 teams began practice with the same dream: to make it to the Final Four on the final weekend of March Madness. The first two weeks of the 2010 tournament were filled with stunning upsets. The sixty-five-team field eventually came down to the following four teams: Butler, Michigan State, West Virginia, and Duke. These teams battled for the ultimate prize to be crowned NCAA Men's Champion for 2010. Here is how the Final Four bracket looked as the teams prepared to play in Indianapolis.

2010 NCAA Men's Final Four Bracket

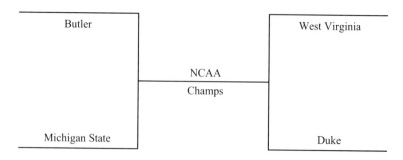

Just as four teams make it to the Final Four each season, there are four things that every person needs to understand about salvation. First, you are wonderfully and uniquely made (Psalm 139:14) by God, and God created a unique plan (Jeremiah 29:11) for your life. In his plan the Creator of the universe wants to get to know you.

Second, you are separated from God when you consciously break one of the Ten Commandments. When you break one, you have actually broken them all. Everyone who has ever lived has experienced this sinful separation from God (Romans 3:23), and if you don't address it, spiritual death (Romans 6:23) will occur.

Third, God loved us so much that even while you and I were sinners (Romans 5:8), he sent Jesus to be the bridge over the sin that separates us from God. Jesus even bore our sin in his body when he went to the cross (1 Peter 2:24). But the good news that we celebrate every day is that Jesus rose from the grave on the third day (Matthew 28:6).

God arranged the first three steps. Now you must take the fourth step and decide to exchange your sinful life for a new life in Christ. You must repent, or turn from your sinful life, and ask God to forgive you (1 John 1:9). After you repent, you must place your trust in Christ and accept God's gift of grace that gives you eternal life (Ephesians 2:8), admitting that your salvation only comes through Jesus Christ (John 3:16). Obey God daily by praying and studying his Word to grow in Christ in all aspects of your life (Proverbs 3:6).

God offers everyone his free gift of grace. You can pray these words to receive Jesus Christ into your life as your Savior. Keep in mind that your attitude and change of heart are more important than these exact words.

Prayer: Lord Jesus, thank you for dying for my sins on the cross. Please forgive all of my sins through your blood that was shed for me. I am so sorry for my sins, and I believe that you died for me. Jesus, I ask you to come into my heart. Thank you for your grace that brings me eternal life in heaven. Thank you for the Holy Spirit who now lives in my heart. Thank you for accepting me as a child of God. In Jesus's holy name I pray, amen.

Now consider these three statements one at a time. You cannot receive Jesus without admitting your sins and vowing to turn away from your sinful life. If you understand each statement and are willing to commit to each, you should pray and ask Christ into your life in your own words. Write your name under *saint*. You should receive the Holy Spirit and eternal life in heaven if you were sincere.

Heaven's Final Four

Step 1) God's Plan for Man	Step 3) Jesus Died for My Sin
Psalm 139:14; Jeremiah 29:11	Romans 5:8; 1 Peter 2:24; Matthew 28:6
(Wonderfully Made; Plan for Good)	(Loved sinner; My Sin His Body; Jesus is Risen)

Saint

Step 2) My Sinful Self	Step 4) Repent, Trust, Obey
Exodus 20:3; Romans 3:23;Romans 6:23	1 John 1:9; Eph. 2:8; John 3:16; Prov. 3:5-6
(Self idol; All sinned; Apart from God)	(Cleansed; Grace: Eternal Life; All Your Ways)

Check box if you sincerely intend to:

☐ Repent (turn from) all of your sin.

☐ Trust Jesus Christ as your Savior and Lord.

☐ Obey God by praying and studying his Word.

If you checked all three boxes, pray now for Jesus Christ to come into your heart. Write your name in the box under *saint*. Welcome to God's family as His child.

BK53: SWAPPING PINE TIME FOR PRIME TIME!

Matthew 28:19-20, Acts 1:8,
1 Corinthians 9:24-27, 2 Timothy 4:2

I don't want to be disqualified.

1 Corinthians 9:27

Deandre Liggins played the two (shooting guard) for the University of Kentucky Wildcats. During the 2008-09 season, Deandre logged solid minutes as the Cats suffered through a decidedly sub-par season. Liggins showed signs of brilliance, but he often took bad shots and played out of control like a frisky colt. A new coach, John Calipari, and three sensational freshmen breathed new life into the 2009-10 Wildcats, who were 25-1 and ranked second in the country. Obviously, three freshmen averaging double digits cut into the playing time of several returning lettermen, most notably Liggins.

One of the biggest surprises of the season was how far Liggins fell on the depth chart. The one thing that a basketball player wants more than anything is PT, playing time. After averaging sixteen minutes per game the previous season, Deandre did not play (DNP) in the first nine games. Every Division 1 basketball team has several walk-ons, and even the walk-ons played in the forty-point blowouts as Liggins rode the bench. Rock bottom came when Deandre sat against lowly Hartford. He had the same speed, quickness, jumping ability, and three-point shot as the previous season. So where was Deandre? Why wasn't he playing? Finally Cal played him against Indiana on December 12 for only one minute.

During the off-season, several players had transferred when the new coach and players came. As fall semester ended, Deandre must have been discouraged and surely considered transferring or quitting. But he stayed and didn't give up. In January, Deandre's playing time increased to twelve minutes per game. In February, it doubled to twenty-three. ESPN GameDay came to Lexington for Kentucky's biggest game of the season against Tennessee before a raucous Rupp Arena crowd and a national prime time audience. Liggins played a season-high twenty-eight minutes and responded with seven points, four assists, four rebounds, and several huge defensive plays, including a diving steal of a 50-50 ball that earned him a chest bump from Cal at midcourt.

Deandre swapped pine time for prime time. His inspired defense and experience paid huge dividends down the stretch as the Cats sought their eighth national title. Deandre *knows* what it is like to sit in the darkness at the end of the bench for over two months, and he practiced hard and followed his coach's instructions to earn his playing time.

Oswald Chambers taught in a *My Utmost for His Highest* devotion that God can choose to play us or bench us. Chambers shared that it is quite possible for God to set us aside if we are not of service to him. The Apostle Paul told the Corinthians that he never wanted to be in a position to be disqualified from sharing the gospel. Paul knew that when sin separated him from right standing with God, he would be DQ'ed (1 Corinthians 9:27) and miss opportunities to share Jesus Christ. Paul didn't want to miss one day sharing the gospel. In fact, Paul urged his fellow Christians to preach Christ urgently under only two conditions: when it is convenient and when it is not (2 Timothy 4:2).

As Christians, God holds each of us responsible for sharing Christ with other people. If we don't follow his game plan, he won't use us. God constantly tries to get us to change so that we can go from darkness to light. As we emerge from darkness into the light, our emotions could range from humiliation and embarrassment to utter relief and joy. When we are on the same page, God gives us more and more playing time in prime time. He puts more opportunities in our path. When we capitalize on these chances, it is possible to get into a wonderful grace spiral that brings joy to our lives and helps God increase his kingdom (John 3:30). It can be as simple as letting our lights shine (Matthew 5:16). When we allow God's light to shine brightly in our lives, we attract others to him.

Just as Cal rewarded Deandre with a chest bump, when we give our all for the kingdom, God is pleased and excited and just wants to chest bump us!

Prayer: Holy Father, thank you for your infinite patience with me. I want more playing time in prime time, and I realize that I need to be obedient. Help me grow through prayer and Bible study so that I will see more opportunities to share my faith and shine my light. Give me playing time today to help further your kingdom, Lord. In Jesus's name, amen.

Note: In 2011 an ESPN story broke that his eligibility was in question due to a former relationship with an AAU coach, and Liggins was eventually cleared to play. Deandre's diligence and perseverance paid off. He was selected in the second round of the 2011 NBA draft by the Orlando Magic.

BK54:
TORN ALLEGIANCE

Matthew 6:23

You cannot serve God and mammon (money).

Becca and I placed our daughters in quite a predicament the way we raised them. When we married in 1981, we owned strong allegiances to our respective flagship universities, UGA for me and UK for Becca. Kentucky won the 1978 national basketball championship, and UGA won the 1980 national football championship. She and I quickly agreed to root for each other's flagship program, which obviously was not a hard decision. Like their parents, Allison and Jillian became fervent UGA football and UK basketball fans. We have pictures of our girls in football stadiums and basketball arenas as we followed our teams around the Southeastern Conference.

Usually, the four of us attend the annual UK-UGA basketball game in Athens. The year 2009 was the eighth consecutive year that we had a daughter at UGA. Allison was there for the first four and Jillian for the last four. In 2007, when Jillian was a freshman, she sat with us at the game. I am incognito at these games, given my Bulldog lineage, but Becca is true Big Blue with a UK clicker shaker and plenty of swagger. In 2007, Jillian sat next to her mother, which made for a pressure cooker situation. Remember the pressure cooker your mom or your grandmother had? There was a pressure gauge that you could adjust to let off steam. At this game, to her left were several thousand of Jillian's newest UGA friends screaming their heads off for the Dawgs. To her right was her blue-bleeding mother yelling for the Cats. Jillian usually cheers vociferously at games, but that night, she was so torn about who to cheer for that she sat motionless throughout the game. Georgia rallied to beat UK in overtime. When Jillian left the arena, her blood pressure must have been up twenty points, and her stomach was in knots. She was tense and miserable because she never cheered for either team. I felt badly for her because she was so torn. Jillian had truly been between a rock and a hard place. Similar feelings must be felt by parents who have strong allegiances to one school, and their child plays at the rival university.

The Georgia-Florida football game has forty thousand in red and black and forty thousand more in blue and orange. There is a continuous buzz of noise throughout the game, but obviously, one half of the stadium cheers a good play while the other half is silent. Everybody in that stadium made a choice. Nobody could possibly cheer emotionally and devote themselves to both teams.

Just as you cannot commit yourself completely to two teams, the Bible teaches us that you can't serve God and money and that the love of money is the root of all evil. When you begin to love your money and hold it too close to you, you cut off the love for giving and helping others that God wants you to have. When you are tight-fisted, you can't accept the blessings that God wants to put into your hands because they are closed. From personal experience, too little money or too much money is a huge distraction. Just enough money seems to do the trick. When money becomes our little g-o-d, or any stronghold is placed above God, realize that more of anything other than God never will be enough. When God is truly our God, he is all that we need.

Prayer: Father God, may I be committed to you and not my money. When I have too little or too much money, help me seek your guidance. May I freely give of my time and my money to help you grow your kingdom. In Jesus's holy name, amen.

BK55:
BRACKET BUSTERS

John 4:7-26, 5:1-9, 8:1-12, 9:1-14

This day when Jesus made the paste and healed his blind-
ness was the Sabbath.

John 9:14

March Madness is one of my favorite events of the year. Office pools
break out all over America, and productivity drops as workers track the
scores of their favorite teams and sneak a peek at March Madness on
demand. I fill out my Final Four bracket, as will millions of basketball
fans who will try to pick the most winners, predict the teams that make
it to the Final Four, and hope for a shot at a $1 million prize with a
perfect bracket.

It's funny how people who don't know basketball sometimes pick
better brackets than the basketball junkies. The challenge is to pick the
teams who will be the surprises of the tournament. The mass appeal of
the tournament is fueled by the buzzer beater wins of the underdogs
that upset the favorites.

Here is a brief tutorial for those who don't follow the NCAA tournament. Play begins with sixty-eight teams. Four play-in games reduce
the field to sixty-four teams. There are sixteen teams seeded 1 (the
strongest) through 16 (the weakest) in each of four geographic regions:
East, South, Midwest, and West. In the first round, the 8 seed meets
the 9 seed, the 7 seed plays the 10 seed, and so forth, with the 1 playing

the 16. The experts call it an 8-9 game or a 7-10 game. A 12 upsetting a 5 is fairly common, and a 13 over a 4 or a 14 over a 3 happens occasionally. Only four times in twenty-five years has a 15 defeated a 2. The underdogs who pull off these stunning upsets are called bracket busters because they blow up your bracket after you picked a higher seed to advance.

But a 16 has never defeated a 1. The 16 seeds have a perfect 0-100 record in the first round. The closest call came when Princeton lost by one to Georgetown in 1989. Close, but no cigar. Below are the 1-16 matchups for the 2010 NCAA tournament: Kansas, Kentucky, Duke, and Syracuse, four of the top basketball programs of all time, versus Lehigh, E. Tenn. St., Vermont, and the University of Arkansas at Pine Bluff (aka UAPB). You can easily see what a mismatch these games are.

2010 NCAA Tournament

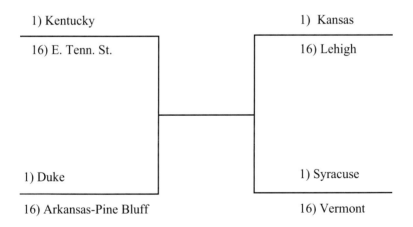

Just as the odds are highly stacked against the lowest seeded teams, the odds were highly stacked against the lowest seeded people of Jesus's day. Here is the way that the lowest seeds would have looked against the top seeds, who were the power brokers of the day.

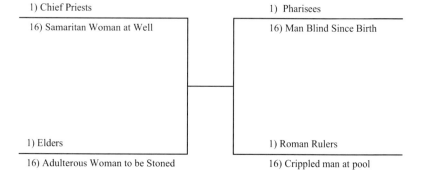

1) Chief Priests

16) Samaritan Woman at Well

1) Pharisees

16) Man Blind Since Birth

1) Elders

16) Adulterous Woman to be Stoned

1) Roman Rulers

16) Crippled man at pool

In a Jewish and Roman world that made outcasts of females, the weak, and the least fortunate, Jesus was the supernatural power behind these four bracket busters. Jesus asked the Samaritan woman for a drink of water and promised her living water if she would only believe. Not only that, but Jesus admitted to her that he was the Messiah, as she rightly guessed. At the Bethesda pool, Jesus raised up a man who had been crippled for thirty-eight years. Then Jesus made the mud paste and gave sight to a man who had been blind since birth. Not only that, but he did it on the Sabbath, which infuriated the Pharisees. Last but not least, Jesus drew in the dirt with his finger and told the self-righteous mob to throw the stones at the adulterous woman if any of them had never sinned. His action rescued the adulterous woman, and Jesus told her to sin no more. These two women and two men, all seemingly without hope, received the greatest upset victories of their lives. Through the love, kindness, and power of Jesus and the mercy and grace of God, countless others continue to have hope.

Prayer: Father God, thank you for sending us Jesus to give hope to the blind, the lame, the outcasts, and to all who have odds that appear to be insurmountable. Through your unconditional love, mercy, and grace, help me remember that all people have hope through Jesus Christ regardless of circumstance. In the holy name of Jesus, amen.

BK56:
GOD LOVES A CHEERFUL GIVER
(AND EVEN SELFISH ME)

Matthew 25:45, 2 Corinthians 9:9

God loves it when the giver delights in giving.

2 Corinthians 9:9

I flashed back to my mission trip with my church family to Cartago, Costa Rica. It was Tuesday afternoon, and suddenly, the temperature dropped about ten degrees, the skies darkened, and the rain poured down. Clouds would swoop in over the mountains into the valley with little warning. I learned to recognize that chilly air meant that rain was on the way. That afternoon, Pastor Danilo's son, David (pronounce Dah-veed), had been on a building supply run when he got caught in the downpour. When he walked into the shell of the church we were building, he was drenched from head to toe. I could see him shivering across the way. That is when I felt the urge of the Holy Spirit to help him. The inner conversation went something like this:

Holy Spirit: "I know that you see David shivering over there. Why, his teeth are chattering! Don't just stand there like a bump on a log. Give him the t-shirt that you are wearing. You have another one in the bag, but the one you have on will fit him. The other one is too small!"

Me: "No!" I said, clutching my University of Kentucky 7-time national champion t-shirt, a very prized possession.

Holy Spirit: "What do you mean, no? Do I need to hit you with a two-by-four? Take your shirt off your back and give it to David."

Me: "Oh, all right! I have learned in the past eight months that you won't leave me alone when I'm supposed to do something."

The t-shirt came off, and I handed it to David. He smiled broadly and said, "A million thanks!"

The next afternoon, David shows up at the work site and he has a gift for me. It's a brand-new shirt that he bought to replace the one that I gave him. He probably spent half a day's wages on it, and it has a great smell that masked the odor of my sweaty body. I could also use it to mask the odor of my sinful, selfish attitude from the day before. Boy, did I feel humble! Here I gave him an old, faded t-shirt for a brand-new shirt. Needless to say, I was completely touched by his generosity and gratitude. I proudly wore the new shirt to church Thursday night, where I gave my testimony to the congregation.

God loves a cheerful giver. He loves it when we help people less fortunate than ourselves. He also loves us when we don't cheerfully give. I seriously doubt that when I get to heaven and I receive my crown, there will be a jewel in the crown for my Wildcat t-shirt. But I learned an important lesson. When God prompts me to give, I don't want to waver. As believers, we have a close and personal Friend, the Holy Spirit, to remind us when we hesitate.

Prayer: Father God, thank you for the people of the Cartago church, who taught me so much about love and warmth during that mission trip. May all who read this devotion have a chance to experience the blessings that come from giving freely of themselves on a mission trip. In Jesus's name, I pray. Amen.

BK57:
WE'RE READY TO FLY

1 Thessalonians 4:14-18, Revelation 21:1-5

Behold, the tabernacle of God is with man, and he will dwell with them, and they shall be his people.

Revelation 21:3

One of the rites of passage of college students on a major college campus is camping out to get tickets to an important conference game. The most famous example of camping out is K-Ville, or Krzyzewskiville, on the Duke campus. Each basketball season, hundreds of students will spend not days but weeks living in a tented village to get the best seats for upcoming games. You have gotta love basketball and your team to spend the night studying and sleeping in sub-freezing temperatures for a two-hour basketball game, but there is no denying the dedication and fervor of the Cameron Crazies. Love them or dislike them, they set the pace when it comes to the degree of hardship endured to be the first inside the arena to watch their team play.

Pastor Bert Neal showed us slides from his trip to the Holy Land. One slide in particular captured my attention. He took a picture of a graveyard with graves above the ground. Now that's common in New Orleans, which is below sea level, but these graves were on a hillside. The hillside was the Mount of Olives, so there were people who carried rocks several hundred feet up the hill to build these graves for their loved ones. The hillside is so crowded with an estimated one hundred fifty thousand graves that there is barely room to walk between the graves.

Why would anyone want to be buried on a hillside? There is a very good reason. The hillside faces the east gate of the Jerusalem wall, and these people believed that when Jesus comes back there will be a new heaven and a new earth. They believed that Jesus will enter the east gate of the new Jerusalem and they wanted to be the first ones to meet him and enter the gates triumphantly with him. First Thessalonians assures us that the bodies of those who went before us will leap from their graves and receive glorious, resurrected bodies like Jesus has.

FFH, a popular contemporary Christian band, wrote a song called "Ready to Fly." The day that Jesus comes back and we meet him in the clouds, we will be united with him forever. That event should be one cool, amazing sight, and while it is a little scary to think about how it will happen, rest assured we will be perfectly safe with Jesus.

Prayer: Father God, thank you for the strong faith of those early believers who not only believed Jesus was the Messiah but were so sure that he would return that they wanted to be first into the new heaven and new earth with him. In Jesus's holy name, amen.

BK58:
TAKING ONE FOR HIS TEAM

1 Peter 2:24

Who Himself bore our sins in His own body on the tree,
that we, having died to sins, might live for righteousness,
by whose stripes you were healed.

My coach friend and golf buddy, A. G. Crockett, shared this coaching story with me. I refereed several games for him in the 1980s, and I was familiar with the subjects of this story. Rockdale Co. played Dodge Co. for the Class AA girls state championship. Dodge scored with a few seconds remaining to take a one-point lead, and a Dodge player called a timeout. Unfortunately, her team was out of timeouts. Traci Waites was a three-time Parade All-American from Rockdale County and one of the great players in the history of the state of Georgia. Traci went to the line and made both free throws, and Rockdale won the state championship.

As you might imagine, the Dodge County girls were distraught, particularly the girl who lost her composure and called the extra timeout. To Dodge County Coach Dick Kelley's everlasting credit, he told reporters afterward that it was his fault and that he had told the player to call a TO. This wasn't true, but Dick couldn't stand the thought of a kid having to answer those questions, so he took the blame. In the midst of major disappointment and sadness, he took the mistake of his player and put it squarely on his shoulders. Who knows how much fruit has and will continue to come from that decision as those girls raise children and grandchildren?

I knew Dick around that time from local slow-pitch softball tournaments because Dodge County was adjacent to my home county of Laurens. The impact of that decision was such that Coach Crockett distinctly remembered the story almost thirty years later in 2009. A. G. wondered aloud how the seeds that were planted in those players and in the one player who called the timeout have flourished.

Just as the coach took the blame and placed it squarely on his shoulders, Jesus took one for his team. Jesus took all of our sins and placed them squarely on his shoulders at the cross. The verse 1 Peter 2:24 tells us that Jesus bore our sins in his own body on the tree, which is another name for the cross. Despite the weight of all future, past, and present sins and his Father turning his back on Jesus because of those sins, Christ managed to keep himself on that cross for three more hours after darkness came over the land. That's how much he loved us and loves us still.

Prayer: Father God, thank you for coaches who make the right decisions in the toughest situations. May we learn from this example when we have people to support who need us to take one for the team, just like Jesus took the ultimate one for us. In Jesus's name, amen.

BK59:
AGAIN

Ephesians 2:8-9, Romans 5:8, 1 Peter 2:24, Acts 2:4

Who Himself bore our sins in His own body on the tree ...

1 Peter 2:24

The 2010 Sweet Sixteen Kentucky High School Athletic Association Boys Basketball Championship was played in fabled Rupp Arena. This state tournament is unique because there are no classifications, which means all high schools, large and small, compete to play in one tournament. Muhlenberg County High School endured a very turbulent ride to get there. Muhlenberg County, one of the most intense basketball counties in Kentucky, opened a new high school in 2009 following the consolidation of Muhlenberg North and Muhlenberg South, who were bitter archrivals. "Imagine Kentucky and Tennessee merging," Muhlenberg Coach Reggie Warford said. Warford encountered sometimes hostile criticism after he was hired as the new coach to come back to his home county from Pittsburgh.

Coach Warford attempted to mesh North players, South players, and his two sons. He was not prepared for the mean-spirited language and fights between some of the players. Some parents and adults were also hostile toward each other. At the end of January, the Mustangs were an ordinary 12-9 team. The team improved in February and closed the regular season with an impressive rout against a tough rival. But when Warford entered the locker room after the game, three players had quit, including a standout sophomore.

That night, the Mustangs became a team. Afterward, the star player, Gabbard, hugged Warford and said, "Coach, this is our team now … I'm going to get you to Rupp." The standout sophomore had second thoughts about quitting and, with the blessing of his teammates, came back, although he endured many wind sprints before rejoining the team. Gabbard and other players joined him in running those sprints, a gesture not lost on Warford, who remarked, "When I saw that, I told the other coaches, 'We're about to be something special.'"

I heard Dr. Charles Stanley explain the difference between mercy and grace. Mercy is not getting what you deserve, and grace is getting what you don't deserve. I gained further understanding of mercy and grace from an illustration by Jay Carty, author of *Coach Wooden: One-on-One*. My interpretation differs slightly from Jay's. The Muhlenberg player who quit the team was shown mercy by his coach and teammates by being allowed to come back. He still suffered the consequences of running many sprints, but when his teammates ran them with him, that was grace. Their love and forgiveness encouraged him to endure and forged a tighter bond among his teammates.

Muhlenberg's wind sprints reminded me of the classic scene in *Miracle on Ice*. In a pre-Olympic exhibition game in Norway, after Coach Herb Brooks saw his players giving a lackluster effort and checking out the girls in the stands, he snapped, "You guys don't wanna work during the game? No problem. We'll work now. Goal line. That one!" When the assistant coach blew the whistle, the team sprinted over and over from goal line to blue line and back, goal line to red line and back, goal line to the other blue line and back, and finally, from goal line to goal line. "Again." Whistle. "Again." Whistle. "Again."

"Herb, this is madness. Somebody's gonna get hurt!"

"Blow the whistle."

"Again!" Whistle. After one hour, the arena lights were turned off by the maintenance crew, and the team sprinted in darkness for another hour. Finally, Mike Eruzione, who became team captain, got it. He told Herb that he played not for Boston University but for the USA. This weary group of prima donnas put aside their selfish interests and bitter college rivalries and became Team USA on the Norwegian ice.

Jesus Christ ran our sprints on the cross as he bore the heavy consequences of our transgressions. He paid the penalty for our sins. We didn't deserve his sacrifice, yet Jesus died for us while we were still sinners (Romans 5:8). But God loves us so much that he allowed his Son to hang for six hours on a cross in excruciating pain with railroad-type spikes driven through his hands and feet. In his holiness, God couldn't look upon the sin that Jesus represented, so God made the sky black. In those three hours of darkness, Jesus labored time and time again to take his next breath as he raked his torn and bleeding back on the rough wooden cross. Again. Again. Again. Why? Because Jesus loves each of us so much. Jesus died on the cross, arose from the grave, and appeared to his disciples, who still hadn't gotten it after three years of coaching. But when an average group of individuals received the Holy Spirit as Jesus had promised, they became the greatest twelve-man team the world has ever known. God gives each of us a choice to join his team by receiving his free gift of grace, which we cannot earn (Ephesians 2:8-9).

Prayer: Father God, thank you for the trials and life lessons that we learn from sports competition. May we use your wisdom, guidance, and instruction to make better teams wherever we work or study. In the name of the One who took our place, amen.

BK60:
ONE AND DONE

2 Corinthians 5:21, 1 Peter 2:24

For He has made Him to be sin for us, who knew no sin; that we might be made in the righteousness of God in Him.

2 Corinthians 5:21

The expression "one and done" is a popular basketball term that has different meanings. First, when the offense shoots and misses and the defense gets the rebound, that's the end of the possession for the offense, which had one shot and only one shot. Too many "one and done" possessions will ultimately end a team's chance of winning the game.

"One and done" also describes an aspiring team's chances in a season-ending tournament such as NCAA March Madness. Some teams are "one and done" by early Thursday afternoon. It's as if they weren't even in the tournament.

The term "one and done" can also be used to refer to a college player who is so outstanding that he is drafted by the NBA after only one season, the freshman season. Carmelo Anthony, Derrick Rose, Tyreke Evans, John Wall, and Brandon Knight come to mind.

The ultimate "one and done" occurred when Jesus took the sins of the world from the garden of Gethsemane, dragged the cross on the Via Dolorosa, and ultimately was nailed to that cross. After Jesus rose from the grave, the animal sacrifices that had been made for hundreds of years came to a screeching halt for thousands of Jews weeks after Jesus ascended to heaven.

The old covenant of animal sacrifices had been replaced by the new covenant. The blood sacrifices and the sprinkling of the doorposts would never have to be followed again because Jesus shed his own blood as the sign of God's new covenant with the people, first the Jews and later the Gentiles. Jesus Christ, who knew no sin but became sin for us so that we might become his righteousness (2 Corinthians 5:21), had delivered the ultimate "one and done."

Prayer: Most wonderful Father, I am so grateful that Jesus had the courage as the Son of Man and Son of God to deliver on a "one and done" for me. In Jesus's name, amen.

BK61:
SECOND CHANCES

Lamentations 3:22-23

The steadfast love of the Lord never ceases, his mercies never come to an end. They are new every morning, great is your faithfulness.

A critical basketball statistic is second-chance points. The ability of a team to gather offensive rebounds and score put backs is a key stat in any contest. When the initial shot is missed, there is a scramble for the ball as the offensive and defensive teams attempt to gain possession. If the offensive player gets it, he or she will shoot the ball for the second time in that team's possession.

The more offensive rebounds the more second chance points that a team can score. Make enough second-chance points, and they will demoralize the opposition and give you a W that you might not have expected.

God usually gives you plenty of second chances to come to know Christ as Savior. After the first time you have a chance to receive Christ and reject him, usually second chances follow in the form of vacation Bible school teachers, pastors, Sunday school teachers, coaches, friends, and parents. Oftentimes, if your heart is hardened, you won't even realize that you passed on many chances. Nevertheless, God constantly puts these people in your path who will share the gospel and demonstrate the love of Christ. God chose to work through other people to advance his kingdom. That's how much trust God places in people who don't deserve the mercy and grace that he so freely gives.

But one day, the last second chance will come in this life, and after that, there will be no more second chances. Once this life passes, we will either be in heaven or in hell. If we are in hell, the Bible promises that there will be eternal torment, remorse, and regret. The remorse will be over all of the second chance opportunities that were missed and ignored. The next time you sense you have been given a second chance, capitalize on it and the gates of heaven will be yours. For eternity, you can celebrate the best decision you can ever make.

Prayer: Most gracious and forgiving God, I don't deserve the second chances, so I thank you for the many times you make it possible for me to accept your free gift of grace, which I could never earn. I am so grateful for your unconditional love, and may I honor you in all that I do. In Jesus's name, amen.

BK62:
PINE TIME IN PRIME TIME

Romans 8:28, Exodus 20:3, 1 John 1:9

And we know that all happens to us is working for our good, if we love God and are fitting into his plans.

Romans 8:28

When I was a high school senior, I discovered a passion when I refereed three middle school basketball games. I loved it. That day began an involvement with officiating that has lasted since 1972. I have long since retired from college basketball officiating, but I still referee our Hoops2Heaven high school games and enjoy training young officials.

After I refereed those three games on a Saturday, my West Laurens team played a weaker opponent, Johnson County (Herschel Walker's high school before his time), that evening. I had averaged about fourteen points and four or five assists per game. Most nights, I got my teammates involved in the scoring and my points would come in the flow of the game. But I decided before the game that I would topple my career high of twenty-three points. I thought a PR (personal record) would be a cinch because I had been shooting well all season. It would just be a matter of getting enough shots.

I rattled in a twenty-footer on our first possession. Hitting your first shot is usually a very good sign, but when I let it go, I had no wrist snap. I fired shots off the iron for the entire first quarter. Seven consecutive misses and several shots were forced. I clanged the rim like the bell of a San Francisco cable car approaching a stop. *Clang! Clang! Clang!* Coach Wildes rarely sat me, but he looked at me in the huddle and suggested very nicely, "Danny, why don't you sit with me for a few minutes?" In reality I benched myself with tired legs, a stiff wrist, and a swelled head! I hurt my team by selfishly going away from our game plan, and my reward was pine time in prime time. I finished with a season low six points as our team won by twenty.

God was, is, and always will be the Head Coach. When we get too big for our britches, he will let us sit on the pine (the bench) with him. We can't afford pine time because it is always prime time in the kingdom. We need to confess the specific sin, energize our prayer life and Bible study, and be ready when he chooses to put us back in the game. God will always forgive us after we admit our mistakes to him. He will remind us of the power of the Holy Spirit within us.

Sometimes, we force the action due to a lack of wisdom and discernment. If we share Christ in a way that isn't aligned with God's will, most likely it won't be effective. I recall several situations that I would have handled differently, but mistakes can teach us valuable lessons. If we allow God to work within us, he will reveal the proper approach and timing in his prime time.

Prayer: Father God, please give me a burning desire to share the good news in complete accordance with your plan and your timing. May I share the good news within the bounds of your eternal game plan. When I share from your game plan, I can be confident that you will bless my kingdom work mightily. In Jesus's name, amen.

BK63:
A TRIBUTE TO
COACH JOHN WOODEN

Psalm 119:100-105, Matthew 12:34, Ephesians 4:29

Drink deeply from good books, especially the Bible.

John Wooden

John Wooden, who won ten NCAA men's basketball titles at UCLA, went to be with the Lord at the age of ninety-nine in 2010. Tribute after tribute praised him as a great man, coach, teacher, father, and husband. My fondest recollection of Coach Wooden is the devotion book that he co-authored with Jay Carty at the age of ninety-three. My niece Darla gave me the book for Christmas, and it became the first book of devotions that I read with regularity. It was a marvelous collection of sixty devotions and unknowingly might have been the seed that was sown that led me to write my sports devotion books. For that seed I am truly grateful. Here are my personal reflections on a man who was a great spokesman and servant of Jesus Christ.

When John was a boy in Indiana, he and his brother were playing in the barn when his brother threw manure in his face. He cursed his brother and went after him. His dad broke them up and whipped both of them, his brother for throwing manure and John for cursing. Coach Wooden said he never used profanity again in eighty-five years. Can you imagine going eighty-five days without cursing? His UCLA players knew Coach Wooden was really upset with them when he would stop practice and say, "Goodness gracious sakes alive!"

Coach Wooden and Press Maravich, Pete's father, had great respect for each other. Wooden thought that Press had a brilliant basketball mind but was too wrapped up in Pete's individual success. Plus, John would cringe when Press would let a good-natured string of expletives fly at the basketball camp at Campbell College. Each day, the coaches would each put a dollar in the pot, and if Press could go the entire day without cursing, the money would be his. He never collected. But surely John Wooden prayed often for Press to know his Savior and Lord personally, and twenty years later, Pete helped lead Press to Christ. Surely Coach Wooden rejoiced that he would meet his good friend, Press, and his prodigal son in heaven one day.

Regarding the devotion book that Coach Wooden co-wrote, what a lesson we can learn from Coach Wooden becoming an author so late in life. When we are obedient to God, we can never tell where he is going to lead us and when he is going to do it. And that's where the real excitement in living occurs.

Coach Wooden once said, "I always tried to make clear that basketball is not the ultimate. It is of small importance in comparison to the total life we live. There is only one kind of life that truly wins, and that is the one that places faith in the hands of the Savior. Until that is done, we are on an aimless course that runs in circles and goes nowhere."

Prayer: Father God, thank you for the legacy of John Wooden, and may his legacy continue to bear fruit for the kingdom for the next ninety-nine years. In Jesus's holy name, amen.

BK64:
SPEAKING THE TRUTH

John 14:6

I am the Way, the Truth, and the Life...

We've been very blessed at summer basketball by a ten-year-old boy that I will call John. John is autistic, and from game to game, we're never quite sure what to expect. But our Hoops2Heaven ministry has never turned a child away who was physically able to play.

One of the highlights of the season was when John scored a basket, and the entire gym erupted in applause as his teammates congratulated him. There was also the day that John refused to play because our sports director, Michelle, placed a girl on his team and it just did not sit well with him. We made a quick adjustment, and the girl graciously moved to the other team without being offended.

At halftime, when the devotions were given, there was no predicting what he would say and when he would say it. Sometimes, John would go on a tangent and take us off course from the message, and his mother and father would squirm anxiously in their seats.

But one night, when Michelle was presenting the devotion, John suddenly blurted out, "I told my friends at school that you need to believe in Jesus to go to heaven. People that don't believe in Jesus are going to hell." Michelle smiled and nodded and continued with the devotion.

The choice of heaven or hell is a truth that Michelle and I will carefully present in a loving way. Every child around him that evening might not have been ready to hear the truth the way that John presented it, but he had indeed spoken the truth. Every adult in the gym might not have been ready to hear it either. Jesus spent more time talking about hell than heaven, but we often take great pains to keep from pointing out the downside to people. John did it very clearly and succinctly, and I'm grateful to him that he had the belief in Christ and the presence to share with us.

Prayer: Most wonderful God Almighty, thank you for the truth that comes from the mouth of babes. In Jesus's name, amen.

BK65:
FOLLOW WISDOM

Proverbs 9:10

The fear of God is the beginning of wisdom.

When I was in my late twenties, visions of greatness danced in my head. I had started a promising career as a college basketball official. I had cut my teeth on some easy small college games for a couple of years, and I began to branch out to get more experience. I attended a basketball official's camp at St. Joe's College in Rensselaer, Indiana, in the summer of 1983. The camp was operated by Dr. Henry "Hank" Nichols, the chair of the English department at Villanova University, the foremost college official of the era, and the referee in numerous NCAA championship games. I had developed pretty good judgment, hustled, and put a lot of flair into my calls; I was kind of a hot dog, frankly, which caught the eye of Nichols. He particularly liked the way that I mimicked his travel signal with a quick one rotation turn of the forearms and then pointing in the opposite direction.

On the final afternoon, Hank and Don Shea made me the referee in the camp championship game, which signified that I had been the top-rated official at the camp. While it wasn't the strongest group, one of my new friends, Terry McAulay, number 77, would later become an NFL official and would work two Super Bowls as the referee.

Before the final game, Hank did me a huge favor. He called me over and said, "Farr, go stand under the basket at the other end of the court. I am going over to talk to Bobby Cremins, the head basketball coach at Georgia Tech. I will point you out to him and recommend that he use you for scrimmages. That will get you some experience calling D-1 ball. When you get back to Atlanta, call him this fall and remind him of the conversation." What a nice gesture. I was on cloud nine as I drove back to Kentucky to my in-laws' home, where Becca was staying while I was at camp.

What happened during the fall with Cremins and Georgia Tech? Well, not much because I never called him. Why? I don't know. Maybe I was too shy. But I probably thought, *I'll just do it my way.* Has that ever happened to you, someone gave you great advice or opened a door for you but you never walked through it? It happens with our relationship with God all the time when we insist on going our way instead of his way. When we are in touch with God's plan and listening for his guidance, he knows what is best for us. It's up to us to be obedient and follow his plan, which is always better than anything we can do on our own. God is for us. He's always using circumstances and other people and directing us to, "Go here. Go there." Find out where God is working and where he is pointing and follow his lead.

Prayer: Father God, thank you for the many doors that you open for us. You must shake your head in amazement when we fail to walk through doors you have opened for us. May I keep my eyes and ears open and recognize where you are at work. In Jesus's name, amen.

BK66:
PETE'S HOOK SHOT

Exodus 20:3

You shall have no gods before me.

The most famous play in the history of Stegeman Coliseum at the University of Georgia occurred on March 8, 1969. Before an over-flow crowd of thirteen thousand, "Pistol Pete" Maravich rallied LSU from fifteen down in the second half with a series of long rainbow jumpers that would have been three-pointers if the three-point line had been in effect then. The game went to overtime, and Georgia was up by two and had possession with only twelve seconds remaining. All Georgia had to do was play keep away from the exhausted LSU players.

But suddenly, a Georgia guard took an ill-advised jump shot and missed. Pete grabbed the rebound, drove the length of the court, and scored to send the game to a second overtime. LSU pulled away in the second overtime, thanks to Pete's free throws and Georgia's cold shooting. There was no shot clock in 1969, so with about forty-five seconds left, Pete went into his *Showtime* dribbling routine, going between the legs and behind the back. Three Georgia players chased him but couldn't catch him.

Just before the buzzer to end the game, Pete threw up a forty-foot hook shot and ran off the court with his index finger in the air, just like Joe Namath leaving the field in Super Bowl III about six weeks earlier. The shot swished for his fifty-seventh and fifty-eighth points of the night. Pandemonium broke out. Immediately, the Georgia male cheerleaders ran after Pete, picked him up on their shoulders, and paraded him around the court to the pleasure of the Georgia fans and to the utter dismay of the Georgia players. Perhaps never before or since have the home team cheerleaders carried an opposing player in celebration around the floor. Such was the magical legend of the Pistol.

As one version of the story has been told, the famous hook shot would have never materialized if the player from Georgia had not tried to steal the spotlight from Pete. When we make selfish plays and take bad shots to increase our scoring total, we hurt our team's chances to win the game. Just as we should always put the team's best interests first, we should place God and others first and our interests last. If Georgia had won the game, there would have been plenty of credit to share all the way around. I believe that Georgia player has thought about that shot many times in the years following the game. I hope that a valuable life lesson came with it.

Prayer: Father God, thank you for the lessons of unselfishness that I can learn from the game of basketball. Forgive me when I am a ball hog in life and want things my way too often. In Jesus's name, amen.

BK67:
NOTHING BUT NET

John 21:3-8

Cast the net on the right side of the ship ...

John 21:6

Larry Bird, Magic Johnson, and Michael Jordan are given credit for revitalizing the NBA during the 1980s and early 1990s. Their styles of play were different, but all three were tremendous leaders. Magic and Larry were friends but were made out to be big rivals.

In 1993 McDonald's sponsored a series of commercials that pitted Michael and Larry making trick shots in a game of horse. With each commercial, the shots became more outlandish.

Larry would shoot the basketball and say, "Off the roof, off the scoreboard, nothing but net." *Swish!*

Michael would shoot and say, "Off the car hood, off the tree, nothing but net." *Swish!*

The array of shots was outlandish for effect. There are many trick shots on YouTube that are nothing short of incredible. In 2010, two University of Georgia basketball players made quite a splash with their incredible repertoire of trick shots.

Jesus had an important "nothing but net" moment with his disciples just before he ascended to heaven. After he had risen from the grave and appeared on several occasions to his disciples, the disciples, who were experienced fishermen, fished all night and caught nothing. Jesus shouted, "Have you any fish?" When they said no, he instructed them to drop their net over the side of the boat. *An outlandish request,* Peter must have thought. "Nothing but net," Jesus told them. Just drop the net. Peter obeyed, and they caught so many fish, 153 to be exact, that the net almost burst.

Sometimes we feel that God makes outlandish requests of us. *You mean it's a sin if I just think bad thoughts? If I cheat on my homework or tell my friend a half-truth, that makes God angry?* God expects us to be perfect in the sense that he wants us to come clean when we do mess up, no matter how small the sin might be. Great rewards await those who stay clean by confessing their individual sins to God.

Prayer: Father God, I know that it is impossible to stay pure, and you and I know that I'm eventually going to slip. But help me give it my best shot, and thank you for disciplining me to help me be more like Christ. In Jesus's name, amen.

BK68:
WHO IS *THAT* KID?

2 Chronicles 34:1-3, Luke 2:40-52,
John 14:12, 1 Timothy 4:12

Did you not know I must be about my Father's business?

Luke 2:49

Twelve-year-old Pete Maravich was already a basketball camp veteran because his dad, Press, took him to every basketball camp that he worked during the summer. Even though Pete was small and frail, his skills were so advanced that he was winning free-throw shooting contests with college all-Americans such as Len Chappell of Wake Forest and scrimmaging with high school players. Soon, he would be dubbed "Pistol Pete" by a sportswriter who interviewed him after an eighth-grade game at Daniel High School in Clemson, South Carolina.

Young Pete was playing in a summer camp game with high school players as Bob Cousy watched from the sideline and chatted with a friend. Cousy was the NBA All-Star point guard of the 1959 world champion Boston Celtics. The "Cooz" was renowned for innovative moves such as his "wrap around the body" pass and an occasional behind-the-back dribble. Cousy was seemingly not paying much attention to the game as Pete came down the court with the ball. At midcourt, Pete threaded the needle with a forty-foot bounce pass through several players with some side spin. The ball ricocheted perfectly into the hands of his teammate for an easy layup. Cousy was so astounded by Pete's pass that he walked onto the court, *stopped the game*, and shouted, "Who is *that* kid?"

Little did Bob or anyone in the gym know that this twelve-year-old prodigy would become to the game of basketball what Elvis was to music. Pete would bring more originality and excitement to the game of basketball than had ever happened. "Pistol Pete" and his father, Press, took their entertaining brand of basketball called *Showtime* to the college basketball world in the late '60s, revolutionizing the game of basketball to this day.

Surely the priests, the Pharisees, and the most learned Jewish scholars of the day were equally astounded by a young prodigy named Jesus, who, at the age of twelve, shared incredible wisdom and insight as he preached in the temple. At some point, one of them must have turned to a friend and exclaimed, "Who is *that* kid?" Little did they know that they were watching and listening to Jesus, the Messiah, the long-awaited Savior of the world. Through the originality of his parables and miracles, Christ brought hope to the poor, to the downtrodden, to the oppressed, to women, and to all who longed for a better life. Many people in the temple failed to recognize that Jesus was the hope of a fallen world that had waited for the arrival of the Messiah for centuries.

Prayer: Oh God, thank you for the lessons that we can learn from our talented youth. May I encourage a youth with a special talent to strive to be all that he or she can be and remind them that Christ is always there to help. In the holy name of Jesus, amen.

BASEBALL

BB28:
FAMOUS TIRADES

Psalm 73

They set their mouth against the heavens, and their tongue
walks through the earth.

Psalm 73:9

A colorful part of major league baseball lore is arguments with
umpires. There is a bang-bang play at first base, and the manager
storms out of the dugout. He kicks the dirt and unleashes a tirade
against the man in blue. There have been some colorful managers in
major-league baseball, such as Tommy Lasorda of the Los Angeles
Dodgers and Earl Weaver of the Baltimore Orioles. But Bobby Cox
of the Atlanta Braves was perhaps the most intense manager, because
he was thrown out of games a record 161 times in his major league
career. He missed the final out of almost a full season of games after
getting tossed.

God understands when we vent to him in anger. King David was
a man after God's own heart, but apparently, he unleashed some real
tirades in his frustration to God. But God understood. The good
news is that God will allow us to tell him exactly how we feel. We
can vent all we want, but we should never question God's judgment.

Sometimes we can get angry when we see others getting the
blessings that we don't believe they deserve. The psalmist lamented

that he was just trying to hang onto his meager lifestyle while the fat cats were wining and dining however they pleased. But the psalmist eventually realized that these fat cats would get their just chastisement in the end if they did not change their evil ways. Let's appreciate what we have and leave the rest up to God.

Prayer: Father God, please forgive me when my anger is about jealousy and not about righteousness. May I leave the judgment up to you. Give me a full appreciation for the countless blessings you send my way. In the holy and precious name of our Savior and Lord, Jesus Christ, amen.

BB29:
DIFFERENT TALENTS MAKE
AN EFFECTIVE TEAM

Romans 12:5-8

Having then gifts differing according to the grace that is
given to us...

Romans 12:6

It takes many talents to merge together to make a successful baseball
team. There is the leadoff hitter whose job it is to get on base any
way he can. The second hitter moves him along with a sacrifice bunt.
The third batter, usually the best hitter for average, drives him in
with a double to the gap. The cleanup hitter blasts a long home run
to open up a three-run lead.

On the defensive side, the infielders gobble up the ground balls
and turn them into double plays. The outfielders use their speed to
chase down long fly balls.

The starting pitcher goes a solid seven innings to give his team a
chance to win. The setup man comes out of the bullpen and pitches
a strong eighth. The closer comes in to slam the door and give his
team the win.

As you can see, it takes a lot of players on the team doing different jobs to win the game. Not all of the jobs are glamorous, but they

are necessary. We are blessed with different talents. Some of us are gifted at speaking. Others are gifted at serving through missions. Some are really good at coaching sports skills. There are others who are really good at teaching kids in vacation Bible school or enjoy singing in the choir. Some naturally radiate the love of Christ and have a special gift for inviting their friends to be a part of their youth activities at church. It is up to each of us to consistently develop and use the special talents that God has given us to reach people for Christ.

Prayer: Dear Lord, help me see the special gifts in my family members and friends. May I remember that their gifts might be much different from mine because you gave us such unique inborn passions. I appreciate your wonderful love for which I cannot fathom the depths. In the name of our precious Savior, amen.

BB30:
KEEP YOUR EYES
ON THE MITT

Hebrews 12:2

Fix your eyes upon Jesus, the author and perfector of our faith, who for the joy set before Him endured the cross, scorning its shame, and sat down at the right hand of the throne of God.

When you watch a major league baseball telecast, you will notice that the catcher will set up where he wants the ball pitched. If he wants it on the inside corner, he sets up near the batter. If he wants it on the outside corner, he will set up away from the batter.

The last thing that some catchers will do is flash the mitt to give the pitcher a clear mental picture of exactly where he wants the ball pitched. The pitcher doesn't just look at the catcher to pitch the ball. The pitcher has a specific target at which he can aim.

In this same way, we need to fix our eyes on Jesus. If we don't keep our eyes on Jesus, we will lose our way and drift off course. During the last twelve hours before his death, Jesus was willing to go through an incredibly painful beating because he loves us so much. He scorned the shame of being openly mocked and ridiculed as he carried the cross through the streets of Jerusalem on the way to Golgotha.

Jesus looked forward to having a relationship with us so much that he had his eyes fixed on us even before we born. When Christ was on the cross, he could visualize us in the future and knew that he was dying for us so that we could know him one day. When we fix our eyes on Jesus and remember how and why Jesus did what he did on the cross purely out of love, it gives us extra determination to serve in the name of Christ and stay focused on him.

Prayer: Dear heavenly Father, thank you for sending us Jesus to live and die and rise from the grave. May I keep my eyes fixed on Jesus and vividly retain the mental picture of the bleeding, beaten Jesus who died on the cross for me. In Jesus's name, amen.

BB31:
MY FIRST BASE HIT

John 3:16

For God so loved the world that He gave his only begotten
Son, that whosoever believes in Him shall not perish but
have everlasting life.

Remember your first base hit as a child? I vividly remember mine. It
was the first year that my town of Cadwell ever had a Little League
team, and our neighboring town of Rentz also fielded a team. We
played twenty-three times against each other that summer. I was
only eight years old, and in our first game, I faced an eleven-year-old
pitcher who could throw sidearm very hard. It was a bit intimidating
to face him, but I managed to hang in there. He pitched a fastball,
and I swung a little late. But the ball felt flush against my bat, and
my line drive went just inside the first base bag! In my first official
bat in a real game, I had my first hit. I was really excited. Before the
day was over, I had gone four for five. What a start to my first season!

The memory of that athletic success is nice, as are many others. But the thrills of our athletic and academic endeavors all added
together could never equal the thrill and joy of knowing Jesus Christ
as Savior and Lord. First of all, there is joy and excitement in knowing that we will spend eternity in heaven with our Savior! Second,
we receive the gift of the Holy Spirit when we come to know Jesus.

The Holy Spirit is sort of like a best friend or another parent who is always there any time of day to help us with any problem that we will ever encounter. Third, when we know Christ, we receive these awesome rewards of fellowship with other Christian brothers and sisters. Finally, as Christians, we also receive a peace that passes understanding that helps us be more content in life. We don't feel pressure every hour of every day trying to fill up our lives with more stuff. All of those reasons are why knowing Christ is more thrilling and satisfying than any athletic performance could ever bring us.

I can describe what it's like to get a base hit or score a basket, but unless you do it for yourself, you'll never experience the excitement personally. I can tell you what a thrill it is that Christ is at the center of my life, but unless you give him a chance, you will never know for yourself. Give Christ a chance to be your Savior and Lord.

Prayer: Father God, thank you for the great memories of our first base hit, or first basket, or first par. It is so much fun to look back at those good times. I thank you most for being able to look back and remember the moment that your saving grace first enveloped me. Hallelujah in the name of Jesus, amen.

BB32:
BLINDED BY THE LIGHT

Acts 9:1-19

And as he journeyed, he came near Damascus; and
suddenly there shined round about him a light from
Heaven... And Saul arose from the earth; and when his
eyes were opened, he saw no man...

Acts 9:3,8

Some of the most popular and funny baseball bloopers on TV are
the pop flies and fly balls that get lost in the sun. Players use all types
of protection to keep from losing the ball in the sun. They wear eye
black to cut down on glare. And caps, of course. They wear sunglasses that they can flip down to shield the glare. Milo Hamilton,
my favorite Braves announcer, would shout, "Felipe Alou, sunglasses
gleaming, one out in the ninth!" The players will sometimes use
their gloves and even their forearms to shield the sun. All of these
actions help, but sometimes nothing helps. Those are the plays that
make the highlight reels. It's a helpless feeling when the player real-
izes that he has been blinded by the sun. You will see them turn away
and literally dive for cover as the ball crashes to the outfield turf and
the runners circle the bases like a merry-go-round.

It was a helpless feeling for Saul, the biggest persecutor of
Christians, when he was on the road to Damascus. Saul asked for

and received orders from the high priest of the Pharisees to travel to Damascus. His mission was to find the Christians, bind them, and bring them back to Jerusalem to be persecuted. However, as Saul neared Damascus, he was suddenly blinded by the brightest light imaginable. Saul heard the voice of Jesus saying, "Saul, Saul, why are you persecuting me?" Saul had no protection against the brightest light, which blinded him for three days. Jesus told Saul to go into Damascus and wait there. Saul made a miraculous recovery when Jesus sent a disciple named Ananias to the house on Straight Street to remove the scales from his eyes and restore his sight. Jesus filled Saul with the Holy Spirit, and Saul received a new name, Paul. He also received new marching orders, which were to share Christ with Gentiles, who were everybody else but the Jews, and the Jewish people.

Once the scales were removed, Saul went from persecutor of Christians to become the apostle Paul, the strongest spokesman for the gospel that the world had ever seen. All of this happened after he was blinded by the light.

Prayer: Father God, I was blind but now I see. I was in the darkness, and thank you that I have seen your Light. May I shine my light brilliantly for you. In Jesus's name, amen.

BB33:
SACRIFICE (BASEBALL)

1 Peter 2:24

Who Himself bore our sins in His own body on the tree,
that we, having died to sins, might live for righteousness;
by whose stripes you were healed.

A sacrifice bunt is sort of a lost art these days. In the American
League, the use of the designated hitter, who bats instead of the
pitcher, means that there is rarely a bunt just to move a runner over.
In the National League, where the pitchers still bat, it's used much
more often. When the pitcher comes to the plate, the first and third
basemen will creep toward the plate, trying to field the bunt as soon
as possible and throw to second to get the lead runner.

After a sacrifice bunt attempt, a rookie catcher shouted to his
veteran pitcher, "Throw it to second!" The pitcher never glanced
at second before he threw to first to get the easy out. The young
catcher was perplexed and couldn't figure out why his pitcher did
not follow his orders. The home plate umpire teased him when he
said, "I guess he considered the source [of the advice]." That wasn't
much solace for the young catcher.

Jesus made another kind of sacrifice, one that influenced the
world for all time. That sacrifice was when Jesus went to the cross
for us. He came to earth to bear our sins in his own body on the

cross so that we could cry out to Jesus and say, "Jesus, I have sinned against you and God. Please forgive me. Come into my life as my Savior!" Even though sometimes you feel like you are a rookie, God will honor your heartfelt plea and grant you his saving grace that you cannot earn.

Prayer: Most High and Almighty God, you loved us so much that you sent the ultimate sacrifice from heaven to earth: Jesus Christ. I cannot earn your grace, nor could I ever repay you. I am so grateful for your daily mercies and gifts. In Jesus's name, amen.

BB34:
YOU'RE OUT OF THE TEMPLE!

Mark 11:15-19

Jesus went into the temple, and began to cast out them that sold and bought in the temple...

Mark 11:15

In major league baseball, there will occasionally be arguments that suddenly turn into bench-clearing brawls. Sometimes multiple people will be thrown out of the game. One of the biggest bench-clearing brawls occurred in 2003 between New York and Boston, when Red Sox Coach Don Zimmer and Yankee pitcher Pedro Martinez scuffled after a batter was supposedly intentionally hit by a pitch. It was a very unfortunate episode that brought out the worst in both teams. Angry does not begin to describe how upset some coaches and players get when their teammates are mistreated.

Jesus did a little bench-clearing of his own. After he had ridden triumphantly into the city of Jerusalem on a donkey to the cries of "Hosanna!" he went to the temple the following day. Jesus was angry from the moment that he stepped into the temple because the Pharisees were selling doves and other wares in the temple. Jesus actually turned the tables over on the Pharisees and ordered them out of the temple. Jesus rebuked the moneychangers and taught them that the temple is a holy place and a house of prayer.

Unlike sinful unrighteous anger in baseball, which leads to bean balls and players fighting and getting hurt, Jesus used righteous anger and chased the sinners out of there. "You're out of this temple!" Jesus said. "You will not desecrate this holy place!"

Prayer: Father God, may I be ever mindful of your presence and understand when the proper time is to demonstrate righteous anger and when the proper time is to hold back. Holy Spirit, please guide me with wisdom and discernment. In Jesus's name, amen.

BB35:
ONE, TWO, THREE STRIKES
YOU'RE OUT!

Matthew 26:36-52, John 3:17

And behold, one of them which were with Jesus stretched out his hand, and struck a servant of the high priest's, and smote off his ear.

Matthew 26:51

At the seventh-inning stretch at fabled Wrigley Field in Chicago, the crowd rises and sings in unison as a guest celebrity leads them in the singing of "Take Me Out to the Ball Game."

Take me out to the ball game,
take me out to the crowd.

Buy me some peanuts and Cracker Jacks,
I don't care if I ever get back.

So it's root, root, root for the home team,
if they don't win it's a shame.

For it's one, two, three strikes you're out
at the old ball game.

Jesus's disciples had three strikes against them when they let him down three times in the same night. When Jesus went to the garden of Gethsemane to pray before he was crucified the following morning, he asked his disciples to stay awake lest they fall victim to temptation. Jesus prayed, and his disciples fell asleep. Strike one! Jesus woke them and asked them to please stay awake and they fell asleep again. Strike two! Finally, Jesus told them to get some rest. Soon, Judas Escariot would betray him and summon the Jews and Roman centurions to the garden to arrest him unfairly. Peter lost his cool and swung his sword, cutting the ear off the servant of Malchus. Strike three! Jesus took the servant's ear and put it back on his body.

Although the disciples had three strikes against them, Jesus did not call them out forever because he came to save them and all people. Jesus summoned the courage to withstand the beatings and abuse and crucifixion, and he arose from the dead to save us, for God sent his Son into the world not to condemn it but to save it.

Prayer: Father God, even when I strike out and I let you down, and it happens much too often, you are still willing to pitch to me. Help me remember that Peter, one of your mightiest apostles, didn't always understand what you wanted. But he became the rock. May my faith be rock steady. In Jesus's name, amen.

BB36:
WARNING TRACK

Exodus 20:18

And all the people saw the thunderings, and the
lightnings, and the noise of the trumpet, and the
mountain smoking.

When I was a slow-pitch softball player, I was plagued by warning
track power. I was a good base hitter, but I wanted to hit the home
runs like the big boys even though I weighed only 155 pounds. I
would hit one home run a month if my timing and swing were perfect. But I had no margin for error. Often, I would fly out just short
of the fence for an easy out. My teammate, Ira, told me one night
after I was not getting on base, "Podnah, you've gotta hit it twenty
feet farther or twenty feet shorter." I learned my lesson and started
hitting singles and doubles so that I could jog around the bases when
Ira would jack it way over the fence.

Those balls that were just short of clearing the fence were landing
on the warning track. The warning track is the bare dirt semicircle in
front of the fence that is about fifteen feet wide. The reason for the
warning track is that it serves as a warning for the outfielders. When
the outfielders race to the fence, they can feel the ground change
from grass to crushed brick. It sends a message to their minds that
they are approaching the fence so that they can slow down or brace

themselves before they collide with the fence. If there was no track, the players would race full speed and crash into the fence, risking serious injury. Many players have had their careers ended by the fence, including Bobby Valentine, former California Angel player and New York Mets manager.

God gives us a warning track to avoid sin in three different ways. First, he gave us the Ten Commandments, the rules to live by. Second, he gave us a conscience to know right from wrong. Third, as believers, we have a boost of a warning track through the Holy Spirit, which gives us a special built-in warning system. But where sin hardens your heart, the warning track blurs and sometimes disappears. When you continue to make bad decisions, eventually, one of those is going to crash you into the wall, and you've really got some problems to deal with.

Prayer: Father God, may I heed your subtle warnings so that I can correct my ways before I crash into the wall. Thank you for the extra warning device that you give me in the form of a person: the Holy Spirit. In Jesus's name, I pray. Amen.

BB37:
COME HOME AGAIN!

Luke 15:11-24

I will arise and go to my father, and will say to him, Father,
I have sinned against heaven, and before you.

Luke 15:18

In baseball, every player begins at home plate as a batter. The first goal is to get to first base, and the ultimate goal is to go all the way around to home plate or come home again. If the player is successful in getting to first base, the next goal is obviously to get to second. Let's say a player gets a single and the second player bunts to move the player to second base. Then the third player moves the runner over with a ground ball to the first baseman. The clean-up batter sends a line drive to left, and the leadoff batter crosses home plate with the first run. So the player comes home again.

The prodigal son began at home plate. When he got his inheritance, his first step was to move to a faraway land, and he blew all of his money on extravagant and riotous living. Then his second step was to find any kind of job because he was broke and starving after a famine ravaged the land. He became so desperate that his third step was to come to the realization that he was so hungry that he would have eaten the husks that he was feeding the hogs. Yet he realized that his father's servants at least had food and shelter. As he came to his senses, the prodigal son confessed that he had sinned against God and against heaven. In a sense, he rounded third and headed for home.

When Bobby Thomson hit a legendary ninth inning home run in 1951 that won the pennant for the New York Giants over the Brooklyn Dodgers, the Giants first base coach did not wait for him to get to home plate to congratulate him. He ran almost to third base to catch him and pummel him on the back all the way to home plate. Likewise, the prodigal's father was so happy to see his lost son that he came running down the road to welcome him home. The father slipped the best robe on his son's back, a ring on his finger, shoes on his feet, and killed the fatted calf. He held a big celebration because his son was lost and now was found.

For all the prodigals who have been estranged from family members, please know how much they want you to come home. God wants all of the prodigals who have not come to know Christ to make that commitment. He wants every prodigal to be saved.

Prayer: Father God, give me a heart to pray diligently and passionately for the prodigals in my extended family, my school, my workplace, and friends of my family. In Jesus's name, amen.

BB38:
A TERRIFIC DOUBLE PLAY
COMBINATION

Romans 8:26, Ephesians 4:30

The Holy Spirit helps with our daily problems and in our praying, for we don't even know what to pray for, nor how to pray as we should.

Romans 8:26

A double play in baseball occurs when you get two outs on the same play. The most common double play is a hard ground ball to the shortstop, who catches and flips the ball to the second baseman, who catches the ball on second base, leaps over the incoming runner from first, and fires the ball to the first baseman just in time to get the batter. It's the 6-4-3 double play. The double play has long been called the pitcher's best friend since he only had to throw one pitch to get two outs.

Two of the best friends we can ever have make a neat double-play combination too. When we truly turn away from all of our sins for the first time and ask Jesus Christ to come into our hearts, that is the first cool thing that happens because we receive eternal life in heaven. Then the second part of the double play occurs. God simultaneously sends us a person, the Holy Spirit, who now lives within us and helps us with our daily problems and our praying. When we are downcast and we don't know how to pray or what to pray for, the Holy Spirit is there to fill in the gaps.

Who hears our prayers as our intercessor and our go-between to God? Jesus and the Holy Spirit, the greatest double-play combination ever.

Prayer: Father God, so often I try to do it myself without realizing that not only are you there to guide me, but you give me Jesus in my heart and the Holy Spirit to help me. Thank you so much. In Jesus's name, amen.

BB39:
THE BIG, BLACK GLOVE

Matthew 11:28

Come to me, all you who are weary and heavy laden, and
I will give you rest.

When Allison was six, we signed her up for girls' softball at the local
park. She was the smallest girl on the team, but she was a good hitter and tried really hard. Girls' softball was new to me, but I quickly
observed that the best players on the team all had big gloves. In fact,
one girl's glove swallowed the tiny glove that I had bought Allison a
couple of years earlier.

I went to the sporting goods store and found the biggest glove
that I thought she could handle, a beautiful, black glove with silver
strings. We brought it to the next game, and it was time for Allison
to take the field. Coach Keith said, "Allison, go to third base this
inning." Allison charged onto the field, and as she ran, I noticed that
she was leaning to her left, her shoulders perched at a precarious
angle. Her new glove was so big and so heavy that it threw her off
balance, and the glove nearly dragged the ground as she ran.

Don't we have circumstances in life that weigh us down? School,
work, meetings at church, family duties, and, oh yeah, gotta carve
out some time to hang with my friends. We've only got so many
hours in the day. If we've crammed too much stuff into our day and

haven't left room for God, those demands will eventually hang on us like a boat anchor. We wonder where the joy in life went.

Trade in that heavy schedule for a lighter one. After only a couple of months of being a believer, I discovered there is beauty and joy in the simpler life of following Jesus. Some anchors disappeared, and my load was lightened. Try letting Jesus control your schedule, and experience the joy of balance returning to your life.

Prayer: Most gracious Father, thank you for helping me discover that a simpler life in Jesus is always a better life. In Jesus's name, amen.

BB40:
HEAVEN'S GRAND SLAM
(BASEBALL)

Jeremiah 29:11, Romans 5:8, 1 John 1:9, John 3:16,
Ephesians 2:8

If we confess our sins, you are faithful and just, and will forgive our sins and cleanse us from all unrighteousness.

1 John 1:9

On July 10, 1968, I came to the plate with the bases loaded, one out in the bottom of the second. My team trailed 5-2, and my friend, Dennis, was pitching. I worked the count to 1-1, and he threw me a fastball down the middle of the plate. I connected, and it was such a terrific sensation to feel the ball hit flush against the barrel of my bat. As I ran down the first base line, I looked up and saw the ball sailing high over the fence in left center field. A grand slam. I had dreamed many times of hitting a home run in competition, and this was a grand slam. How do I remember the date? When you pitched no-hitters or hit home runs in my Little League, the league director would give you the baseball as a souvenir. I wrote the details on the ball with a pen, and I still have it in my closet.

Just as my grand slam home run plated four runs on one play, and there are four bases in baseball, there are four points to understand about salvation. At first base, you are wonderfully and uniquely made by God (Psalm 139:14), and there is no one exactly like you. God created a unique plan (Jeremiah 29:11) for your life so that you can enjoy his special blessings. The unique plan doesn't mean everything that happens to us will be wonderful and that we will live without problems.

At second base, each person is separated from God from the first time that he or she consciously breaks one of the Ten Commandments. Each person inherits a sinful nature at birth (Psalm 51:5) and is destined to commit his or her first sin at an early age, which separates us from God. Everyone who has ever lived has experienced this sinful separation from God (Romans 3:23), and if we don't do something about it, spiritual death (Romans 6:23) will be the end.

At third base, God loved us so much in spite of our shortcomings that even while we were sinners (Romans 5:8), he sent Jesus to be the bridge over the chasm of sin that separates us from God. Jesus even bore our sin in his body when he went to the cross (1 Peter 2:24). But the good news that we celebrate every day is that Jesus left the tomb and came back to life (Matthew 28:6).

God did all the work to get you safely to third base. Now he wants you to come home. God wants you to score the winning run for eternity, but you must exchange your sinful life for a new life in Christ. You must repent, or turn from your sinful life, and ask God to forgive you (1 John 1:9). After you repent, you must place your trust in Christ and accept God's gift of grace to receive eternal life (Ephesians 2:8), admitting that you cannot earn God's grace and that salvation only comes through Jesus Christ (John 3:16). Then you must commit to obey God by praying often and studying his Word daily to grow in Christ in all aspects of your life (Proverbs 3:6).

God offers everyone his free gift of grace. I invite you to pray this prayer to receive Jesus Christ into your life as your Savior. Your sincere desire to transform your life is more important than these exact words.

Prayer: Lord Jesus, I need you. Thank you for suffering on the cross and dying for my sins. I want my life to change. Please forgive all of my sins through Christ's blood shed for me. I turn away from my sinful life and put my trust in you who died for me. Jesus, please come into my life. Thank you for your free gift of grace that brings me eternal life in heaven. Thank you for the Holy Spirit that now lives in my heart. May I grow in my love for you through prayer and your holy Word. Thank you for accepting me as your child into the family of God. In Jesus's holy name, I pray. Amen.

Now consider these three statements one at a time. If you understand each statement and really want to commit to each, you should pray and ask Christ into your life in your own words. Write your name under *saint*. You should receive the Holy Spirit and eternal life through Jesus Christ if you were sincere and understood your commitment.

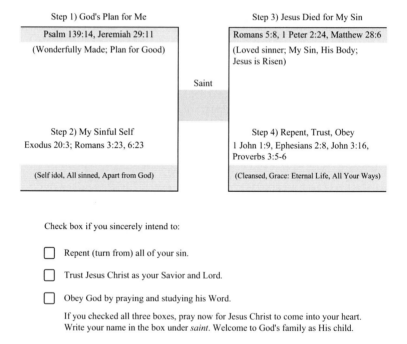

Heaven's Grand Slam

Step 1) God's Plan for Me		Step 3) Jesus Died for My Sin
Psalm 139:14, Jeremiah 29:11		Romans 5:8, 1 Peter 2:24, Matthew 28:6
(Wonderfully Made; Plan for Good)		(Loved sinner; My Sin, His Body; Jesus is Risen)
	Saint	
Step 2) My Sinful Self		Step 4) Repent, Trust, Obey
Exodus 20:3; Romans 3:23, 6:23		1 John 1:9, Ephesians 2:8, John 3:16, Proverbs 3:5-6
(Self idol, All sinned, Apart from God)		(Cleansed, Grace: Eternal Life, All Your Ways)

Check box if you sincerely intend to:

☐ Repent (turn from) all of your sin.

☐ Trust Jesus Christ as your Savior and Lord.

☐ Obey God by praying and studying his Word.

If you checked all three boxes, pray now for Jesus Christ to come into your heart. Write your name in the box under *saint*. Welcome to God's family as His child.

BB41:
I AM COUNTING ON YOU

Matthew 28:19-20, Galatians 4:6, Ephesians 2:8

Therefore, go and make disciples ...

Matthew 28:19

A giant in the world of baseball and sports died on July 13, 2010. George Steinbrenner, the owner of the New York Yankees and a man of great contrasts, died of a heart attack at the age of eighty. He was nicknamed the Boss because everybody knew that he was in complete control. George made his fortune in the shipbuilding business before buying a once-proud-but-fallen Yankee franchise at bargain basement rates in 1973. Steinbrenner made a $9M purchase and turned millions into billions, as the Yankee franchise is now worth over $1.5 billion dollars.

Steinbrenner had a passion for winning and settled for nothing less than excellence day in and day out for over thirty-five years with the Yankees. His drive fueled the Yankees to seven world championships, his most recent coming in 2009. My first recollection was how many Yankee managers he had fired and how many free agents he had signed for exorbitant sums of money. But the stories of George's behind-the-scenes generosity, his handwritten notes of encouragement to players, and his mellower attitude during his last few years painted a more complete picture of the man.

Derek Jeter, the Yankee all-star shortstop and future first-ballot Hall of Famer, shared a story that happened when he was an eighteen-year-old rookie in the Gulf Coast League, the lowest Yankee farm club. Seemingly bigger than life, George came up to Derek, put his arm around him, and said, "Derek, we're really expecting big things from you." Derek couldn't believe that George knew his name, and the story obviously stayed with Derek like an epiphany. Jeter certainly delivered big-time for the Yankees. A second story was that Steinbrenner believed that there was 10 percent more in every man than the man thought he was capable of delivering. George sought to find it one way or another.

We all know that the real boss, our heavenly Father, is so much, much bigger than anyone. Yet God loves us so much that he yearns to have a personal relationship with each person. God's plan became crystal clear when Jesus uttered the Great Commission (Matthew 28:19-20). Through Jesus and the Holy Spirit, God firmly and lovingly wraps his arms around each believer and says, "We're really expecting big things from you."

God is the generous giver of all gifts, mercies (Lamentations 3:22-23), and grace (Ephesians 2:8). Our primary desire should be to know him as well as we possibly can. As an outpouring of our love, God expects us to demonstrate and share the good news, day in and day out (2 Timothy 4:2), with people that we come into contact with. God gave us way more than 10 percent extra because he poured the Spirit of his Son into our hearts (Galatians 4:6), and he sealed us with the Holy Spirit for eternity (Ephesians 4:30). We don't have to try to do it all by ourselves (John 15:5) because he equipped us with the power of the Holy Trinity, the best team ever. God wants our availability much more than our ability.

Prayer: Oh magnificent and most holy I AM, thank you for the life lessons that I can glean from the world of sports and the world of business. Through these lessons learned, I can share them with a world that needs to know that you were, are, and always will be the boss. In the precious name of the One who took my place at Calvary, amen.

BB42:
3-6-3

Matthew 26:58-75, 27:35-50; Mark 16:1-14

Then he began to curse and to swear saying, "I do not know the Man!" And immediately a rooster crowed. And Peter remembered the word of Jesus who had said to him; "Before the rooster crows, you will deny Me three times." So he went out and wept bitterly.

Matthew 26:74-75

The 3-6-3 double play is the most difficult double play to turn in baseball. The 3 is the shorthand notation the scorer uses for the first baseman, and the 6 is the shorthand notation for the shortstop. With a runner on first base, a sharp ground ball is fielded by the first baseman. The first baseman must make an accurate, strong throw to the shortstop covering second base, being careful not to hit the runner in the back. After the first baseman throws to the shortstop, he must scurry to the first base bag, find the bag with his foot, and look up just in time to catch the return throw. First basemen who can make this play consistently are few and far between.

There was a very unique and interesting 3-6-3 combination involved in the resurrection. Peter bragged that he would never forsake Jesus, but Jesus told Peter that after Peter denied him three times, a rooster would crow. After Jesus was wrongly accused and arrested, Peter indeed denied Jesus three times, the cock crowed, and Peter wept bitterly.

Then Jesus clung to the cross for six hours to prove how much he loves us by dying for our sins. After Jesus was on the cross for three hours, the sky turned pitch black, and Jesus spent the next three hours in darkness, separated from the Father who could no longer look upon the sin that Jesus had taken in his body to the cross.

After the stone covering the tomb was rolled away on the third day, signifying that Jesus had defeated the grave, three women discovered that he was no longer in the tomb. According to the gospel of Mark, Mary Magdalene, Mary, the mother of the disciple James, and Salome were at the tomb. What is unusual about the women telling Peter and the disciples that Jesus had risen is that women were viewed as second-class citizens, and their witness would have been discounted in a court of law at that time.

Three times Jesus was denied by Peter. Six hours he stayed on the cross to demonstrate his perfect love. Three women found the empty tomb, which represented his resurrection from the grave. That's a 3-6-3 combination for eternity.

Prayer: Dear Father God, thank you for the courage and dedication of the early men and women followers of Jesus, and thanks most of all for Jesus, who defeated Satan's attacks and overcame the grave. In Jesus's name, amen.

BB43:
EXCITEMENT IS AT
A FEVER PITCH!

Luke 24:1-12, Mark 16:1-14

Why are you looking for the Living One in a cemetery?
He is not here, but raised up ...

Luke 24:5-6

One of my favorite scenes from a baseball movie occurred in *Fever Pitch*, starring Jimmy Fallon and Drew Barrymore. Jimmy plays the character of Ben, a teacher and an obsessed Red Sox fan. Drew is a successful young executive who believes that she can cure her boyfriend Ben of his Red Sox obsession.

In an attempt to show his girlfriend that she was more important to him than baseball, Ben gives away his tickets to a crucial Red Sox-Yankees game to go with her to a Great Gatsby party. He has a great time and, even upon finding out the Red Sox trailed 7-0 in the late innings, takes the disappointing news in stride.

Later, Ben is awakened from a deep sleep by the telephone. He can barely hear the caller because of very loud background noise.

His friend screams, "You won't believe it! It's the most amazing comeback in the history of baseball! The Sox were down 7-0 and scored eight runs in the bottom of the ninth! You missed the greatest game in the history of Fenway Park!"

Startled, Ben didn't believe his friend. He reached for the TV remote and clicked on the local newscast. Sure enough, there stood a newscaster outside Fenway Park, describing the revelry as something you would not believe and that a gigantic conga line had broken out. Indeed the Sox had won 8-7.

If such a win really happened, there would be different degrees of happiness and joy. If a Red Sox fan only read the final score "Boston 8, New York 7," the person would say "Great!" but couldn't appreciate the thrilling details. If a person saw the game on TV, there would be much more excitement and elation. But to the longsuffering Red Sox fans at the game who had seen the despised Yankees win world championship after world championship, this victory would have been the sweetest and triggered the greatest celebration.

Consider the reaction of Mary, the mother of the disciple James, Salome, and Mary Magdalene upon finding the empty tomb. These loyal women traveled with Jesus and suffered with him as he endured the horror of the crucifixion on the cross. Imagine their unbridled joy and excitement after hearing the angel proclaim, "He is not here. He is risen!"

Surprised by Mary Magdalene's emotional account that the three women had seen Jesus alive and well, the disciples didn't believe her (Mark 16:10-11). Later that evening, Jesus appeared to the eleven and scolded them for not believing her (Mark 16:14).

There are still mixed reactions to the empty tomb. Many people who attend church only on Christmas and Easter value the empty tomb like the person who only read the final score. Their excitement quickly fades. But people who have a personal relationship with Jesus Christ should be joyous not only on Easter but throughout the year. Believers understand the painful price that Jesus paid for our sins to give us hope of eternal life in heaven. Where does your hope reside?

Prayer: Father God, may my joy be rekindled not only on Easter Sunday but each day by the excitement of knowing that Christ is risen and that I will be with both of you one day. In Jesus's holy name, amen.

BB44:
GOD KNOWS HOW
JIM JOYCE FEELS

John 11:35, Romans 8:26, Hebrews 13:5

Jesus wept.

John 11:35

An extraordinary story suddenly unfolded on June 2, 2010, at Detroit's Comerica Park when the Tigers faced the Cleveland Indians. Tiger pitcher Armando Galarraga retired the first twenty-six Indian batters, including the leadoff batter in the ninth that was robbed of an extra base hit in left center field. The play was eerily reminiscent of the bobble and catch in the ninth inning of Chicago White Sox pitcher Mark Buehrle's perfect game in 2009.

With the entire crowd on its feet and screaming for an out, the twenty-seventh batter grounded a ball between first and second. The Tiger first baseman backhanded the ball, hesitated for a moment, gained control, and fired the ball to Galarraga covering the bag. Armando caught the ball and stepped on the bag almost a full step ahead of the runner.

Perfect game. No! What? The umpire called him safe? No way! Over two hundred thousand games have been played in the major leagues, and this game would have been only the twenty-first perfect game in history. The blown call was made by Jim Joyce, fifty-four, a veteran of many World Series and playoff games. With his rough, gruff persona and Fu Manchu moustache, if you look up umpire in the dictionary, you would find Joyce's picture. Everybody in Comerica Park knew it was an out except Jim Joyce.

How could it happen? Only if you've refereed or umpired can you begin to understand. As the first baseman gloved the ball and hesitated slightly, perhaps Joyce anticipated the runner would be safe instead of concentrating on the play and his mechanics. Officials are taught to anticipate the play, not the call. Whatever happened, in the next three seconds, Jim Joyce made arguably the worst call since the sixth game of the 1985 World Series. In that game, umpire Don Denkinger blew a similar call that likely cost the St. Louis Cardinals a world championship.

I debated that the home plate umpire could have rescued his buddy by going over to Jim and saying, "Jim, you didn't see the pitcher step on the bag well ahead of the runner, did you?" The home plate umpire winks at Jim for emphasis.

Jim would say, "Nope."

The home plate umpire would shout, "Batter's out! Ball game!"

But Jim was left on an island.

After the game, Jim Joyce saw the replay. What did the tough, gruff, veteran umpire do? He wept because he felt so bad. Joyce apologized to the pitcher, who accepted his apology and said in a totally classy statement that everybody makes mistakes.

No doubt Jim Joyce tossed and turned and grieved over his terrible call throughout the night. There was probably little that anyone could do for him as he replayed it over and over in his mind, willing to give just about anything if he could change it. He wouldn't have wished the sinking feeling in his gut and the overwhelming shock that went through his body when he saw the replay on anyone.

Jim Joyce was certainly not the first person to be remorseful over a mistake. You and I have made terrible mistakes and felt deep remorse in different situations. I know it's not life or death, that it's just a ball game. I assure you that Joyce was absolutely sick over what happened. But God gives each of us unique passions and abilities. When God knitted Jim Joyce in the womb, he gave him a love for baseball, the ability to concentrate in pressure-filled situations, the perseverance to survive years of long car rides in the minor leagues, and the fortitude to ignore catcalls and threats.

When we suffer disappointments, setbacks, heartbreaking losses, and personal trials, we can draw on the promises that God cares deeply for his children when they're hurting. Jesus, the Son of Man and Son of God, came into our world so that he could experience every hurt we will ever experience and understand the exact emotions we're going through (John 11:35). Jesus specifically experienced the emotions of hatred, betrayal, rejection, and ridicule on his journey to the cross. I pray that Jim Joyce was reminded often of God's love and faithfulness (Hebrews 13:5). God will never leave nor forsake us.

Prayer: Most gracious and loving God, may I always be aware of how deeply you love me, especially when I'm down in the dumps. In the depths of despair, may I remember that Jesus has been there and done that. Give me the unshakable faith that there is One who really understands what I'm going through. In the precious name of the Lamb, amen.

BB45: EPILOGUE OF THE JIM JOYCE SAGA

Lamentations 3:22-23

The steadfast love of the Lord never ceases, his mercies never come to an end. They are new every morning, great is your faithfulness.

I hoped that Jim Joyce, the umpire who botched the call at first base that cost Detroit Tiger pitcher Armando Galarraga a perfect game, would be able to experience God's mercy and grace soon. I had no idea that it would happen so quickly and so thoroughly. Here are the mercies and acts of grace that Jim experienced in the next twenty-four hours. Remember that mercy is not getting what you deserve and grace is getting what you don't deserve.

The first act of mercy was the umpire's rotation in the next game. Instead of being on third base and waiting for hours for a call to come his way and the pressure that would come from that call, he was the home plate umpire. That position got him into a groove by forcing him to concentrate on every pitch. Second, the game was in the afternoon, which meant that Joyce was able to get up early, eat breakfast, go straight to the ball park, and get into his pre-game routine. A night game would have meant waiting for hours and dwelling on the play. Even worse would have been an open date. Third, the afternoon game lessened the national scrutiny on him because it was over before most people got home from work. Finally, the Tigers won easily 12-6, so there was plenty for Tiger fans to cheer about and little to jeer about. I call those good examples of mercy.

But the grace was the coolest part. After the previous night's game, several players commented that Jim Joyce was one of the umpires that you could actually talk to, so those good deeds had already begun to work in his favor. As Joyce and his crew strode through the tunnel to the playing field, fans near the tunnel applauded a man who had blown one of the biggest calls in baseball history. When he entered the field, you could tell he had been crying because there was one umpire with a red face. As he walked to the plate for the pre-game lineup card ceremony, who walks to the plate but Armando Galarraga? Now Joyce is really struggling to hold back the tears. He checked the lineup cards, but I doubt he could read them through his watery eyes. He handed the lineup card back to Galarraga and gave him a playful swat on the shoulder. As Galarraga returned to the bench, his same Tiger teammates who screamed bloody murder at Jim Joyce the previous night were also applauding.

If you asked Joyce, he would tell you one of the worst days of his life was followed by one of the greatest days of his life. It was a day that he didn't deserve, but he got it because he had treated people fairly. Let's face it. There are a lot of people with forgiving hearts who are willing to give others a second chance.

We have an incredible God who loves all of his children and extends us mercy and grace at totally unpredictable times. May Jim pass that mercy and grace along to others as he plays out the rest of his career.

Prayer: Wonderful and most gracious Father, thank you for the encouragement that you send my way when I need it most. Just when things appear to be the bleakest, you bring out the sunshine to remind me that there is always hope. In Jesus's name, amen.

BB46:
GOD'S MERCIES
ARE AMAZING

Zechariah 9:12, 1 Timothy 1:15-16

I promise you two mercies for each of your woes.

Zechariah 9:12

The mercy story of Umpire Jim Joyce continues. First base umpire Joyce made one of the worst and most ill-timed calls in baseball history that cost Armando Galarraga a perfect game. It was soon revealed that he is one of the umpires in baseball who will listen to the player's point of view when there is a disputed call. Players and fans rallied to his side the following day after he tearfully admitted he blew the call.

ESPN interviewed a hundred baseball players and asked them to rate the best umpires in baseball. Less than two weeks after making one of the worst calls in baseball history that made him the target of threats and abuse all over the country, Joyce was named by fifty-three players as one of the best umpires. The most votes received by another umpire was thirty-four, an astounding nineteen-vote advantage for Joyce. Again, players lauded Joyce's ability and his willingness to allow players to question calls and receive explanations.

Joyce's fair treatment of players was never intended to be money saved for a rainy day. He loves the game, and he appreciates the player's right to know why he made a call. After the biggest screw-up of his career, Joyce has received mercy after mercy, which has surely hastened the healing that this scar could leave.

Recall that Joyce immediately confessed that he blew the call and how badly he felt. I believe that God looks for us to confess specific situations that we foul up and express real remorse for our actions. Joyce never wants to repeat the call that he made. It would be too painful. God doesn't want us repeating bad mistakes and suffering the inevitable consequences. God will forgive us every time we ask him. Jesus taught that we are to forgive our brothers seventy times seven if necessary. God promises us a clean heart when we confess our sins. Then God gives us mercy, often multiple mercies, to move us through the healing process.

Jim Joyce could never have anticipated the good fortune that he received after he blew it. When you blow it and you think you are the worst person and the biggest screw-up ever, remember that the Apostle Paul was granted some of the greatest mercies after killing Christians and trying to destroy the early church. After Saul was blinded on the road to Damascus so that Jesus could have his undivided attention, Jesus showed him great mercy by restoring his sight. Also, instead of condemning Saul, who became known as Paul, Jesus appointed him to be his chosen person to share the gospel with the Gentiles. There is nothing that you've done that God won't forgive. God will restore you completely after you confess your sins, and God will take you from worst back to first as a result of his forgiveness. What a great promise, and God never breaks promises.

Prayer: Heavenly Father, thank you for your mercies that are new every morning. In Jesus's name, amen.

BB47:
GOD IS ALWAYS
WATCHING

1 Peter 5:7

He is always watching everything that concerns you.

I have two good friends, Fred and Tim. Fred coached Tim in high school, and Tim later became a coach. One afternoon Tim's baseball team played at Sprayberry High School, whose outfield fence backs up to Sandy Plains Road, a busy, four-lane road perched above the playing field. Fred was driving home from a meeting and was stopped in traffic behind the left-field fence. He observed a coach and an umpire having a discussion in the middle of the diamond. Suddenly, the umpire whirled his arm in the classic motion and tossed the coach, Tim, out of the game for arguing too vehemently. "You're outta the game!"

Fred called Tim that evening and the conversation went something like this.

"Hey, how did the game go today?"

"Oh, it was fine."

"Is there anything that you need to tell me?"

"Well, I sort of had a problem with an umpire."

Oftentimes, our actions are shaped by who is watching. I could be watching a TV show that someone I respect wouldn't approve of, and I will flip the channel if that person comes into the room. So what is the difference between that behavior and the fact that God is watching me all the time? The Bible says in 1 Peter 5:7 that he is always watching us and concerned about everything that impacts us. A good checkpoint for all of us is to behave like Jesus is in the room, on the baseball diamond, on the conference call, or with us in the car. If we are conscious of Jesus throughout all of our activities, our behavior will be more Christlike.

Prayer: Father God, you must chuckle when you see me behave as if you are not watching. Help me always be cognizant of your presence so that I honor you by turning from temptation no matter who is around. In Jesus's holy name, amen.

BB48:
YANKEE STADIUM
GIVEAWAY

Matthew 7:7

Ask, and you will receive...

My daughter Allison took a trip with friends to New York City. The four of them took in a game at the new Yankee Stadium in the Bronx. Allison proudly shared how she helped negotiate tickets from the scalpers outside the stadium. She remains a chip off the old block. They took the subway to the Bronx on Friday night and sold their tickets because her boyfriend couldn't join them and then bought tickets prior to Saturday afternoon's game. All in a day's work.

Her bartering adventure reminded me of my only trip to the old Yankee Stadium where the Bronx Bombers won so many titles. In 2000 I was in New York with my AT&T team to close a contract with a vendor and our attorneys in Manhattan. One evening, we used the firm's Yankee tickets. There were three of us, and we had six tickets, so we debated what to do with the remaining tickets. We decided that since they were free for us, we would just give them away.

The search around the stadium began for someone "worthy enough" to claim the tickets. Here came two young couples who obviously needed tickets as they headed for the ticket booth. I called out to them and explained that we had three free tickets. Maybe it was my Southern accent or the sheer surprise of being offered something for free in New York City with no strings attached. But one of the young men, who turned out to be Brooklyn Law School students, literally recoiled and took a small step backward. I wanted to tell him, "They're Yankee tickets, not snakes!" Eventually, a level of trust developed that we weren't scamming them, and they were very appreciative.

It reminded me that often God wants to give us what is *best*, but we recoil, begin to take inventory, and weigh his offer against our feeble choices. The closer we walk with God the more obedient we will be and the more ready we are to recognize and accept the wonderful surprises and favor that he wants us to have. God loves us so much that he would do anything for us, including sending his Son to die an awful death only to rise resurrected, defeating the grave forever. That's God's ultimate gift that I pray each of you will receive one day.

Prayer: Father God, thank you so much for the favor that you extend me. I don't deserve it so many times, but I am so grateful for your surprises. In Jesus's name, amen.

BB49:
TRIPLE PLAY!

John 14:16

And I will pray the Father, and he shall give you another
Comforter, that he may abide with you forever.

A triple play is when you get three outs on the same play. It's very
unusual to get three outs on one play. It happens in the major leagues
a couple of times a season. Sometimes it's a hard line drive to the
shortstop for the first out, who flips the ball to the second baseman
standing on second base to get the runner who drifted away from
second, and then the second baseman fires to first in time to get the
runner who wandered off first base. On a rare occasion, a shortstop
will make an unassisted triple play by catching a line drive near second base, stepping on the base, and tagging the runner coming from
first. Three outs on the same play.

The Holy Trinity, three in one, makes up a neat, faith-based triple play. First, God is our Judge, the Maker of the Universe, and
sent Jesus Christ from heaven to earth so that he could experience
our emotions and human hearts. God loves us so much that he sent
Jesus to save us from ourselves. Second, when we confess our sins for
the first time and ask Jesus to come into our lives, we receive Jesus
as our Savior and begin to strive to make him Lord of our lives. The

most wonderful benefit is that we receive eternal life immediately and are guaranteed to live in heaven with God and Jesus forever.

Now here is where the triple play comes in. To connect us eternally with him, God gives us the Holy Spirit, who is the same Holy Spirit whom Jesus sent after his ascension to live inside the twelve disciples. Through the power of the Holy Spirit, these disciples were able to change the world for Christianity even though Jesus was back in heaven. God, Jesus, and the Holy Spirit. It's the triple play for all time.

Prayer: Thank you for the Holy Trinity of you, Father, your Son, and the Comforter, who enable us to overcome anything that Satan can throw at us when we place our total trust in the Trinity. In Jesus's name, amen.

BB50:
WHAT IS YOUR
ROOKIE CARD WORTH?

Job 11:23, Colossians 3:17, 1 Peter 2:2

Like newborn babies, crave pure spiritual milk, so that by
it you may grow up in your salvation.

1 Peter 2:2

Almost forty-three thousand fans rocked the Ted on a Monday night in
2010 as the Atlanta Braves exploded for five runs in the seventh inning
to hand rookie phenom pitcher Stephen Strasburg the second loss of his
young career. Most of the forty-three thousand came to see Strasburg,
who brought tremendous excitement to baseball in the first season of his
major league career.

Braves fans experienced a similar phenomenon in 2010 in Jason
Heyward, another "can't miss" young star. Or can he? Heyward went
on the DL with a bad thumb and dropped to .251. We recall the huge
excitement around Jeff Francoeur's debut in 2005 when he hit .400 for
the first month. But Francoeur would become one of many outfielders
with average stats.

Long-time Braves fans will remember another rookie sensation, Brad
Komminsk, who was reputed to be the next Henry Aaron. Komminsk
also wore number 7 as Francoeur did, but think of an even bigger and
stronger version of Francoeur. Komminsk had ransacked minor league

pitching, but he could never hit the major league curve ball consistently. Komminsk played for seven major league clubs in eight seasons with only 23 HR, 105 RBI and a .218 lifetime average.

Hall of Famers like Hank Aaron produce consistently outstanding results for fifteen to twenty years because they have a tremendous work ethic, physical ability, and mental toughness. One indication of a baseball player's lasting greatness is the value of his rookie card. A mint 1954 Topps Hank Aaron rookie card sold for $100,000. An eBay auction for the *only* Stephen Strasburg "Superfractor" card in the 2010 Bowman Chrome set exceeded $10,000, but I wonder what it will be worth in ten years. What is the Brad Komminsk 1984 rookie card worth in 2010? You can buy one on eBay for a solitary George Washington.

Every believer started out as a rookie, a first-year player, in the Christian walk. Most arrived on the scene quietly with little fanfare while some created tremendous excitement by bursting onto the scene with their Damascus road experiences and flashy testimonies. Perhaps others have experienced memorable mission trips, but now the thrill is gone. The mountaintop experience faded. Now what? How do you maintain steady performance day in and day out in the kingdom or else become a flash in the pan?

Similar to the current value of the Aaron, Strasburg, and Komminsk rookie cards, our contributions to God's kingdom are measured over our lifetimes. Hold up your virtual Christian rookie card. What is its current worth to the kingdom? Perhaps you had the potential to influence thousands for Christ but instead have reached hundreds, or several, or just yourself. Wherever we stand, the challenge for each Christian is to increase the value of his or her "rookie card" through daily prayer, obedience, and Bible study. Find your niche where God can use you to great advantage.

Prayer: May I consistently perform for you and your kingdom, day in and day out, so that the value of my rookie card increases. Remind me when I am struggling that apart from you, I can do nothing, and may you receive all of the glory for my kingdom efforts. In Jesus's name, amen.

BB51:
THE KEYS TO VICTORY
IN JESUS (BASEBALL)

Romans 7:7-9

I had not known sin, but by the Law...

Romans 7:7

There are three keys to winning any World Series. Invariably, the team that excels in these three areas will have an excellent chance of being victorious. First, the winning team must have great pitching. The starters must be able to keep the team in the game, and the relievers need to shut the opposition down in the eighth and ninth innings. Second, the pitchers need good support from the defense with very few errors and some outstanding catches that demoralize the opposition. Third, the team must be able to score runs. Oftentimes, scoring is lower than the regular season because of better pitching, which makes timely hitting with two outs even more important. If any of these facets of the game is off, it will place tremendous pressure on the team and reduce the chances of winning the World Series.

There are three keys to leading a victorious life. You must first set the table for Jesus so that he can get the "save." The way you set the table for Christ is by confessing your sins, which is called repentance, and asking God to forgive you in an attitude of godly sorrow. Instead of being sorry that you got caught, you are truly sorry and never again intend to be bound by sin in your life. You've now opened the door for Jesus to get the save. The second key is when you turn toward Jesus and ask him to come into your life. The third key is when you place your trust in Jesus Christ and put him and other people first.

Even after you commit your life to Christ, the evil one will tempt you constantly to get you to sin, which moves you away from God. When you break one of God's rules, confess your specific sin to him immediately. He will always forgive you and restore you to a full relationship with him.

Prayer: Father God, thank you for clearly giving me the three keys to living a victorious life through Jesus Christ. May I love you with my whole heart and be obedient to you each day. Thank you for loving me unconditionally and for the abundant mercy and grace that you give me, a sinner. In Jesus's precious name, amen.

BB52:
THE UNFORGIVEABLE SIN

Ephesians 4:30

And grieve not the Holy Spirit of God…

Baseball has a rich tradition, and strategy is a very important part of each game. Part of the strategy is avoiding critical mistakes when the risk should have never been taken. These mistakes have traditionally been called cardinal sins. I call them forehead slappers, the types of mistakes when you slap the heel of your hand against your forehead. You scream, "Why did you do that?"

For example, it is a cardinal sin to be thrown out at third base for the first out of an inning. The reason is that you can still score from second base on a base hit. Another cardinal sin is when the pitcher gets ahead in the count and grooves an 0-2 pitch. The pitcher should throw at least two pitches off the plate to see if the batter will chase a bad pitch. A third example is to get thrown out going from second to third on a ball hit to the left side of the infield. The risk is simply too great to try it.

Dr, Michael McQueen, senior pastor of St. James UMC in Alpharetta, Georgia, explained that the one cardinal or unforgiveable sin in the Bible is to grieve, which means to sadden, the Holy Spirit. The Holy Spirit reveals our sinful nature to us and the need to turn from a sinful life and trust in Jesus. As each year advances and sin accumulates like another layer of shell around a pearl, the heart becomes hardened more and more until the Word of God bounces off the heart. Without the penetration of the Holy Spirit, we can never receive the forgiveness that is necessary for eternal life in heaven. If we never allow the Holy Spirit to work, we will have no hope to be with Jesus for eternity.

Prayer: Father God, help me convey to others the need to follow the calling of the Holy Spirit. In Jesus's name, amen.

BB53:
THE SALARY DRIVE

2 Timothy 4:2, Colossians 3:17

Whatever you do, in word or deed, do everything in the name of our Lord Jesus Christ.

Colossians 3:17

Until the late 1960s, baseball players renegotiated their contracts after the end of each season. There was no such thing as free agency until Curt Flood of the St. Louis Cardinals successfully tested the waters, and that ruling changed the face of baseball and sports forever with players moving from one team to another and signing multi-year guaranteed contracts.

When there were no guaranteed contracts, there was a saying for a player who had underperformed all season but suddenly got on a hot streak in September, the last month of the season. The games in September were called the salary drive because the player hoped his improved statistics would drive up his salary when he sat down with the owner.

That is not the only example of a salary drive. In basketball, padding your stats in the last couple of minutes of the game happens during garbage time. The losing quarterback pads his stats late in the fourth quarter after the game has long been decided. In high school, students will loaf all semester and then cram during finals to achieve a better letter grade. In business, some employees will try to make a big accomplishment in December, but it's too late to help their ratings because many companies only consider the January through November accomplishments.

What is common in all of these examples is a lack of urgency from the beginning. When we as believers are lackadaisical with an "I will do it next year" attitude, we are not following the urgency with which our generation needs to see or know about Christ. The second book of Timothy makes it clear that we are to be urgent about sharing the gospel with others. Second Timothy 4:2 instructs us that we are to share the gospel urgently whenever we get the chance, even when we don't feel like doing it or it isn't convenient.

For example, let's say you were on a summer mission trip and became friends with a local person, who asked you why you would spend a week working in the hot sun. That question would be a great opportunity to share what Christ means to you. If you failed to speak up, you might never get another chance to share with that person. Colossians 3:17 tells us to do everything in the name of our Lord, Jesus Christ. We need a sense of urgency each day because we encounter people who are walking in darkness, and they need to be drawn to the Light that comes through Christ Jesus.

Prayer: Father God, today is the first day of the rest of my life. May I commit it to sharing your light, your love, and your gospel with people who need the hope that I have. In Jesus's name, amen.

BB54:
ARE YOU IN A VALLEY?

Psalm 23, Romans 8:18, Colossians 1:27

Christ lives in you. This gives you assurance of sharing his glory.

Colossians 1:27

My friend Bob and I were talking baseball, and I mentioned Atlanta Brave manager Bobby Cox's National League farewell tour. Bobby retired following the 2010 season after an illustrious career as manager of the Atlanta Braves, who fought hard to get him into the playoffs one last time. I thought it was cool that Delta painted a big red 6 on the plane used for Bobby's last regular season charter flight when the Braves faced the New York Mets. When he was a kid, Bob saw Bobby Cox play as a third baseman for the New York Yankees in the late '60s and even saw him hit a few home runs.

When we think of the Yankees, we think of the Bronx Bombers, the Babe, Joe D., the Mick, Derek Jeter, and the classic pinstripes. The Yankees are twenty-seven-time World Champions and are perhaps the most storied franchise in sports history. But during the period from 1965 to 1967, after appearing in five consecutive World Series from 1960 through 1964, the Yankees lost forty-nine more games than they won, even finishing last in 1966.

All of the best sports teams eventually go through valleys after their championship runs. Perhaps you have been in a personal valley for a while and can't see your way out.

You might feel like your situation is never going to improve. But Jesus Christ understands exactly where you are and how you feel because he experienced every possible valley as the Son of Man. God sent his Son to die a brutal death for our sins, and the Son of God defeated the grave forever, which gives us hope for eternity in his presence. No matter who you are or what you have done, there is always hope in Christ.

Prayer: Father God, when I am down or despondent or discouraged, may I realize that you're walking through the valley with me and that you will lead me out of the valley, to the promised land, and to the other side. In Jesus's name, amen.

GOLF

GOLF29:
DUSTIN'S WARNING SIGNS

2 Timothy 3:16, Psalm 119:100-109

All scripture is given by inspiration of God, and is profitable for doctrine, for reproof, for correction, for instruction in righteousness.

2 Timothy 3:16

Make no mistake. The game of golf is alive and well. For those who were concerned that there were no exciting players beyond the post-Tiger/Phil era, the 2010 PGA Championship was truly a changing of the guard. The back nine play at Whistling Straits generated riveting drama. Six players, including three who were twenty-five or younger, had a great chance to win over the last three holes, producing one of the most thrilling shootouts since Jack Nicklaus won his final major championship in the 1986 Masters.

Nick Watney, a twenty-something rising star, entered the last round with a three-shot lead, but his game fell apart on Sunday's front nine. Steve Elkington, a member of the old guard at forty-seven, missed two easy putts that would have given him the lead. Bubba Watson, the crowd-pleasing bomber wearing his emotions on his sleeve, blasted 390-yard drives and displayed the deft touch of a safe cracker. Golf's next superstar, twenty-one-year-old Rory McIlroy, finished one shot back along with Zach Johnson, winner of the 2007 Masters. Eventually, twenty-five year-old Martin Kaymer of Germany beat Bubba in a three-hole playoff.

The playoff was somewhat anticlimactic because the lead story of the 2010 PGA Championship was twenty-five-year-old Dustin Johnson, another prodigious long-ball hitter. Dustin came to the eighteenth hole with a one-shot lead after tremendous birdies on sixteen and seventeen. He drove outside the ropes into a bunker that had been trampled all week by spectators. Dustin grounded his club in the bunker and was assessed a two-shot penalty by the PGA rules officials, thereby missing the playoff by one stroke.

Much to his credit, Dustin reacted like a gentleman when he received the ruling. He didn't go ballistic or blame the PGA officials, saying that they had their job to do.

Whistling Straits is a unique golf course because there are hundreds of sand bunkers outside the ropes on this links-style layout. Prior to the beginning of play, the PGA ruled that all sandy areas would be played as bunkers. That ruling meant that a player cannot touch the sand in the bunker with his club before striking it. The two-shot penalty, viewed as too harsh by many people, should not have been a surprise to Dustin or any golfer in the field because the PGA officials posted a sheet of tournament rules in large font on the players' locker room mirrors.

Watney commented afterward that the players generally don't read the rules much. Usually, when a player is concerned about committing a rules infraction on tour, he simply summons a rules official.

Think about someone posting a message on the front door so that you couldn't possibly miss it in the morning. The reminder on the locker room mirrors read in part: "Bunkers: All areas designed and built as sand bunkers will be played as bunkers (hazards). Many bunkers will likely include numerous footprints, heel prints, and tire tracks. No free relief will be available."

Initially, I felt tremendous sympathy toward Dustin regarding the ruling, especially considering the chaos in the gallery surrounding him on eighteen. Nevertheless, he failed to ask for a rules official, consult his rulebook, or confer with his caddie before grounding his club. Dustin obviously failed to heed the special warnings that the PGA posted in the locker room. Admittedly, he had not taken time to read and understand the warning. The oversight cost him a shot at winning the ensuing playoff of golf's final major of the year. Dustin clearly suffered the consequences for his mistake.

Many people don't read God's rules much either. Certainly God blessed us with a conscience to know right from wrong, and believers have the additional advantage of the prompting of the Holy Spirit when we are about to mess up. When we hit the ball into trouble, we can consult the Rule Book (God's Word) or call in the Rules Official (Holy Spirit) to help us make the proper decision. Back in the day, God gave the people of Israel special warnings through the pleas of a dozen major and minor prophets. These men told the chosen ones to repent or face the consequences of eternal separation from God. Jesus spoke often in the Gospels of the eternal consequences of failing to heed the warnings of the prophets. God still places people and circumstances in our paths. These events are warnings that we need to turn to God, whether we recognize them or not.

Have you heeded the special warnings? Take time now to respond to the warning signs. Your response could make the difference in winning or losing your final major.

Prayer: Father God, when you woo me to change, thank you for giving me many warning signs. Help me heed these signs so that I am assured of winning my final major, where one of my rewards is eternal life in heaven with you. In Jesus's name, amen.

GOLF30: MISSED OPPORTUNITIES? REFOCUS!

Luke 9:62, Acts 20-24, 1 Corinthians 9:22

Life is worth nothing unless I use it for doing the work assigned me by the Lord Jesus, the work of telling others the Good News about God's mighty kindness and love.

Acts 20:24

Although I had been a Christian for almost five years, I missed some opportunities one summer when I got consumed by golf. I made my first hole in one, and two weeks later, I matched my best golf round ever when I shot 65 with a ball in the water. Hey, I found the secret. Visions of the Champions Tour paraded in my head.

I proceeded to hit several thousand balls on the practice tee over the next month, and I ignored God leading me to have open gym in order to play more golf. I reassured myself, "It won't matter. The boys won't miss it." I believe that God noticed. Luke 9:62: "Jesus told him, 'Anyone who allows himself to be distracted from the work that I plan for him is not fit for the kingdom of God.'"

Later that summer, I partially tore a tendon in my left elbow and had painful tendonitis for six months. I was amazed how often that pain in my elbow reminded me of where I should have been spending more time. But during my down time, I got in touch with God's plan through the youth sports ministry at my church. I believe that God's plan is for me to use my passion for sports to help reach someone who could miss spending eternity with him. That's one reason that I wrote this book.

When was the last time that you cried for someone who is unsaved? If you're a Christian and you envision a family member or friend spending eternity separated from God, it should bring you to tears. Evangelist Charles Spurgeon once issued this challenge: "Have you no wish for others to be saved? Then you are not saved yourself. Be sure of that." Paul said in Acts 20:24, "Life is worth nothing unless I use it for doing the work assigned me by the Lord Jesus, the work of telling others the good news about God's mighty kindness and love!" John Wesley, the founder of the Methodist church, stated, "You have nothing to do but to save souls. Therefore spend and be spent in this work."

If you feel lukewarm for Jesus, pray now that God will rekindle your heart for the unsaved and reach out to your lost friends. If you are not sure how to share, you can always ask a Christian brother or sister for guidance.

Prayer: Dear Father God, may I realize that nothing is as important as reaching the lost. Help me recognize and take advantage of the opportunities you give me to share Christ with my friends in words, deeds, and actions. In Jesus's holy name, amen.

GOLF31:
IS IT JUST LUCK?

Matthew 7:7

Ask and you will receive, seek and you will find, knock and
the door will be opened to you.

The par-3 twelfth hole at Augusta is one of the most nerve-racking
holes in golf. Only 155 yards long across Rae's Creek, the narrow
green is positioned diagonally to the right, and the steep bank slopes
dangerously toward the water. When the wind swirls, it's very hard
to detect which way it is blowing. Short right is in the water, long
left is up in the foliage on the hill. Many Masters have been lost at
this dangerous hole.

One year, the Thursday round was interrupted by weather.
Play began on Friday at 7:30 a.m. to complete the first round. Jack
Nicklaus had only played ten holes on Thursday, and being the big
Jack fan that I was, I talked my brother, L. E., into getting up at
4:30 a.m. and meeting me in Augusta at 7:00 a.m. We needed thirty
minutes to walk to Amen Corner, the farthest point on the course,
to see Jack Nicklaus complete his first round.

When the weather is cold in the early morning, golfers have trouble staying loose. When you are tight, you miss shots to the right.
On a clear but chilly forty-degree morning, Jack pushed his opening
tee shot on eleven to the right and missed the green to the right

with his approach but managed to chip close and get his par. When he came to the twelfth tee, there couldn't have been more than a dozen people down there to watch the four-time Masters champion. I was within five yards of Jack. The flagstick was on the right edge, the most dangerous hole placement. I could see Jack aiming for the center of the green to play safe, but he blocked his tee shot. He had enough club though, and the ball finished six feet from the hole.

Everyone applauded, and the guy next to me yelled, "Great shot, Jack!"

Under my breath, I muttered to him, "But he wasn't aiming there."

Jack heard me, turned around, and said with a wry smile, "You're right about that!"

In 1992, Masters champion Fred Couples hit his tee shot on the twelfth hole short to the right. The ball landed on the steep bank, which was wet from overnight rain, somehow grew teeth, and didn't roll back into the water. He made a par and won by two shots.

Sometimes we receive unexpected blessings and don't even realize they came from God. Certainly, Jack and Fred were blessed with fortunate breaks on these shots, but oftentimes, when we get a blessing from God, we call it good fortune, good luck, or a small world. There is nothing small about God's world.

Once I was obedient with a couple of small things that I had been struggling with. Afterward, I felt peace about the situation and thanked God for the special blessing that I believe that he sent my way. Do our good fortunes happen by chance? I don't think so. Not when blessings come from a God who put the entire universe together in six days.

Prayer: Father God, sometimes I am not sure if it is you that just blessed my life. May I improve my discernment so that when you send a blessing my way, I see it and give you immediate thanks. In Jesus's name, I pray. Amen.

GOLF32:
USE THAT FIFTEENTH
CLUB IN YOUR BAG

Romans 8:26; Acts 1:8; Ephesians 4:30, 6:10

Be strong in the Lord, and in his great power!

Ephesians 6:10

From 1992 through 1994, Ben Crenshaw's game had been deteriorating as he slipped farther down the money list. To list him as a serious contender for the Masters green jacket in 1995 would have been purely a sentimental choice, even for his most ardent supporters. On Monday night of Masters week, Ben received distressing news that his longtime coach, Harvey Penick, had passed away in Austin, Texas. Crenshaw and his close friend, Tom Kite, who was another Penick student, flew from Augusta to Austin for Harvey's memorial service. Ben arrived back in Augusta on Wednesday night, obviously feeling a deep sense of loss.

Working with his veteran caddie, Carl Jackson, Ben found a swing key on the range before his Thursday round. After three days of driving the ball consistently and making his usual bushel basket of putts, Ben found himself in contention on Sunday. He so desperately wanted to win the tournament in memory of Harvey Penick that he could have allowed his emotions to get the best of him.

However, Gentle Ben fired a great final round and left himself the luxury of being able to make bogey on the last hole. After cleaning up a one-foot putt, he buried his face in his hands and wept uncontrollably as Carl gave him a hug.

After the green jacket ceremony, Ben spoke of the peace that he felt during the madness of a frantic Augusta back nine finish. Crenshaw was quoted that he felt like Harvey was there with him during the round and how that memory gave him strength, almost like having a fifteenth club in his bag. Perhaps the spirit of Harvey Penick was right there with Ben, whispering in Ben's ear to take dead aim. It was one of the great final round finishes in Masters history.

You and I have a fifteenth club in our bags that we rarely use, and that is the power of the Holy Spirit. Recall that Jesus said to the disciples just before he ascended into heaven that you will receive the power of the Holy Spirit and that you will be witnesses to me in Jerusalem and in all Judea and Samaria and to the ends of the earth (Acts 1:8). The Holy Spirit resides within us to help us with our daily problems, just as Harvey's memory kept Ben focused. Let's take advantage of the power of the Holy Spirit, which God sealed us with at our redemption (Ephesians 4:30). In times of turmoil and stress, let's be strong in the Lord and in his great power (Ephesians 6:10).

Prayer: Dear heavenly Father, may I remember that I have the power of the Holy Spirit within me to do great things for your kingdom. May you receive every bit of the glory. In Jesus's name, amen.

GOLF33:
GO FOR IT LIKE ARNIE!

2 Timothy 4:2

Preach the Word of God urgently at all times, whenever you get the chance, in season and out, when it is convenient and when it is not.

Arnold Palmer is considered by many golf experts to be the most popular golfer to ever play the game. His passionate, swashbuckling, go-for-broke style endeared him to legions of fans for over fifty years. So popular was Arnie during his heyday that he remains a beloved icon.

Arnold won eight major championships, including four Masters titles. Augusta is where Arnold took the game of golf to another level as TV televised his dramatic win in 1960 when he birdied the last two holes to win his second green jacket. The popularity of golf and the rich purses in professional golf have their roots in Arnie's success at Augusta.

Arnold had powerful blacksmith arms and swung at the ball with all of his might with a club-twirling finish. He played out of trouble quite often and hit some amazing recovery shots that wowed his followers, called Arnie's Army. Sometimes it worked out, and sometimes it didn't, but Arnie played with a passion for the game and never backed off.

Leading the final round of the 1964 Masters by a comfortable six shots, Arnie went for the green in two on the par-5 fifteenth hole with a mighty smash of a 3-wood and tore a huge divot out of the fairway. Squinting into the sun, Arnie said, "Did it get over [the water in front of the green]? Did it make it?"

His playing competitor Dave Marr deadpanned, "Arnold, your divot got over."

What can Christians learn from the legend of Arnold Palmer? First of all, Arnie had incredible charisma and an engaging smile. He was incredibly gracious with everyone that he met. He constantly made eye contact and shook hands with the gallery. According to some, he could make a complete stranger feel like a longtime friend. But most of all we can learn from the passion with which he tackled the game of golf. God doesn't want a bunch of wimpy Christians. He wants believers to witness for Christ with passion. If we witnessed for Christ with a passion equal to that displayed by Arnie in his workplace, the kingdom around the world would grow much more quickly and the second coming of Jesus would happen much sooner. Paul taught us to "Go for it!" when he urged believers to share Christ urgently at two times: when it is convenient and when it is not.

Prayer: Father God, may I tap the passion with which Arnie played the game of golf and Paul preached your gospel. May I hang with people who have a passion for living and a passion for reaching others for Christ. In Jesus's name, amen.

GOLF34:
SINGLE-MINDED FOCUS

2 Timothy 4:2

Preach the Word of God urgently at all times, whenever
you get the chance, in season and out, when it is convenient and when it is not.

Some golfers are legendary for their ability to focus on the task at
hand. When Nicklaus needed to hole a putt, he would crouch over
the ball for what seemed like an eternity. Then, once he was absolutely sure that he had the line down, he would stroke the putt and
invariably find the bottom of the cup, particularly if the putt was
a big one. Who can forget the forty-footer he holed in the 1975
Masters as he leaped around the green with his putter thrust high
into the air as a disconsolate Tom Weiskopf watched from the six-
teenth tee. Then there is the 1986 Masters seventeenth hole, the
replay we've seen a million times when Jack holes the putt to take
the lead and Verne Lundquist shouts, "Yes, sir!"

Perhaps no golfer had more of a reputation for possessing steely
concentration than Ben Hogan. Affectionately nicknamed the
Wee Ice Mon by the Scots after his 1953 British Open triumph at
Carnoustie, Hogan rarely spoke during a competitive round because
he was so into his game. At the 1947 Masters, his playing partner,
Claude Harmon, made an ace, a hole-in-one, on the treacherous

twelfth hole. Hogan made a deuce by holing a birdie putt. When Hogan reached the thirteenth tee, he asked Harmon, "What did you make?"

If there was any apostle that had Hogan's steely focus in golf, it had to be Paul. Look what Paul endured yet remained steadfast in his desire to see the Jews and the Gentiles of his day come to a personal relationship with the Savior that Paul had once persecuted. If we simply live with an eternal focus each day, whether or not it rivals Paul's focus or Hogan's on the links, we will be much more prepared to spread the good news of the gospel of Jesus Christ.

Prayer: Dear Father, I thank you for the amazing Apostle Paul and what I can learn from his passion for sharing the gospel each day. May I have a daily awareness of eternity and the opportunities that you place in front of us each day. In Jesus's name, amen.

GOLF35:
NEED A MULLIGAN?

Romans 10:13

For whosoever shall call upon the name of the Lord shall
be saved.

It is a fairly common practice on some American golf courses that
businessmen will rush to the first tee without a warm-up and take
two and pick the best drive. Take two refers to the first tee ball and a
second tee ball called a mulligan. There is a story about an American
who played The Old Course at St Andrews, Scotland, for the first
time. As he reached for his second ball, the caddie said, "You will
now be playing your third shot." The American got the hint, picked
up his tee, and played his first ball.

In 2008, with the help of many friends from church, I founded
the Golf for His Glory tournament that benefits our youth, missions, and ministries at Mt. Zion UMC and serves as an evangelistic
outreach to share the gospel of Jesus Christ. As I sought ways to
share the good news of Christ with the 115 golfers who played the
first year, my good friend, Robert, introduced me to Pocket Power
Testaments. This booklet of the gospel of John includes commen-
tary that comes in a variety of themes, including golf. On the cover
is a picture of a golf ball in the woods in thick grass behind a tree,
and the caption reads, "Do You Need a Mulligan?" Very clever I

thought, and most of the golfers seemed to enjoy the gift of the gospel of John.

Do you ever feel sometimes that you just don't have a lot going for you? It's easy to get frustrated when things aren't going well. Perhaps you are feeling the burden of expectations or your family is struggling financially or emotionally. Have you continued to struggle to do it by yourself? Right now, do you feel that you are four down with four to play? If this situation describes you, have you looked up to the Ultimate Caddy and said, "God, I can't do this by myself anymore. I desperately need a mulligan, a second chance. Can you please send me Jesus?" How would it feel to know the peace that passes understanding? If you turn from your self-centered ways and confess Christ as your Savior, not only will you receive eternal life, but you're on your way to finding the peace that comes from knowing that this world is not all there is. You get the mulligan of all time when you receive Christ. The Holy Spirit will help you with your daily problems and help you pray when you ache and can't possibly put your thoughts into words.

Prayer: Father God, thank you for the clean, fresh start from our selfish efforts that always leave us wanting more than this life has to offer. Jesus Christ, your Son, is the mulligan each one of us needs at some point in our lives. Thank you for the saving grace that is available through Jesus. In his holy name, I pray. Amen.

GOLF36:
HOW SHOULD CHRISTIANS
REACT TO TIGER?

Luke 17:3-4

If your brother trespass against you, rebuke him; and if he repent, forgive him. And if he trespass against you seven times in a day, and seven times in a day turn again to you, saying, I repent; you shall forgive him.

Everyone in the world of golf had their eyes on Tiger Woods at Augusta National Golf Club in April 2010. Tiger returned from a self-imposed exile from the PGA Tour after he admitted sexual misconduct and impropriety. Certainly there were mixed reactions to Tiger's return, but generally the galleries treated him like any other player. Certainly there was not the adulation to which he had grown accustomed. Upon his return most golf fans wanted him to be gracious to the galleries like Arnie and Jack and Phil had been, and to exhibit better self-control when his tee shot went wayward.

In 2009 Kenny Perry, at the age of forty-nine, was a yipped chip from being the oldest man to win the Masters. Certainly he has enough game to put on that green jacket. However, Kenny made a statement without his golf clubs. He put someone else ahead of himself in a demonstration of Christian love and brotherhood. Kenny told the Masters committee that he would play with Tiger the first two days of the 2010 Masters. He felt empathy for the man even though Tiger let his family, a lot of kids, and the golfing world down. You couldn't expect other golfers to follow Kenny's lead. Obviously, they didn't want to get caught up in the circus and hurt their games and the only chance some might ever have to win a Masters.

Regarding Tiger's situation, let's leave the judgment to God. He has proven that he is perfectly capable of judging all of us. There has not been nor will there be a sin that God cannot forgive when someone comes with a repentant heart. Neither should there be one that we cannot forgive. Forgive your brother seventy times seven (Matthew 18:22).

Recall the example of Jesus drawing in the dirt to take the icy stares away from the adulterous woman. The Pharisees sought to stone the woman for her sins, but Jesus said, "Let him who is without sin cast the first stone (John 8:7)." The eldest Pharisee dropped his stone and walked away. The others followed suit until only Jesus and the grateful woman remained. Jesus told her to go and sin no more. Surely Tiger appreciated anything his playing partners and the galleries did to help make him feel welcome.

Prayer: Dear Father, it's easy to take pot shots at people who have committed worse sins than I have. Or have they? Help me realize that sin is sin in your eyes and that I need to keep my house clean through frequent confession of my sins, and thank you for your wonderful forgiveness. In Jesus's name, amen.

GOLF37:
RYDER CUP MAGIC
AT BROOKLINE

Mark 9:34; Acts 1:8, 26; Hebrews 11:1, 6

What is faith? Faith is the confident assurance that something you want is going to happen.

Hebrews 11:1

Every two years, the best twelve golfers from the United States and
the best twelve from the European continent compete in an intense
three-day competition called the Ryder Cup, which was named after
the founder of the competition, Samuel Ryder, in 1927. The competition thrills golf fans around the world, and it gives players who are
accustomed to competing for individual honors, money, and titles,
the chance to win or lose as a team.

On the eve of the Sunday singles final at Brookline Country
Club in the 1999 Ryder Cup, the Americans trailed 10 to 6 and had
been roundly criticized by the American press for being a disparate
group of individuals. The American captain, Ben Crenshaw, saw
something in his team that the media experts were not seeing. At
the press conference following the matches on Saturday, Crenshaw
pointed to the media and said, "I'm a big believer in fate. I have a
good feeling about tomorrow. That's all I'm gonna say."

You might or might not believe in fate, but certainly Captain Crenshaw had faith in his team. Despite the fact that no team had ever erased a four-point margin on Sunday, he had a confident assurance (see Hebrews 11:1) that they would come through in the clutch. Crenshaw still believed his individual stars would come together as a twelve-man team.

In a brilliant strategic move on Sunday, Crenshaw front loaded his lineup and put his top six golfers out first in the singles matches. Roars erupted all over the course as the Americans quickly made up lost ground by winning the first six singles matches, followed by Justin Leonard's forty-five-foot bomb on the seventeenth hole. Leonard's putt won the Ryder Cup for the Americans and had Crenshaw on his knees kissing Mother Earth. Ben kept the faith in his team.

Near the time of Jesus's crucifixion, after almost three years of following Jesus, seeing the miracles, and hearing the message, remember how the disciples argued with each other about who was the greatest (Mark 9:34)? It was still all about individuals. Judas Escariot would soon betray Jesus. When Christ was led to the cross, the eleven remaining disciples, except John, scattered like a covey of quail.

But Christ kept the faith in them. After all, the future of Christianity rested in the hands of these eleven average human beings. Matthias was selected to replace Judas Escariot (Acts 1:26) as the twelfth disciple. After Jesus ascended into heaven, that average group of individuals received the Holy Spirit as Jesus had promised (Acts 1:8). Collectively, they became the most important twelve-man team the world has ever known.

Prayer: Most wonderful Father God, when I look at all that the twelve disciples were able to accomplish, I am in awe that you would trust them with the future of the world. Please entrust me to do the small things that can further the kingdom. In Jesus's holy name, I pray. Amen.

GOLF38:
MY ROUND AT AUGUSTA:
WHAT I LEARNED

1 Peter 5:7

He is always watching everything that concerns us ...

It was the first full weekend of 1974. I had gone to Augusta with my roommate, Tim, to play golf for the weekend. On Friday night I called my friend, Bob, to see how he was doing. I had played college golf with Bob the previous year, and he had gotten married and landed a dream position at Augusta National. When he invited us to come play on Saturday, I couldn't believe it. I was going to play Augusta National! I could hardly sleep, given my anticipation.

What a thrill to drive down Magnolia Lane in Fulcher's 1967 Chevy! The caddies met us in the parking lot on a dreary, drizzly, forty-five-degree day. We teed off around noon, and my first tee shot went straight down the middle. I had a decent front nine, and having a caddy read the greens and make my club selections really helped.

Unfortunately, the wheels started to come off. I bogeyed ten and eleven, and hit in the water on the tough par-3 twelfth. I laid up for my third shot on the par-5 thirteenth, and my caddy suggested a pitching wedge. I had a bit of a side hill lie and had hit my last shot fat. I hesitated and asked him for a nine-iron, which I smoked over the green for another bogey. That was the last piece of advice that I received that afternoon.

I should have taken his advice. My caddy had many years of experience and knew my distances by the second hole. I should have listened to him instead of being hardheaded and hitting a different club. Even though my caddy offered no more advice, he still walked beside me and carried my clubs.

We would be smart to take God's advice. After all, God knew us before he knit us, and he invented time. So that's a lot of experience right there. When we become self-centered and stop taking God's advice, he can go silent on us for a time. He might leave us alone for a season, but he will not abandon us because he will come back for his children. If we shout out for his help, he is only a single prayer away. No matter the situation, God loves us and will always pull the right club for us.

Prayer: Father God, may I seek your guidance so that I pull the right club much more often than trying to do things on my own. Thank you that you love me so much and that you are always there when I need to talk to you. In Jesus's name, amen.

GOLF39:
MY MOST PAINFUL DAY
ON THE GOLF COURSE

Isaiah 53:4

Surely he has borne our griefs, and carried our sorrows...

It was the final round of the 1974 Georgia Junior College State Tournament at the University of Georgia golf course. My team from Middle Georgia College was right in the thick of it to win it all. I turned the front side in thirty-eight after hitting eight of nine greens on a tough golf course. But I slipped up with bogeys on two relatively easy par 4s and came to the par-5 twelfth hole. After a bombed drive, I was in position to hit the peninsula green in two for a sure birdie and a possible eagle. I lined up my three-iron carefully and gave it all that I had. I flushed it, and the ball flew high in the air on a line just left of the flagstick.

That's when the nightmare occurred. The ball landed no more than thirty feet from the front right pin placement. Instead of bounding onto the green, the ball caught the top of the bank and fell back into the water. I made double bogey on my way to an inglorious 43 on the back nine. We lost the state title by only two shots, which meant that if I had simply shot 40 on the back side, the title would have been ours. I was crestfallen and felt that I was the one who cost us the state title.

That shot happened over thirty-five years ago, and I still have the same vision of my ball hitting the bank and toppling into the water. What I would have given at the time for that ball to make the green. A birdie would have renewed my confidence, and who knows what would have happened. It was the most disappointing and painful day on the golf course that I ever had.

God hurts when we hurt. Jesus Christ came to this earth from heaven so that he could know exactly how we feel, no matter the disappointment nor the pain. When we feel like we've hit rock bottom in a relationship, or in school, or in a job, or in a sporting event, we can rest assured that Jesus has felt any emotion that we could possibly feel. Through Christ, we can find solace in our disappointments and failures.

Prayer: Father God, I appreciate you sending Jesus so that he could know what it's like to hurt when we hurt. When I feel so low, help me remember that Jesus felt depths I could never imagine. Thank you for always caring and watching everything that concerns me. In Jesus's name, amen.

GOLF40: THE KEYS TO VICTORY (GOLF)

Romans 7:7-9

I had not known sin, but by the Law...

Romans 7:7

At most major golf tournaments, particularly the US Open, the champion invariably excels in three key statistical areas. First, the winner must drive the golf ball into the fairway the majority of the time. The Open rough is so deep and wiry that stray tee shots often lead to bogeys. Second, the winner must be at or near the lead for the week in hitting greens in regulation. Once the player is on the green, he needs to get down in two putts, which is the regulation number for a par. If any of these facets of the game is off, it will place so much pressure on the player's other facets that any chance of winning will disappear. Rory McIlroy, the 2011 US Open winner, drove the ball long and straight, led the field in greens in regulation, and three-putted only once on his way to a stunning eight-shot victory!

Just as the US Open places golfers under tremendous pressure, the devil constantly keeps the pressure on you to keep you from a relationship with Jesus Christ. You can win that battle and come to know Christ by executing the three keys to victory in Jesus. The first key is that you must come to the realization that you need to exchange your sinful and self-centered life for a selfless one devoted to Christ. When you achieve that realization, confess your sins to God and vow to turn away from sin and turn toward him going forward. God will honor your confession and cleanse you of all the sins you have ever committed. What amazing news it is that you can be freed from the tyranny of sin that plagued you for your entire life!

The second key is to trust that Jesus Christ died for your sins on the cross, and that through his blood it is possible to go to heaven. Trust means believing with all of your heart, mind, and soul that Jesus is your Savior and Lord.

Once you have committed to live your life to Christ, the third key is to practice the following spiritual disciplines to grow as a disciple of Jesus Christ. Be obedient to God by reading your Bible daily and praying, which is simply talking to God and listening for his inner voice to guide you. Obedience to God also includes attending worship services each Sunday and hanging with other believers to learn from each other.

Prayer: Father God, thank you for so clearly giving me the keys to victory in Jesus. May I love you with my whole heart and be obedient to you each day. Thank you for loving me unconditionally and more than I can understand and deserve as a sinner. In Jesus's precious name, amen.

GOLF41:
TAKE MORE CLUB

Acts 1:8, Romans 8:26

You shall receive power when the Holy Spirit comes upon you…

Acts 1:8

The most common mistake that most golfers make is to try to hit the ball too hard into a strong wind. A strong wind against you will magnify the margin of error of your shot, and your mind plays tricks on you. You think, I can swing ten percent harder and hit it ten percent farther. But what happens is that when you grip the club tighter, trying to hit it farther, your big muscles tighten because you are not as confident, and you get off your natural rhythm. The result is usually a mishit shot that falls short and right of the green into the bunker or the water hazard.

What is the key to playing a shot into a strong wind? Take one or two more clubs. Instead of taking a seven-iron, use a less-lofted club such as a six-iron or even a five-iron. Swinging easier with a less-lofted club allows you to swing smoother and keep the ball under the wind. The extra power of the less-lofted club propels your ball where it needs to go. Tap the power of the stronger club when you're going against the wind.

Oftentimes, we try to do it by ourselves in our personal lives. We believe that we can force the action by just trying harder or by cramming more activities, more e-mails, and more calls into our day. But when we try 10 percent harder, it doesn't always produce better results. Sometimes our extra effort is counterproductive, and we can actually cause ourselves more problems.

We believers often neglect the Holy Spirit, the person who lives within us. This is the same Holy Spirit that Jesus promised the disciples that came upon them on the day of Pentecost. Talk about going into a strong headwind. How could twelve ordinary, flawed individuals have changed the world with their strength alone? Their efforts would have been futile. When our efforts are futile or we feel overwhelmed, we need to tap into the awesome power of the Holy Spirit. The first phrase in Romans 8:26 tells us, "The Holy Spirit helps us with our daily problems." When we consistently invite God to be present throughout our day, God gives us the extra power we need to overcome obstacles through the presence of the Holy Spirit.

Prayer: Father and most Holy God, may I realize that just gritting my teeth harder and climbing into a bunker mentality mode is not the answer. May I step back and take the time to bring you into the decision-making process when I face difficulties. In Jesus's name, amen.

GOLF42:
MAKE IT LOOK EASY

Romans 5:8

God proved his great love for us in this way; Christ died
for us while we were still sinners.

Watch the pros on the practice range at the Masters or other major
golf tournaments. There are hundreds of years of collective experience there, and a ton of sweat equity went into honing the skills of
their craft. We marvel as we watch the repetitive ease with which
these men power the golf balls three hundred plus yards and hit
irons so accurately with so little effort. Their skills around the green
as they strike precise chip shots, amazing bunker shots, and pressure
putts leave us shaking our heads in wonderment. When we compare
their swings to our uncoordinated efforts, it is evident why we struggle to shoot anywhere close to par.

Speaking of repetitive ease, at the Masters in 1973, the players
would hit their personal practice balls on the range. Their caddies
would stand 150 to 200 yards away and catch the soaring iron shots
on one hop and place the balls in the bag.

Once Lee Trevino hit irons one after another just perfect as a
woman gushed in awe behind him, "Oh, that is beautiful! How
amazing!" Trevino finally turned to her and teasingly said, "Lady,
what do you expect from the US Open champion, ground balls?"

The pros make it look easy because it cost them so many thousands of hours of practice to get them where they need to be. God made our salvation easy because it cost him so much when he sent Jesus Christ to the cross to die for our sins. No matter how much sweat equity we put into good deeds trying to earn our way into heaven, it will never work because by grace we have been saved through faith. By placing his Son on the cross, it is as if God played this incredible round of golf and left us with only having to make a straight in two-footer up the hill. It's right there for the taking if only we will pull the putter out of the bag and finish it off by repenting of our sin and confessing Christ as our Savior and Lord.

Prayer: Most holy and gracious God, I can never fathom the amount of effort, blood, sweat, and tears that Jesus undertook for me so that I could have an easy way to the cross. Thank you for your unending love for me. In Jesus's name, amen.

GOLF43: GOD HAS NO WAITING LIST

John 14:6

I am The Way, The Truth, and The Life ...

As the Masters rolls around each year, I get a slightly sinking feeling occasionally when someone brings up how hard it is to get badges to the Masters. I have been so fortunate since 1973 to use the badges that my aunt and uncle first purchased in the 1950s. In the 1970s, Augusta National Golf Club closed the waiting list because there were thousands of people who wanted badges, and so few badges became available. So I didn't bother to pursue the waiting list. I had the false assurance that the badges would always be there.

But I cringed when I heard a story of a person who had been on the waiting list for twenty-one years and finally received badges in 2010. I did the math. Let's see. He got on the wait list in 1989. I could have been on it years before and didn't bother. What was I thinking? All it would have taken is several minutes to write a letter to Augusta National and a 37 cent stamp. Don't get me wrong. I am grateful to have attended over thirty Masters tournaments. But I knew the situation, had the knowledge, and didn't act on it. So mentally, I give myself a kick because they could have been used by me, my daughters, and my wife.

In some ways, that can be similar to the unwillingness of people to heed the warning that there is only one way to heaven. The only way is by confessing our sins, which is called repentance, and placing our faith in Jesus Christ as Savior and Lord. Perhaps you hear the story of a person who received Christ later in life and you say to yourself, *I need to get around to doing that one day.* But you can't come to Christ when you want to. You must be drawn by the Holy Spirit. Mentally, you will give yourself a kick when you eventually make the decision. *What was I thinking? Why didn't I do that earlier?* All it takes is a few minutes for a confession of your sins to God and asking Jesus to be at the center of your life. You know the situation and you have the knowledge, but you haven't acted on it. What about now?

Now here's the difference in the Masters wait list and God's list. On God's list, you don't have to wait for somebody to come off. You can leapfrog everybody on the list and come immediately into God's family because of his free gift of grace through faith in Jesus Christ. No wait list for eternal life, the greatest gift of all time.

Prayer: Father God, I thank you that you have no wait list to come to know Christ and become a believer. You also have no unreachable list. Help me remember to pray for those who are still waiting to come to Christ. In Jesus's name, amen.

GOLF44:
THE BIG THREE

Matthew 17:1-2; Mark 5:37, 14:33

And he took with him Peter and James and John ...

Mark 14:33

Arnold Palmer, Jack Nicklaus, and Gary Player were called the "Big Three" because they were the three dominant golfers of the 1960s. These three Hall of Famers won nine consecutive Masters from 1958 through 1966. Fans of the era enjoyed seeing them play so much that eighteen-hole made-for-TV showdowns were created, which made them even more famous. The show was called Big Three Golf.

Palmer, Nicklaus, and Player were distinctly different golfers and personalities. Arnold was the most popular with the fans because of his big strong forearms, swashbuckling persona, and go-for-broke style. Palmer oozed charisma like few athletes in sports. In 1963, the Masters limited ticket sales for the first time. Why? It was due to Arnie's popularity. Jack was the big kid with a crew cut from Ohio seeking to dethrone Palmer as the best player in the game. Despite incurring the wrath of some fans that were jealous of him overtaking Palmer, Jack eventually won the fans over with his big booming drives, towering irons, and deft putting. Gary was the little South African, much smaller than the two giants of the game but the first physical fitness fanatic among golfers. Player used his scrappy, bulldog determination to win two Masters titles during this time. Since that time, there have been dominant golfers, but none went head-to-head for a decade as these three golfers did. During their illustrious careers, Nicklaus, Palmer, and Player won thirty-five major championships.

Peter, James, and John were the big three disciples for Jesus, who took them along for his majors like the raising of a girl from the dead, the transfiguration, and the garden of Gethsemane. Their personalities were certainly different. Peter emerged as the leader among the disciples but was often headstrong and had conflicting ideas about how Jesus ought to do things. Yet Jesus told Peter that he would be the rock upon which his church would be built, and Peter became a key leader in the early church. James and John were fishermen and brothers, James being the older. They once argued who should sit at the right and left hand of Jesus, and this debate infuriated the other disciples. For this and other similar acts, the two were nicknamed sons of thunder. But their bravery could not be questioned in the end.

Prayer: Father God, thank you for the early disciples and for the contributions of the big three. Even though they didn't always get it, their record improved after the Holy Spirit came to reside in them. For their courage and loyalty to Jesus, we give you thanks. In Jesus's name, amen.

GOLF45:
MASTERS QUALIFICATION

Matthew 10:32-33, John 14:6

Whosoever acknowledges me before others, I will also acknowledge before my Father in heaven.

Matthew 10:32

Every spectator at the Masters is given a spectator's guide, which shows you how to get around the course and provides profiles of each golfer. In each profile, there is one number or multiple numbers to the right of the player's name. The numbers are codes that indicate how the player qualified for the Masters. In fact, there were eighteen different ways that a golfer could earn a trip to the 2010 Masters. Some of the qualifications include being a past Masters champion, finishing in the top eight at the 2009 US Open, finishing in the top fifty in the world golf rankings, and winning a PGA tournament since the 2009 Masters. In 2010, Phil Mickelson met nine of the eighteen qualifications.

Some folks are under the mistaken impression that there are at least eighteen ways to get into heaven. Those fallacies include the following: "I've been good enough to make the cut." "I'm no adulterer or murderer." "God is not the kind of God who would keep me out of heaven. He's a loving God." "I make the cut compared to my friends, who are much worse than me." "Look at all the ways I've helped people. Surely that counts for something."

Jesus made it abundantly clear that there is only one qualification that will ever enable you to see the true Masters, God and Jesus, in heaven. Jesus said, "I am The Way, The Truth, and the Life. No one comes to the Father except through me." You cannot earn the grace of God, which is free to all who turn from sin and confess that Jesus Christ is Lord.

Prayer: Most holy and magnificent God, may I be ever aware when my friends and family members believe there is more than one way to the Father. Help me share your good news in ways that they will truly understand what it takes to see the Masters in heaven. In Jesus's name, amen.

GOLF46:
GOT AN AMEN CORNER?

Matthew 26:34-49

Stay here while I go over there and pray.

Matthew 26:36

Even at ninety-eight years old, my dad could still recount stories from his youth in north Alabama. It is amazing to think that he knew people who lived during the Civil War, and yet here he is, living in the age of blogs and Twitter in the twenty-first century. One of my favorite stories is to hear him describe the amen corner of his boyhood church. He told me that the women and children would sit in the center pews in front of the preacher, and the men folk would sit on the side pews. When the preacher made a good point as judged by one of the men, the man would say, "Amen." Dad said that the louder the men said, "Amen," the louder the preacher would get, feeding off the congregation.

Another type of amen corner was named in 1958 by Herbert Warren Wind, the famous golf historian and writer. Amen Corner at the Augusta National Golf Club consisted of the dangerous second shot to the eleventh green, the par-3 twelfth, and the daring drive on thirteen with Rae's Creek lurking to the left. Seeking to capture the excitement of Palmer's first Masters win in 1958 where Amen Corner played such a huge role, Wind made reference in his

Masters article to "Shouting in the Amen Corner," a popular big band jazz tune.

According to masters.org, Palmer embedded his tee shot in mud on the twelfth hole in the final round. He was allowed by the rules official to play two balls, the original ball with which he made a double bogey, and a second ball as a free drop with which he made a par. Palmer eagled the thirteenth hole, and when he was on the fifteenth hole, word came that his free drop had been honored. Immediately, he took the lead and held on for his green jacket.

There is another type of amen corner that each of us needs. It is that quiet corner or place that each believer should go to start each day with God. My time consists of a couple of devotionals, including *My Utmost for His Highest*, prayer time, and meditation. In the solitude of the early morning, so often God speaks to us through quiet utterances in our minds. My amen corner has varied from place to place, but my recent amen corner is the corner of our sofa in the living room.

It is with even more certainty that you can meet God in your amen corner compared to seeing the top golfers in the world at Augusta National's Amen Corner each April. How can I be so sure? Because Augusta National became a pasture for four years during World War II. God didn't take days off from anyone's amen corner during that time.

Prayer: Father God, most precious Lord, may I realize that the precious time that I spend with you each day in my amen corner keeps me from making bogeys and double bogeys during my day. Thank you for the blessing and the privilege to make a tee time with you any time that I wish. In Jesus's name, amen.

GOLF47:
PRACTICE BEFORE
YOU PLAY

Joshua 1:8

This Book of the Law shall not depart from your mouth,
but you shall meditate in it day and night...

The brand-new Masters practice range built in 2010 was incredible
to see. It was built on top of the gravel parking lot that had been
adjacent to the first hole for more than fifty years. One pro said that
he just wanted to stay there and practice. Pros could practice shaping
their drives left to right and right to left because trees lined pretend
fairways out on the range. The vast, semicircular tee box was several
hundred yards long and allowed the pros to practice shots against
any type of wind. For jaded professional golfers to be giddy over a
practice range when they had seen hundreds before, it was obviously
quite special.

Typically, a golfer competing in the Masters will go through a
standard warm-up routine. The golfer will stretch his muscles and
hit numerous short wedges to find his rhythm. Soft wedges are followed by short irons, middle irons, long irons, metal woods, and
finally, the driver. The ball-striking practice is followed by many

chips, pitches, bunker shots, and putts before moving to the first tee to begin the round.

A top golfer warms up thoroughly before each round. With that preparation, the pro ensures he will be fully prepared for each shot, saving himself several strokes on each round. If a particular club gives him grief during the round, then the pro will spend extra time after the round addressing that particular flaw.

As believers, we would be well served to get into that type of routine before and after the activities of our day. The practice range or warm-up for the believer is with a devotion that is taken in a quiet place. Scripture reading is geared to that devotion, prayer, and meditation. Without that preparation, our day simply will not go as well as it could have. By spending extra quiet time in the morning, we save ourselves several headaches each day and ensure that we will be prepared for the shots that Satan takes at us. If a particular problem surfaces during the day such as anger, impatience, or greed, that problem can be addressed by specific Scripture study before we retire for the evening. Ground work in the morning, followed by specifics in the evening, is a winning combination that will help you play many par and sub-par "rounds" for him during your lifetime.

Prayer: Father God, help me spend time with you in the Word each morning to prepare for my day, just as a golf pro at the Masters spends time on the practice range before playing his round. Grant me the discipline to maintain good daily habits. In Jesus's name, amen.

GOLF48:
ARNIE, YOU DON'T
HAVE A CHANCE

John 3:16-17

God sent His Son into the world not to condemn it, but to save it.

John 3:17

After the third round of the 1960 US Open at Cherry Hills Golf Club in Denver, Colorado, Arnold Palmer trailed by seven shots with a total of 215. As he glumly ate a sandwich before going out for the afternoon round to complete thirty-six holes on the final day, he asked his sportswriter friend, Bob Drum, of the Pittsburgh Post-Gazette, what it would take to win the tournament. The Drummer told him that 280 wins the Open, and he implied that Palmer didn't have it in him to shoot a 65, and, therefore, didn't have a chance to win. Clearly miffed, Palmer finished his sandwich and stormed out of the clubhouse.

It might have been a psychological ploy to fire him up. Palmer threw caution to the wind and hit driver on the tight first hole instead of the iron he had laid up with the first three rounds. He burned a low scorcher through the rough up onto the first green almost 350 yards away. That was the first of six birdies that Arnie would make. With each birdie, his gallery grew larger, and word of the charge that Arnie was so famous for swept back to the clubhouse. When an out-of-breath Drum made his way to the ninth tee, Arnie saw him and smirked, as if to say, *No chance? I'll show you!* Palmer shot 65 and won the Open by two shots over a young phenom named Jack Nicklaus and a fading superstar named Ben Hogan. Great stuff.

Speaking of Nicklaus, in 1986, the late Tom McCollister handicapped the Masters field in the *Atlanta Journal-Constitution* the prior Sunday and essentially wrote that Jack was too old and didn't have a chance to win at age forty-six. Nicklaus used the article as motivational fodder and fired a final-round 65 to win the Masters for a record sixth time.

Who has ever told that you can't do something? You might have reacted angrily, with an "I'll show them" attitude with added determination. But if your discouragement came at the wrong time from the wrong person, it could have had a tremendous negative impact on you and deterred you from being all that you could be.

On the other hand, who have we ever written off as not being able to do something? With respect to a person becoming a Christian, have you ever told someone verbally, or with body language, or with a lack of prayer that there is no way they can come to Christ? We must remember what sinners we were when Jesus cleansed us in the blood of the Lamb for the first time and that there were people who might have prayed for many years for us to come to Christ. "No matter the circumstance, there is no one on God's unreachable list," I once heard Mark Hall of Casting Crowns say. So we must keep praying for those who are, as far as we can tell, not walking with the Lord yet. Everybody has a chance to come to Christ, because God is constantly reaching out to them by placing people in their paths. You could be one of those people.

Prayer: Father God, may I not be quick to pass judgment on someone by remembering that at one time, I was a miserable sinner condemned by my past. But through your free gift of grace and my intercessory prayer, each of my friends and family members can come to know Christ. May I do my part in sharing the good news. In Jesus's name, amen.

GOLF49: *$#@*%! (HOW JESUS CURED MY CURSING)

Exodus 20:7

Thou shalt not take the Lord's name in vain ...

When I was a teenager, I had a red-hot temper that was fueled by not having Jesus Christ in my life. I was a club-throwing, foul-mouthed, angry young man, and these bad habits carried into my young adult years. When things didn't go my way, I would just go ballistic. I shot 67 one day and broke two clubs. It's not a course record that I'm at all proud of.

Many times, I blamed God for my bad shots, yet he never swung a club. I tell the story that my wife, Becca, gave me a Bible for our third anniversary, perhaps because of a tantrum that I threw on the golf course one day.

Another factor was that it was commonplace and funny to curse on the playing fields or in the dugouts. It was fun to crack jokes, and it seemed harmless at the time, but I later realized how offensive it was to God. I cursed every day for years, either inwardly or outwardly. It seemed to be an incurable habit.

But an amazing thing happened with my temper and with my foul mouth in the first two weeks after I was saved. The Holy Spirit had come into me, but I still needed some time to kick my bad habit. When a car would pull in front of me or I would be surprised, I would let a curse word go before I realized what I had done. But the reactions became fewer and farther between until several weeks later, I was no longer bound by my anger and cursing. I had given up thirty-five years of cursing just as the Jews had given up traditional sacrifices after receiving the Holy Spirit. It was an amazing and almost immediate transformation. Whenever I have doubts or need reassurance, all I need to do is to look back at my transformation, and I know beyond a shadow of a doubt that I have been redeemed.

Tiger Woods took steps to control his behavior on the golf course by going back to Buddhist self-control techniques, but it became quite evident during the final round of the 2010 Masters that he still has a long way to go. A person might try any number of self-improvement techniques, but I speak from truth in my life. The only surefire way to eliminate your unrighteous anger and cursing is to make Jesus Christ the focal point of your life. The power of the Holy Spirit will help you with your daily problems, and one of those problems is certainly cursing, a violation of one of the Ten Commandments. Only Jesus Christ can truly change your life.

Prayer: Father God, I thank you each and every day for the fruit of the Spirit that enables me to keep a lid on it when someone does an injustice to me, or I stub my toe, or I hit a bad shot. Thank you for your mercy, which I do not deserve, and for forgiving me for all the times I took your name in vain and cursed. In Jesus's name, amen.

GOLF50:
YOU REALLY DON'T WANT
TO MISS IT HERE!

2 Timothy 3:16

Every part of Scripture is God-breathed and useful one way or another—showing us truth, exposing our mistakes, correcting our rebellion, training us to live God's way.

In the 1960s a man began measuring the golf courses that the pros play a week in advance. He would draw intricate diagrams of each hole with many different yardages that he personally measured. The pros and caddies paid $20 for each of his special yardage books because they were extremely valuable and saved them hours of work at each tour stop. If he sold 150 books at $20 each for forty courses a year, he made some pretty good money.

The most unique features of the book were the special notations for the different places on each hole that a player needed to stay away from, such as deep pot bunkers, water hazards, or impossible places to pitch close from around the green. He had a rather unique acronym that I don't care to repeat here, but in essence, the acronym meant, "You don't want to end up here!" and "You really don't want to end up here!" What do the pros call it when they miss it in these places? They call it dead, meaning they have no chance to par the hole.

The Bible has great advice for living, including rules to live by such as the Ten Commandments. The Bible also makes it clear that there is pleasure in sin for a season, but the bitterness far outweighs the pleasure. Jesus spent more time talking about the place you don't want to wind up rather than heaven. He used many analogies that the people of the day could relate to, such as wheat and weeds called tares, bridegrooms with no oil in their lamps, and the sheep and the goats. Some will heed the warnings, turn from sin, and turn to Christ, but very sadly, many will not turn.

Have you heeded the warnings? God and Jesus desperately want you to end up with them in heaven, so much so that God is constantly trying to bring you to a relationship with Jesus Christ. Please realize and internalize that the Bible is indeed God-breathed truth.

Prayer: Most holy and precious God, may I realize that there are some places that I shouldn't be. Give me discernment to stay out of those places, and help me ensure that I will permanently stay out of the ultimate place you really, really don't want us to go for eternity. In Jesus's precious name, amen.

GOLF51:
BAILOUT!

Matthew 5:27-32, James 4:7, 1 Corinthians 6:18-20

Flee from sexual sin!

1 Corinthians 6:18

A great golf architect builds courses that test the skills of the best players in the world, and he will also make the course playable for the novice golfer from shorter tees. On each hole, the seventeenth at TPC Sawgrass notwithstanding, the architect will design the hole so that there is danger lurking on one side of the fairway such as deep bunkers, out of bounds, or water hazards that threaten to swallow your golf ball. On the other side, the architect will leave a safe landing area that is farther from the green. When the golfer plays to the safe area, the second shot will be much more difficult to land on the green for a potential birdie putt.

Oftentimes, the pin placement will be directly over a bunker or near the water hazard. The golfer risks bogey or worse by going directly for the pin to get a birdie, but there is usually a wide area of the green that is accessible. However, the golfer is much more likely to three-putt for bogey after playing safe to the wide area because the putt will be a long one.

The safe areas are called bailouts because the golfer can avoid a serious mistake by bailing out to the safer landing area. Do you realize that God equips us with bailout areas when Satan tempts us with lust? God will never allow us to be tempted beyond our capability to escape. First, God gave us brains to realize that the lure of someone who is not our spouse can be avoided by using the door that God placed in the room. Perhaps one reason God allowed us to invent doors was to give us a way out. Second, he gave us hands to flip magazine covers and to change the TV channel. Third, he gave us necks so that we can turn our heads and avoid taking second looks. Fourth, he gave us legs so that we can run from the temptation of sexual sin. Finally, he gave us Scripture that we can memorize and use against Satan.

It can't happen to you? Yeah, right. No man or woman is immune from succumbing to temptation. Remember that Jesus taught his disciples in the Sermon on the Mount that even thinking about sex outside of marriage is the same as committing the act. But with God's help and the leading of the Holy Spirit, you can find the bailout areas.

Prayer: Father God, help me realize through the Holy Spirit when I am too close to the precipice. I thank you for giving me ears, eyes, hands, and legs that keep me from crossing the edge. In Jesus's name, amen.

GOLF52:
CAREER DECISION

Proverbs 3:5-6

Trust the Lord with all your heart, and do not rely on your
own understanding.

Proverbs 3:5

Englishman and journeyman golf pro Brian Davis was in a great
position to win his first PGA Tour title as he teed off on Harbour
Town's tough eighteenth hole in a playoff with veteran Jim Furyk.
Davis pulled his second shot into the hazard to the left of the eighteenth green and faced a difficult recovery shot. Being careful not to
ground his club, which would have resulted in a two-shot penalty,
Davis carefully swung and played a shot onto the green. As soon
as the ball finished rolling, Davis called PGA Tour official Slugger
White over.

Even the TV announcers were not sure what had happened. But
as Davis took his backswing, he barely nicked a weed in the hazard.
The nick was imperceptible on TV, but Davis told White that he
felt the shaft brush the weed. Davis incurred a penalty because your
club cannot touch anything in a hazard during the backswing.

What a display of integrity! As Davis rode to the eighteenth
tee for the playoff, he must have been thinking that if he won the
playoff, he would be in the Masters for the first time. Calling the

two-shot penalty on himself immediately assured Davis that he would miss the Masters. Also, his second-place prize money was $400,000 less than Furyk's winning check. But when the pressure was on, he did the right thing immediately. What an absolutely commendable and honorable decision!

When pressure builds for a golfer, the player will often revert to his or her worst habit under pressure. For Tiger and Phil, it's getting stuck on the downswing and slicing the ball. For Kenny Perry, it's the yips with the chips that cost him the 2009 Masters. For Scott Hoch, it was a missed two-footer than cost him the Masters in 1990.

There are times when we are all placed in pressure situations. Who's your daddy when that happens? If your daddy is Satan when the pressure is off, it's likely going to be Satan when the pressure-filled moment comes. Around the house, it could be yelling at your family members. On the road, it could be yelling at the driver who cut you off. On the job or at school, it could be telling a half-truth to protect yourself. But walk in God's presence daily, and you'll make more Christlike decisions when the pressure is on.

Prayer: Father God, help me rely on your strength and the guidance of the Holy Spirit when I must make decisions that could conflict with what I know is the right thing to do. In Jesus's name, amen.

GOLF53:
CUTTING PHIL
BY ONE SHOT

Isaiah 40:22, 25-26; John 3:30

It is He that sits upon the circle of the earth, and the inhabitants thereof are as grasshoppers…

Isaiah 40:22

Suppose you had an opportunity to play the Pebble Beach Golf Links when it was in US Open condition. The course runs firm and fast, and some of the hole locations are almost impossible to access. Golf Digest holds a contest annually when several celebrities and a random golfer are drawn from thousands of entries to see if they can break 100. A 10-handicapper would probably break 90 on Pebble Beach during normal conditions, but in Open conditions, the golfer would be hard pressed to break 100.

Now suppose the 10-handicapper was paired with Phil Mickelson in the white-hot cauldron of Open pressure. Phil will most likely post a score that is two strokes on either side of par. But 10-handicapper Joe Golfer would do well to break 100. Joe Golfer would immediately recognize the difference in their abilities to play tournament golf and know that he's fortunate to be on the same course with Phil. If you took the best score by Phil or Joe on each of the eighteen holes, Joe would likely play just one hole where his score was one stroke better than Phil's. If Phil shot 71, their best ball would be 70.

It's that same way with God when we think we're doing it all or it's all about us in bringing people to Christ. God chose completely fallible human beings to spread his gospel, but it doesn't happen because of our grandiose plans and positioning. The Holy Spirit is used by God to bring new Christians into the kingdom, yet he chooses to use us as bit players and let us help him out with a shot here or there. Louis Giglio reminded us in his book *I Am Not but I Know I AM* that God is *very, very big* and that we are very, very small. Certainly it is a tremendous honor and privilege whenever someone comes to Christ through an effort we were involved in. But it's the power of God, the saving blood of Jesus Christ, and the drawing of the Holy Spirit that gets the job done. It is the power of God working in us and through us.

Prayer: Father God, help me recognize that it's not the oratory skills that help a person receive Christ, but it is through the power of the Holy Spirit that you use our feeble attempts to bring people to Jesus Christ. Thank you that you allow me to play a small role in the growth of your kingdom, which you and you alone create. In Jesus's name, amen.

GOLF54:
I DON'T LOOK AS GOOD
AS I THINK I DO

Romans 7:18-19

For the good that I would do I do not; but the evil which I would not, I do.

Romans 7:19

Allison and Jillian took golf lessons from a golf pro who used video to show them the proper angles for proper ball position, backswings, and downswings. The video replays were very helpful for them to see exactly what their faults were so that they could correct them.

I once played to a 3-handicap and broke par several times a year. I had not had my swing videotaped for years until Chris offered to put my swing on video. I hit eight to ten iron shots and hit the last few flush. Feeling very confident, I waited for the video to rewind so I could admire my swing on the videotape.

What I saw shocked me. As I took the club back, my head dipped about three inches as I lurched away from the ball. When my back-swing completed, my club was well past parallel, and the clubface pointed to the right instead of slightly left of the target. In fact, the club pointed a good thirty degrees too far to the right. Then I made a nice correction to get the club on line and managed to hit a flush shot, except for the last shot, when I came completely out of the shot and the ball went right. I walked away feeling much more humble about my golf swing.

We can groove a bad swing and get by most of the time. But in pressure situations, our worst habit will pop up at just the wrong time, and we're in deep trouble. In pressure situations, we can lose our temper or make selfish outbursts, and we wish that we hadn't said it, but it's too late. The damage has been done.

Sometimes we think we're looking good, but we don't realize how sinful our lives are. We have lowered our standards and look all right compared to our peers, but we do not hold our lives up to the standards exemplified by Christ. When we really look at ourselves, and especially our thought lives, we can be confident that we aren't measuring up. That's when it is time to make a confession of our specific flaws and ask God to remove those flaws.

Prayer: Father God, just when I think I am sitting pretty, I can know for sure that I have exalted myself in a prideful manner. Please allow me to make those swing corrections before I have to undertake one of your painful overhauls. In Jesus's name, amen.

GOLF55: THE SPIRITUALITY OF ST. ANDREWS

Matthew 13:36-50

The tares are gathered and burned in the fire...

Matthew 13:40

The 150th anniversary edition of the British Open was played at the hallowed Old Course at historic St. Andrews, the birthplace of golf. Phil Mickelson said that the course had a spiritual feel to it. Bobby Jones was given the key to the city in 1958. His love affair with St. Andrews was such that he remarked that he would have had a rich and full life even if all he had were his experiences at St. Andrews. The course has a number of quirks. The players play a blind shot over a railroad shed to the fairway on number seventeen. The fifth hole sports a green that is 101 yards deep, longer than a football field. Imagine putting the length of a football field. The seventh and eleventh holes actually cross as the course loops back toward the clubhouse. The numbers on the flagsticks on the double greens always add up to 18. The course is laced with pot bunkers that are like a one-shot penalty since players must play sideways or even backward because of the steep faces. A fellow with a long-toothed rake walks with the players during the round to rake the bunkers for them.

The spiritual feel that is inescapable comes from a little different twist than the ethereal beauty of Augusta National, which has Amen Corner. Here, the experiences of the players, which often occur in driving rain or howling winds, are described by names that have been given to landmarks on the course. The first hole has a fairway 130 yards wide, and the green sits on the precipice of a creek called the Swilcan Burn. The fourteenth hole par 5 has a ghastly looking bunker shaped like a boomerang that is aptly named Hell Bunker. Jack Nicklaus once took five shots to escape on his way to a 9. The seventeenth hole has a pot bunker that is called the Road Hole bunker. Tommy Nakajima once made a 13 on this hole, finally escaping what are now called the Sands of Nakajima. The final hole, the eighteenth, is a short par 4 with the most famous bridge in golf, the Swilcan Bridge, and a devilish crevice in front of the green called the Valley of Sin.

Certainly it behooves each of us to escape the Hell Bunkers and the Valleys of Sin and the eternal burn by turning from our sins, trusting in Jesus Christ as Savior and Lord, and staying obedient to God. Jesus Christ is the bridge over the eternal burn. Some competing players have avoided the burn and will escape before their lives are up here on earth. Sadly, some will fall victim to the wages of sin and never escape. In which group do you reside?

Prayer: Father God, thank you for the spiritual context in which these St. Andrews landmarks were named. May these hazards serve as reminders to golfers of the eternal pitfalls that can envelop them without a relationship with Jesus Christ. In Jesus's name, amen.

GOLF56:
WHEN OUT OF BOUNDS
IS TOTALLY IN

Galatians 5:22-23

But the fruit of the Spirit is love, joy, peace, patience, goodness, kindness, faithfulness, gentleness, and self-control...

Here is a story of incredible sportsmanship and grace. Two colle-
giate golfers, Grant Whybark and Seth Doran, were vying for a spot
in the 2010 NAIA National Championship.

Grant's team had wrapped up the conference championship and
a trip to nationals, but he found himself in a playoff against Seth
for individual honors. The winner would advance to the national
tournament. Grant realized that if he won, his opponent and friend,
Seth, would not advance. So Grant made a huge decision before he
got to the tee box.

Whybark purposely hit his first tee shot out of bounds to the
right of the fairway. Amazing! Seth made par and advanced to the
national tournament. Grant explained that he did it because Seth is
a great player and a great person. Seth had never been to nationals,
and this season was his last as a senior. Grant felt like Seth deserved
to go to nationals and that he couldn't feel good about taking the
chance from him.

What lesson can be learned from Grant? Clearly, he cared more about how his competitor would feel getting to go to nationals than how he would feel if he won the tournament. It was a very self-less act.

This was a great example of grace because Seth received a gift so wonderful that, no matter what a good guy he is, he didn't deserve it. In essence, Grant took one for Seth when he hit his ball out of bounds so that Seth could advance.

Jesus did a similar but much bigger thing for all of us on the cross. He took one for us and paid the penalty so that we could advance to the ultimate tournament: our home in heaven.

Prayer: Father God, in this world of dog-eat-dog competition and win at all costs, thank you for this story that warms our hearts. May I exhibit a similar form of grace to the people that I meet. In Jesus's name, amen.

SPORTS

S35:
BATTLING IN THE TRENCHES

Matthew 28:20, Hebrews 13:5,
John 15:5, Philippians 4:13

Apart from Me you can do nothing.

John 15:5

The flashy scorers and speedy athletes receive most of the attention from the media and fans. The Heisman Trophy typically goes to a quarterback or running back. The slam dunkers receive the most highlights on ESPN each evening. In hockey, the most popular players are the goal scorers and the great passers.

But it's the battles in the trenches that make the offensive highlight reels possible. The big uglies in the offensive line open the holes and protect the quarterback from sacks. It's a very physical battle for the rebounds in the lane by the big men, who trigger the outlet passes for the fast breaks and alley-oop slam dunks. It's the scuffles for the puck in the corner that create opportunities for exciting goals.

It's battling in the silent trenches with daily blocking and tackling of prayer and Bible reading that gets us ready when tough times come. If we wait until the tough times to cry out to God without having the relationship, then we won't be in the relationship position that we need to be. By putting substantial roots down through daily communications with God, we won't be blown away when the storms come. There will be no wavering. We will know that God didn't cause the problems, and that he will be there to see us through them. He promised that he will never leave nor forsake us and that he will be with us until the end of the age. We must be prepared to call on God and remember Scripture to pull us through tough times.

Prayer: Dear Lord, help me have the daily discipline to pray with you and study your Word. I need you during the good times and the bad times. When the bad times come, help me know that you are always there with me. In Jesus's name, amen.

S36:
"THE CITY" ON A HILL

Matthew 5:14-16

You are the light of the world. A city that is set on a hill cannot be hidden.

Matthew 5:14

There have been some bizarre pro uniforms. In 2009 NFL teams wore their fifty-year anniversary uniforms, and the Denver Broncos undoubtedly took the prize for the worst with their vertically striped brown-and-white stockings. The vintage jerseys of the Capital Bullets (now the Washington Wizards) with their vertical stripes and tiny, odd lettering were very unusual and are apparently coming back for the 2011-12 NBA season!

One of my all-time favorites was the NBA's San Francisco Warriors jersey in the '60s. The jersey was gold with navy trim and was one of the first non-white home jerseys. The number on the back was surrounded by a cable car climbing diagonally up the back of the jersey. On the front was the Golden Gate Bridge and the words "The City" representing the city of San Francisco. Very cool! San Franciscans proudly believe their city with its unique blend of cultural charm, breathtaking hillsides, and jaw-dropping bay vistas is second to none. Having traveled there several times, I am sure that the team wore "The City" jerseys with pride.

When I recall "The City" jerseys, it reminds me of the charge from Jesus's Sermon on the Mount that his followers are to be the salt and light of the world. A city on a hill such as San Francisco cannot possibly be hidden. It would be impossible not to see San Francisco with its bright lights if you were hundreds of feet above the Bay area. God challenges us to shine our light through our words, deeds, actions, and especially our attitudes in ways that are visible to other Christians, who recognize us as brothers or sisters in Christ. The light also needs to be visible to unbelievers who will hopefully ask us one day, "How do you not lose your temper even when things are not going well?" It's important that we let our light shine through good works and give our Father the glory. As the children's song goes, "This little light of mine, I'm gonna let it shine."

Prayer: Dear Lord, I love you and I appreciate your blessings each day. May I reflect that appreciation in my face, my words, and my actions to show people in darkness that there is another Way, another Truth, and another Life. In the holy name of Jesus, I pray. Amen.

S37:
C'MON AND HIT ME WITH YOUR BEST SHOT!

Ephesians 6:10-20

Be strong in the Lord, and in His great power!

Ephesians 6:10

Two of the most successful offenses in college football have been the run-and-shoot and triple option. The former is geared toward passing, and the latter is geared toward running. Texas Tech and Oklahoma have had great success with the run-and-shoot, and Air Force and Navy have had great success with the triple option. Defensive coordinators burn the midnight oil to figure out how to stop these prolific offenses.

In a heavyweight championship boxing event, when a boxer takes the best shot from his opponent, withstanding the blow gives him confidence that he can win the bout. Muhammad Ali deployed an innovative tactic that he nicknamed Rope-a-Dope in his 1974 title fight with George Foreman in Kinshasa, Zaire. Ali trained with sparring partners for weeks to toughen him to withstand body blows. He would cover his face with his gloves and his chest with his forearms, hang on the ropes, and let Foreman punch him at will. Ali had prepared himself to take Foreman's best shots. Foreman literally punched himself out, and Ali finished him off in the eighth round for a surprise victory.

If you've had recent success in leading people to Christ, Satan is gearing up to stop you because God has used you to take market share from the evil prince. After I spoke to an FCA huddle, I received a wonderful note from the FCA student leader, who wrote that the kids talked all day about the Pete Maravich video and message. Satan had taken a whipping in the hallway. There is no doubt that the hallway chatter ticked off Satan. He doesn't mind when the Christians are behind closed doors. But when they invade his territory, the devil is going to fight back like the devil. Get ready to protect your blindside.

Satan looks for your weak areas and the chinks in your armor like the soft underbelly of an armadillo. Satan will explore every angle, much like those defensive coordinators finding a way to stop the potent offenses.

When I refereed college basketball, an interesting phenomenon occurred. The head coaches would never waste their time yelling at all three officials, or even two for that matter, as they attempted to gain an advantage. Based on the experience level of the officials and who missed the most calls against their teams, the head coaches would pick on that official and try to influence his calls. It was always a good night when the coaches worked somebody besides you.

Here is how Satan operates. He's going to try to sidetrack those who have weakened themselves by letting their guards down against spiritual warfare. He's also going to pick on the people who are hurting him the most. Consider that there is so much pressure from Satan on pastors because caring for hundreds or thousands of church members far outweighs what you and I encounter. That's one reason pastors need our prayers daily. I encourage you to stop now and say a prayer for your pastors.

In 2 Corinthians 12:10, Paul reminds us that "...For when I am weak, then I am strong." Our earthly strength is weak, but our eternal strength comes from God, who helps us take Satan's best shot and still come away victorious.

Prayer: Most holy and gracious Father God, help me take daily checkpoints to make sure that I've got my shield up, my breastplate on, my helmet securely fastened, and that my feet are shod with the proper protection. I need all of that protection so that I can take Satan's best shot and continue to serve you and the kingdom. I ask you for special protection for my pastors and church staff. In Jesus's name, amen.

S38:
DOESN'T GOD CARE
WHO WINS?

Psalm 73, Job 21:7-11, Jeremiah 12:1, 1 Peter 3:12

> For the eyes of the Lord are over the righteous, and his ears are open unto their prayers: but the face of the Lord is against them that do evil.

> 1 Peter 3:12

Why do the bad guys win instead of the good guys? Why do the bad guys seem to prosper? Many Christians who follow sports have surely harbored similar thoughts. When evil faces off against good, why does evil come out on top so often? Shouldn't God reward those who have followed his guidance and worked just as hard, or harder, than those who are driven by their selfish desires? When the final pass is thrown to decide the game or the championship game is played with millions watching, why do the bad guys seem to win so often? After all, God could control the outcome if he desired.

These emotional vocal expressions and questions prompted me to recall the teachings of the Old Testament. In Psalm 73, an oppressed man almost lost his faith when he saw how much better off the fat cats were compared to him. "They are not in trouble as other men, nor are they plagued like other men. Therefore pride serves as their necklace, violence covers them like a garment" (Psalm 73:4-5).

After Job was admonished by his friends for not blaming God for his woes, he replied:

> Why do the wicked live and become old, Yes, become mighty in power? Their descendants are established with them in their sight, And their offspring before their eyes. Their houses are safe from fear. Neither is the rod of God upon them. Their bulls breed without failure; Their cow calves without miscarriage. They send forth their little ones like a flock, And their children dance.
>
> Job 21:7-11

Pleading with God, the weeping prophet Jeremiah said, "Why does the way of the wicked prosper? Why are those happy who deal so treacherously? So now we call the proud blessed, For those who do wickedness are raised up, they even tempt God and go free" (Jeremiah 12:1).

Certainly we live in a fallen world and evildoers seem to triumph over do-gooders more often than not. Whose prayers does God answer when Christians pray to win? Someone once remarked that God usually appears to answer the prayers of the team with the best players. Why doesn't God seem to favor the Christian coaches and players on the grand stage? The good guy receives harsh criticism from the fans and press when his team loses while the bad guy celebrates another championship, reaps the monetary rewards, and receives accolades from the press. When people operate unethically to the spirit of the law or the rules of accepted behavior, God is never glorified. When these same people win, they are placed in the national spotlight. Inevitably, there is a negative message that is transmitted to young people and adults that being unethical is how you win games and how you get ahead in life.

I would never pretend to have the wisdom to answer these questions. But here are some points to consider. I don't think that God feels that he must constantly reward mature Christians, certainly not as often as baby Christians who are likely to become discouraged. The prophet Isaiah reminded us, "For as the heavens are higher than the earth, My Ways are higher than your ways" (Isaiah 55:9). Romans 8:18 assures us that what we suffer now is nothing compared to the glory we will receive later. God needs Christians who will exhibit grace in defeat and courage when dealing with adversity. If the Christians won all the time, that grace would never be demonstrated, would it? Romans 5:3 proclaims, "Tribulation produces perseverance, and perseverance, character, and character, hope." Christians who lose an important game have a tremendous opportunity to demonstrate eternal hope through their faith in Jesus Christ.

Consider that our lives are "as a vapor that appears for a little time and then vanishes away" (James 4:14). Take a moment and snap your fingers. *Snap!* That sound is the equivalent of a normal lifespan compared to the time that we will spend in eternity. Consider the eternal fate of those who have been callous in their dealings and have broken the rules for wanton gain. Clearly, on the day of judgment, God will address the shortcomings of those who have not been washed in the blood of our Precious Savior. "And I saw the dead, small and great, standing before God, and books were opened. And another book was opened, which is the Book of Life. And the dead were judged according to their works, by the things which were written in the books" (Revelation 20:12). Only those who receive God's free gift of grace have their names written in the Book of Life, and "not because of works" (Ephesians 2:9).

When our final whistle blows, will we have been solely purposed for temporary gain while losing our souls in the process (Matthew 16:26)? The key question will be the same for each of us. During our brief stay on earth, did we turn from our sins with godly sorrow and ask Christ to blot out our transgressions? God's judgment will always be fair and just. So the next time evil appears to triumph over good in a sports contest, know that this game was but one move in the chess game of life. When "checkmate" ends the game on earth, evil always loses in the end. Good will reign victoriously forever with Christ and our Father in heaven, and evil will lament forever what could have been. The existence of personal relationships with Christ, or the lack thereof, will determine the final victors and losers.

So does God care who wins? God's will intends for us to use our talents and interests, athletic or otherwise, to the utmost. When we play hard, give our all for a team, and completely use our gifts, the kingdom of God wins. What he cares about most is daily obedience and surrendered lives. To those who are obedient and surrendered to him, all of the money and championships in the world pale in comparison to knowing Christ as Savior and Lord.

Prayer: Our most gracious Father, when I become frustrated after seeing people succeed who appear to be ethically challenged, help me know that this type of worldly success is fleeting and that the ultimate success comes from knowing you as my Lord. In Jesus's name, amen.

S39:
A FIRST FOR THE AGES

Matthew 5:1-12

Blessed are the pure in heart, for they shall see God.

Matthew 5:8

Becca and I bought a Wii one Christmas, and our favorite game is bowling. Wii bowling is very realistic the way that you can simulate a roll and make the ball hook. It's great fun. As I flipped channels after church one Sunday, looking for the NFL game, I came across professional bowling on ESPN. I don't know the names of three pro bowlers and probably would not admit it if I did. But I heard that Kelly Kulick, a thirty-two-year-old woman from Union, New Jersey, was one of the final four bowlers. I thought that was unusual and then heard that she had a chance to become the first woman bowler to win a PBA tour event.

That piece of information intrigued me because I have followed golfer Michelle Wie's quest to compete on the men's PGA tour. Michelle made much ballyhooed appearances in several tour events and almost made a cut in Hawaii as a sixteen-year-old. But she has never come close to winning any men's pro event. Annika Sorenstam, considered by many to be the best woman golfer of all time, missed the cut by five shots in a PGA event in Fort Worth and never tried another men's tour event. The exception is Danica Patrick, who won the Indy 300 race in Japan and became the first woman to ever win an Indy car event. But what about women competing in tennis, basketball, baseball, hockey, swimming, and bowling? The top men are more powerful and swifter than the top women and have obvious physical advantages.

On the final day of this PBA tour event, Kulick went into the bowl-off in third place and won her head-to-head match by only five pins to make the finals. She then faced a bowler who had competed in sixty-eight finals. This was her first. Her opponent was more powerful and rolled the ball with more speed and spin. What happened next was one for the record books. Kelly rolled ten strikes and destroyed this fellow by an unbelievable 69 pins, 265-196. She had become the first woman to win a PBA tour event, and incredibly, it was a major, which meant she had defeated the strongest possible field. Her margin of victory was akin to winning the Super Bowl by six touchdowns, Wimbledon 6-1, 6-2, 6-1, or the Masters by twelve shots. Kelly gave thousands of young girls and women renewed hope that they can compete with men, and she changed the norms of her sport. A woman had won a men's major sports championship, which many people believed was impossible because the norm of competitive sports is that women cannot compete with men.

Jesus forever shattered the religious norms of the day. Never before had someone preached that anything but religious superiority and power was necessary. The meek will inherit the earth? What about the powerful Romans? I'm supposed to pray in silence in a private place? Why, nobody will see or hear me. When I give my alms, I shouldn't tell anyone because it should be done in secret? I receive a blessing when I mourn? I am supposed to be content with what I have? How can this man's teachings stick without the authority and power of Caesar? Yet the obedience of Jesus to do the work of his Father rocked the world of the Pharisees.

His teachings especially brought hope to the desperate, the poor, the shunned, the underprivileged, the downtrodden, and, yes, to women who were terribly treated and disrespected then. I find it interesting that the three people at the empty tomb were all women. Jesus came as a helpless baby born to a teenage virgin and was never a member of the powerful hierarchy. How could Jesus ever get ahead? Yet he established a system of belief and trust that grew rapidly and has lasted for two thousand years, despite entrusting twelve common fellows who had trouble understanding and applying his teachings. In fact, one betrayed him and ten died as martyrs. In a much more significant historic first for the ages, Jesus turned the world upside down in a way that removed the old biases and precedents forever. With God, all things are indeed possible.

Prayer: Father God, it is so exhilarating to see the hard work and determination of an underdog pay off. Jesus came into the world as an underdog, but I praise you for the way that he taught us and turned the tables on the Pharisees. May I follow his teachings to help you advance your kingdom on this earth. In the holy name of Jesus Christ, amen.

S40:
A-T-T-AAA-C-K!

Ephesians 6:10-20, Romans 8:3

… the sword of the Spirit, which is the Word of God.

Ephesians 6:17

In seventh and eighth grade, our daughter, Jillian, cheered for the middle school football team. One of their staple cheers went like this. "A-T-T-AAA-C-K! A-T-T-AAA-C-K! Attack, attack, attack!" The cheer was designed to inspire the offense to take the ball down the field and score a touchdown. If you don't score, it's impossible to win a game.

The book of Ephesians, chapter 6, inspires us to put on the whole armor of God. The helmet of salvation, the belt of truth, the breastplate of righteousness, and the shoes of peace are some of the essential armor pieces. These particular elements are designed to protect you from the arrows of Satan. But there is one offensive weapon, the sword of the Spirit, which is the word of God (Ephesians 6:17). My friend, Danny, preached an awesome sermon in which he challenged his congregation to be conquerors. Satan never takes a day off, so we must be clothed with the armor of God to protect ourselves. But we also need to come out on the offensive, armed with Scriptures that we have memorized for all occasions. So when Satan comes at us, we're not just taking blows, but we're giving them too.

Danny is a big soccer fan, and he shared with his congregation how the US men's soccer team kept falling behind in games in the 2010 World Cup because they were playing back on their heels. The US team spent most of the games trying to climb out of the holes they dug for themselves. Danny shared how his father and brother played on a soccer team that went undefeated three consecutive years and had a different approach. Their team's philosophy was to be on the attack from the opening whistle, put a couple of goals into the other team's net, and watch the other team fall apart or scramble to catch up.

We don't have to scramble to catch up or just stay afloat when we have God in our corner. God is with us, for us, and in us. He gave us his awesome, perfect Word that we can use to come out swinging from the moment we get out of bed until we put our heads on the pillow. To use the Word, we must be in the Word daily, seeking God's special guidance. Brandish your sword, the mighty Word of God, and use it to become conquerors for the kingdom.

Prayer: Dear Father, may I walk out the door knowing that I can tap your mighty power when I get ready to face the challenges of the enemy. Through your mighty and Holy Word, help me arm myself in such a way that I am easily recognized by those I meet as being from your kingdom. In Jesus's name, amen.

S41:
HEAVEN'S WORLD
CUP (SOCCER)

Jeremiah 29:11, Romans 5:8, 1 John 1:9,
John 3:16, Ephesians 2:8

But by grace you have been saved through faith…

Ephesians 2:8

Every four years, the best soccer clubs in the world compete for the World Cup. The interest in the tournament is unprecedented, as more than two hundred nations are enthralled by the competition. Qualifying for the World Cup begins the previous year with matches held in more than a hundred countries, and the best thirty-two teams qualify to compete in the World Cup, which is a month-long tournament. The first World Cup was won by Uruguay in 1932. The World Cup was held for the first time in the country of South Africa in 2010. The final four teams were Spain, Germany, Uruguay, and the Netherlands.

Just as the soccer World Cup is won by one of the last four teams in the tournament, there are four facts that every person needs to know. First, God created a unique plan (Jeremiah 29:11) for your life so that you can enjoy his special blessings. The unique plan doesn't mean that we will never have problems or trials in life.

2010 World Cup Pairings

Spain

Netherlands

Spain 2010

World Cup Champion!

Germany

Uruguay

Second, each person is destined to commit his or her first sin at an early age, which separates us from God. Everyone who has ever lived has experienced this sinful separation from God (Romans 3:23). We must resolve this separation from God, or spiritual death (Romans 6:23) will be the result.

Third, God loved us so much that even while we were sinners (Romans 5:8), he sent Jesus to die and pay the penalty for our sin that separates us from God. Jesus even carried our sin to the cross (1 Peter 2:24). As Christians we should rejoice that Jesus rose from the grave (Matthew 28:6).

Finally, you alone must decide to exchange your sinful life for a new life in Christ. You must repent, or turn from, your sinful life and ask God to forgive you (1 John 1:9). After you repent, you must trust in Jesus Christ as your Savior and Lord and accept God's gift of grace to receive eternal life (Ephesians 2:8), admitting that you cannot earn God's grace and that salvation only comes through Jesus Christ (John 3:16). Then you must commit to obey God daily by praying and studying his Word to grow in Christ in all aspects of your life (Proverbs 3:6).

God offers everyone his free gift of grace. I invite you to pray this prayer to receive Jesus Christ into your life as your Savior. Your change of heart is more important than these exact words.

Prayer: Lord Jesus, I know that I am a sinner. Thank you for suffering on the cross and dying for my sins. I want my life to change. Please forgive all of my sins through Christ's blood that was shed on the cross for me. I have repented of my sins, and Jesus, I ask you to come into my life and make me a new person. Thank you for your forgiveness of my sins and your free gift of grace that brings me eternal life in heaven. Thank you for the Holy Spirit that now lives in my heart to help me with my daily problems. May I grow in my love and obedience to you through prayer and Bible study. Thank you for accepting me as a child of God. In Jesus's holy name, I pray, amen.

Consider the following three statements. If you understand each statement and really want to commit to each, you should pray and ask Christ into your heart in your own words. Write your name under *saint*. You should receive the Holy Spirit and eternal life through Jesus Christ if you meant it.

Heaven's World Cup

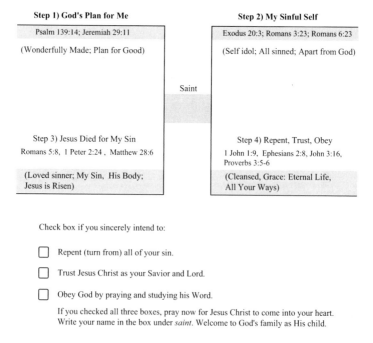

Step 1) God's Plan for Me

Psalm 139:14; Jeremiah 29:11

(Wonderfully Made; Plan for Good)

Saint

Step 2) My Sinful Self

Exodus 20:3; Romans 3:23; Romans 6:23

(Self idol; All sinned; Apart from God)

Step 3) Jesus Died for My Sin
Romans 5:8, 1 Peter 2:24 , Matthew 28:6

(Loved sinner; My Sin, His Body; Jesus is Risen)

Step 4) Repent, Trust, Obey
1 John 1:9, Ephesians 2:8, John 3:16, Proverbs 3:5-6

(Cleansed, Grace: Eternal Life, All Your Ways)

Check box if you sincerely intend to:

☐ Repent (turn from) all of your sin.

☐ Trust Jesus Christ as your Savior and Lord.

☐ Obey God by praying and studying his Word.

If you checked all three boxes, pray now for Jesus Christ to come into your heart. Write your name in the box under *saint*. Welcome to God's family as His child.

S42:
DUDE, THAT IS SOME SERIOUS HANG TIME!

1 Thessalonians 4:14-18, Revelation 1:7

Oh, we'll be walking on air!

1 Thessalonians 4:17

The most exciting players in basketball seem to have a unique ability to stay in the air longer than other players. While others are coming down, they are still hovering near the basket. It's actually an illusion. A scientific study of basketball players was conducted, and the actual time that the stars hung in the air was less than a second. What the best players can do is contort their bodies so that they wait until the last possible moment to pass or shoot, thereby extending the time they have to make unbelievable plays. Michael Jordan and Vince Carter come to mind as hang-time artists.

Football punters strive for hang time, but even the best punters are able to keep the ball airborne less than a second more than the average punters. But a half second means that their kick coverage team can cover five more yards, which is the difference in the ability to make the tackle or watch the speedy returner sail down the sideline behind a wall of blockers.

We were thrilled in the Winter Olympics to watch snowboarders like Shaun White hang in the air at the apex of their leaps as they contorted their bodies to perform a 720 or even a 1080. From the time they leave the half-pipe until they returned was no more than three or four seconds. As they hang in the air, it feels like they are there much longer.

Speaking of hang time, did you know that the most serious hang time will happen when Jesus triumphantly returns? I don't want to frighten you, and it's difficult for us to imagine. When Jesus returns, the Christ followers who have passed away will be safely united with Jesus in the sky in the blink of an eye. Immediately the Christ followers walking the earth will follow. All who hang with Jesus in the air will receive glorified, resurrected bodies in place of earthly bodies, and our next stop will be heaven to be with our Father God forever. Hanging on the rim after a bodacious slam dunk? That's nothing compared to hanging in the clouds with Jesus!

Prayer: Father God, it is so exciting that one fine day, I will get some serious hang time in the clouds with your Son, who promised me that he would come back for those who trust in him as Savior and Lord. What an awesome time that will be. In Jesus's name, amen.

S43:
LIVING IN THE PRESENT

Philippians 3:13-14

I am focusing all my energies on this one thing, forgetting the past...

Philippians 3:13

My Friday morning men's group that meets at Roswell UMC discussed the pressures that young athletes face as they strive to make their local high school teams. Hundreds of kids vie for a few slots each season on the varsity team. Often, it is not the talent that separates them but the mental approach of being ready, being in the right place, and making the right play at the opportune time. It is very difficult for the young shortstop who boots a double-play ball with so much riding on it to forget the mistake, refocus, and get ready for the next play.

The best athletes have the ability to forget and refocus. A professional golfer has been known to display a temper from time to time, but when a champion makes a mistake, he quickly puts it aside and doesn't look back. Quarterbacks cannot look back at the last pass that turned into a pick six if they are going to lead their teams down the field to victory. Life's experiences can make us look back over our shoulders and wish that we had a do-over. Paul made it clear that he was focused on forgetting the mistakes of the past and looking forward to what lies ahead. He was looking forward to the next opportunity to share Christ, not back at what had happened in his life when he persecuted Christians and watched in glee as Stephen was stoned.

How many events are you constantly looking back on, wishing you could change things? Paul urged the Philippians to push ahead toward the prize that awaits each believer. This is great advice for us. We need to know how important it is to keep pushing ahead and that when things don't work out the way we want, God still has an eternal plan. Believers ought to be focused each day on kingdom goals, the only goals that matter for eternity. Don't look back and miss the kingdom opportunities that await you.

Prayer: Most gracious God, help me in the present, at this time, right here, right now. Please cleanse me from my hidden faults so that I can experience you fully and see it when you plop an opportunity in my lap. Thank you for entrusting a small part of your kingdom work to me. In Jesus's name, amen.

S44:
FILL OUT YOUR
SCORECARD

Colossians 3:23

Work hard and cheerfully at all you do, just as though you
were working for your Lord and not just for your masters.

When I was ten years old, I began keeping score of baseball and
basketball games that were broadcast on the radio. Our radio recep-
tion in our home in rural Georgia was poor, so after I finished supper
and homework, I would go out to our 1963 Chevy Bel Air, turn the
key to accessory power, lock the doors, and tune the radio to one of
my favorite stations in the South and Midwest. There was WSB in
Atlanta for the Braves, Hawks, and Bulldogs, KMOX in St. Louis,
WLW in Cincinnati, WCAU in Philadelphia, and on really clear
nights, my favorite, WBZ in Boston and the gravel-throated Johnny
Most of my beloved Celtics. If the weather was chilly, I would bun-
dle up.

Mom would say, "Be careful out there."

Dad would say, "Don't run the battery down," because he didn't
want to deal with a dead battery in the morning.

For the next several hours, I would keep score on my specially
constructed score sheets. I would use three different-colored pens:

red, green, and blue. I recall adding the number of points of each player. I loved it when six or seven players would score in double figures or when the score was 143-126. The games came alive as I imagined the exploits of Oscar Robertson, Bill Russell, and Jerry Lucas performing in distant arenas as I sat in a clear, moonlit Georgia night.

When the game ended, I would run inside and get ready for another school day. What a blessing it was to have parents who never questioned why I did what I did. They understood what enjoyment I received from listening to the games. What I would give to have copies of those score sheets to show Becca, Allison, and Jillian. Perhaps they were lost when we moved when I was fourteen or are in some obscure folder in a closet. But I still have vivid memories of doing what I loved to do with my passion for sports and numbers.

I've been fortunate to tap my passion for sports for Christ. Think back to what you loved to do as a kid or what you enjoy doing now. Find a way to channel that energy for Christ. Colossians 3:23 teaches us to work hard and cheerfully at all we do as if we were working for Christ. Our music minister, Bob Fraumann, often tells our choir that he feels that he's never worked a day in his fifty-plus-year career in music. The reason is that Bob has served Christ through his music and interwoven his ministry into his life activities. A Christian is very fortunate when he or she can live out his or her inborn passion for Christ. God understands our passion because he made us that way. Our passion is the special inner drive that comes from doing what we love to do and doing it to grow the kingdom of God.

Prayer: Father God, I appreciate so much the inner drive and passion that I was born with. Thank you for making me part of a family that understood and nurtured my passion for sports that I can use to help you share the gospel. In Jesus's name, amen.

S45:
THE DRONE OF
THE VUVUZELAS

Ezekiel 37:1-14, Psalm 46:10

Again he said to me, "Son of man, can these bones live?"
And I answered, "Lord God, you know." Again he said to
me, "Prophesy upon these bones, and say to them, 'O you
dry bones, hear the word of the Lord.'"

Ezekiel 37:3-4

If you watched any of the 2010 World Cup games, you undoubtedly
heard the vuvuzelas (vu-vu-zay-las), the plastic horns that the soccer
fans blow time and time again during the game. The decibel level
reaches that of an airplane taking off.

When I was a young boy, you could buy a horn that was very
similar to a *vuvuzela* at Atlanta Stadium. Our Little League team
went to see the Braves and the Giants, and half of us on the team
bought one of those long, blue horns that looked and sounded very
much like the *vuvuzelas*. The following week, my creative friend,
Darryl, modified his horn. He shortened his horn by two inches
and positioned aluminum foil inside the horn. I don't how he did
it, but he had the loudest horn in Cadwell. You could hear it downtown practically.

Back to the *vuvuzelas*. They are as annoying as can be when you are watching the game and trying to listen to the announcers. But after a few minutes of concentrating on the game, you become unaware of the incessant noise.

The chosen people of Israel were oblivious to their sin despite the constant droning of Isaiah, Jeremiah, Ezekiel, Daniel, and the minor prophets. Because they disobeyed God, he allowed the Northern Kingdom (Israel) to be captured by the Assyrians in 722 BC. God also allowed the Southern Kingdom (Judah) to be captured by Babylon in 586 BC. Judah should have learned from Israel's experience!

Even today, we become oblivious to the drone of sin in our lives and don't even notice it after a while. We need to take checkpoints periodically to see if sin is sucking us into its powerful current that threatens to overwhelm us. One great way to take a checkpoint is through daily Bible reading, prayer, and meditation. These daily devotions bring stillness to the soul and peace to the heart. "Be still, and know that I am God" (Psalm 46:10). If God has something to say to you, you've got a much better chance of hearing it when you sit down with him each day.

Prayer: Father God, the hectic pace and incessant noise of the secular world can drown out your voice just like those *vuvuzelas*. Help me find time to meet with you each day so that I can hear your guidance. In Jesus's name, amen.

S46:
HOW MUCH INJURY
TIME IS THERE?

Matthew 28:19-20

Therefore, go and make disciples in all the nations…

Matthew 28:19

It's an interesting phenomenon to watch a World Cup game. In all other sports, the clock ticks down from 20:00 or 15:00 or 12:00 to 0:00. But in soccer, the clock ticks from 0:00 to 45:00. In the second half, the clock ticks from 45:00 to 90:00, but usually that's not how much time is left in the game. There are usually several stoppages of play for players who are shaken up or injured. For the length of time that it takes to get the player off the pitch (aka field), the referee adds injury time. So when the clock ticks 90:00, instead of game over, there are typically two to four minutes of extra time or injury time. The players have no idea when the game will actually end. But they can sense that there is not much time. If their team is down a goal, they urgently try to score a tying goal. Only the referee keeping injury time knows, and he blows the whistle to signal the end of the game.

Often we procrastinate, or wait until the last minute, to take action. Becca and I talked for weeks about applying for Masters single-day tickets. The deadline was midnight on June 30 to apply online. Becca came into the living room and said, "I just completed the online application for the tickets." It was 11:58 pm! We had plenty of time and almost blew it.

Just as the players are unsure how much time is remaining, we don't know the length of our life or the lives of others on earth. It is easy in our busyness to become complacent about sharing the gospel and performing acts of kindness in the name of Christ. Let's be urgent about his work *now*, just as if we need to make that tying goal! When Jesus said to make disciples in all the nations (Matthew 28:19), that includes the good ole USA.

Prayer: Dear heavenly Father and Creator of the universe, may I be acutely aware of people who need your saving grace. Give me the compassion to follow through and the guidance for how to reach out to them in word or deed. In Jesus's name, amen.

S47:
70-68. 'NUFF SAID

Hebrews 12:1

Since we are surrounded by such a great cloud of witnesses,
let us throw off everything that so easily entangles us, and
let us run with perseverance the race marked out for us.

The first week of the Championships at Wimbledon in 2010 was like none other in sports history. An extraordinary tennis match lasted over eleven hours over three different days with no rain delays.

If a match goes five sets, Wimbledon requires the player to win the fifth set by two games. It took more than eleven hours, but UGA graduate John Isner won the longest Grand Slam singles match ever played, breaking qualifier Frenchman Nicolas Mahut's serve in the 138th game of the fifth and final set. Surely that's a typo. You meant thirty-eighth game in the fifth set, right? No, the 138th game. The final score was 6-4, 3-6, 6-7, 7-6, 70-68. An astounding 138 games. The 138 games alone were equal to playing eleven 7-6 tiebreaker sets. Added to the first four sets, the match was the equivalent of fifteen full sets.

In the 2009 final, Roger Federer defeated Andy Roddick 5-7, 7-6, 7-6, 3-6, 16-14, an epic battle for the ages with the most games (seventy-seven) in a men's final ever. Some called the Federer-Roddick battle the greatest match ever, but the Isner-Mahut battle surpassed it. Federer, the fifteen-time grand slam winner, said, "It's beyond anything I've ever seen and could imagine. For them to serve the aces they served and stay there mentally is a heroic effort."

Manny Diaz, UGA men's tennis coach, said, "The scoreboard isn't even working; [it doesn't] even know how to get to these numbers. Physically, they are being asked to do things that they have never done before."

The equivalent in major league baseball would be a sixty-inning game, or an NBA game lasting twenty overtimes, or an NFL game lasting eight extra quarters, or an eighteen-hole US Open golf playoff lasting fifty-four holes.

These were truly uncharted waters. Nobody even knew that players could play that many sets and sustain such a high level, with a hundred aces apiece, without serious injury. Mahut held serve sixty-two consecutive times when, if he had lost the game, the match would have been over. The players played with incredible heart to surpass what was previously believed to be physically possible.

What will these two tennis pros take from this amazing experience? Plenty. The next time they are tired in a third set or fifth set, they can look across the net and know their opponent hasn't been down that road.

Many of us plunge into uncharted waters when devastation hits. Some of us have never played a five-setter, much less a three-setter. We can't relate to the courage and strength that is required. Clearly, God is always present to give us courage and strength when we feel like we cannot go on.

Here is a takeaway for our lives. God calls for us "to run with perseverance the race set out for us" (Hebrews 12:1). Some personal races are far more difficult emotionally, mentally, physically, and spiritually than others. For those of you who have been far beyond where you thought you could possibly persevere due to personal problems or challenging family situations, I encourage you to share your story of perseverance with friends who need to hear it now or later. You have a personal testimony that only God can provide you. God is constantly making lemonade out of lemons. Only God can take disastrous consequences and create hope.

Prayer: Father God, may I realize that you and I can do far more than I alone can do. May I share my story of perseverance with grace and humility. May I recognize where my strength comes from, which is from you, Father, and from your Son, who went through far more than I will ever face. It is all because of your immeasurable love, which I do not deserve but am so grateful to experience. In Jesus's name, amen.

S48:
ISNER'S SEQUEL

Galatians 6:9

And let us not be weary in well doing, for in due season,
we shall reap, if we faint not.

The previous devotion referenced John Isner's riveting three-day
match over eleven hours at Wimbledon that set tennis records that
will last for generations. In his next match, Isner was easily defeated
in straight sets as he battled a stiff neck, which required a physical
therapist to treat him between games. Isner set a Wimbledon record
of 108 aces in his marathon match, but on this day, he had exactly
108 fewer aces. His serve was more than 10 miles per hour slower
than the previous day. Isner knew he was in trouble as he was warm-
ing up. But he showed up to do battle for thousands of his new fans,
even though he didn't even have his C game.

God expects us to give our best effort each day. The Lord knows
that some days we just don't have it due to injury, illness, fatigue,
or just being human and mistake prone. When we don't have our
best and the odds are against us, when the wind is howling in our
faces or the sun is in our eyes or the rain is pelting down, we are still
supposed to show up and give it our all. With the help of the Holy
Spirit, we can make it through the problems of the day and still

remind people of Christ despite the struggles. We can count on God to richly bless us for our efforts under duress.

Prayer: Father God, for those days I don't want to get out of bed and face the music, help me remember that Jesus faced all the music that I will ever encounter and much, much more. May I have the courage to never duck a day and give it all that I have so that I can give you the glory. In Jesus's name, amen.

S49:
BEFORE THE CROWN
CAN BE WORN

Romans 8:18, 1 Peter 5:4,
2 Timothy 4:8, Philippians 4:13

The cross must be carried before the crown can be worn.

Morning & Evening, Charles Spurgeon

In mid-November the top-tier college football teams are still in the hunt for the Bowl Championship Series (BCS) national championship trophy. The second-tier teams can still win their conference championships and get into a BCS or New Year's Day bowl. The third-tier teams scrape to get into any bowl to reward their players and earn an extra fifteen days of practice for the next season. The bottom-tier teams hope to pull an upset in their rivalry games over the next two weeks to cap otherwise dismal campaigns.

All of the teams that vie for the BCS national championship trophy took basically the same steps for the season. There were strenuous off-season conditioning workouts for the players. Teams concentrated on the fundamentals in spring practice and endured two-a-day practices in the stifling August heat and humidity. Players suffered season-ending injuries, and others played through the pain of bruises, cuts, and scrapes throughout the season. Late in the season, there is never enough time to heal, and players must find a way to keep going. Eventually, one team will find a way to endure and be crowned the national champion in the second week of January.

Why are some teams more successful than others? Top-flight talent and great coaching are always two important keys to success. But perhaps some team members didn't pay the price by following the team rules, or completing the voluntary summer workouts, or studying film to prevent the blown assignment that made the difference between winning or losing a crucial game in November.

Certainly no team has ever received the championship crown without practicing the fundamentals each day. Nor can a person expect to reap the rewards of heaven without enduring some trials and tribulation. Christ took no short cuts on his way to the cross or on the cross. Charles Spurgeon, the wonderful English evangelist from the late nineteenth century, wrote, "The cross must be carried before the crown can be worn." Believers need to stay true to Christ daily to endure the challenges of life and the enemy. Some will endure more steadfastly than others.

Very few will get to heaven without going through some trials. But the rewards are great now and in heaven for those who are committed to carry their cross daily in the name of Jesus Christ, regardless of circumstances. Jesus went through all the bad stuff and wore the crown of thorns so that we could have the faith to persevere by "depending on Him" (Hebrews 11:6) and, one day, wear the eternal crowns of life (Revelation 2:10), glory (1 Peter 5:4), and righteousness (2 Timothy 4:8).

When the victory is achieved, whether it is coming back from an illness, or from a tough start in a class to get that B, or coming back to help your team after an injury, the battle will have been worth it as you give God the glory for all that he has brought you through. "Yet what we suffer now is nothing compared to the glory we will receive later" (Romans 8:18). Rest assured that you "can do all things through Christ who strengthens" you (Philippians 4:13). In John

16:33, Jesus provides the assurance that "there will be tribulation, but be of good cheer, for I have overcome the world."

Prayer: Most merciful God, help me realize that the real victories are won in the trenches of everyday life when I choose to endure. I have the choice to endure because Jesus endured all of our sin on the cross to achieve the ultimate victory. I put my total trust and faith in Christ and believe that I can do all things through him who strengthens me. In Jesus's holy name, amen.

S50:
AVOID THE RED CARD

Romans 8:28, Exodus 20:3, 1 John 1:9

And we know that all that happens to us is working for our good, if we love God and are fitting into his plans.

Romans 8:28

During the 2010 World Cup, it was apparent that the teams clearly understood which players had received yellow cards. When a player receives a yellow card from the referee, he is allowed to stay in the game. However, a second yellow card in the same game is the equivalent of a red card, which would remove the player from the game and also keep the player out of the next game.

Often, a player will receive a red card from the referee by going after an opponent too aggressively, or tackling a player in the goal box, or having a hand ball inside the box as a player from Uruguay blatantly did. When any of these plays happen, it not only hurts the player but also his or her team. A red card means that your team plays ten on eleven for the remainder of the match. The man disadvantage led to Netherland's loss in the finals.

God was, is, and always will be the referee, and he will show us the yellow card when we begin to slip away from his plan. If we continue to play out of control and outside his game plan, God might red card us and let us sit on the sideline. Clearly, we can bench ourselves by putting ourselves above God and others (Exodus 20:3), through unconfessed sin (1 John 1:9), and allowing strongholds to separate us from God. When we go through the dry season, we wonder where God went. He hasn't gone anywhere. God never leaves the field (aka throne). He will discipline us because he loves us, and he could give our minutes to others who are obediently following his game plan. God's action is similar to how a coach might substitute for us if our actions are hurting the team's chances to win the game.

But there is good news. When we confess the specific sins and ask for forgiveness, God will forgive us, forget that it ever happened, and put us back in his game. When we get back in the game, eternal things are waiting to happen. We will sense the power of the Holy Spirit at work in us and through us when we are in step with God.

Prayer: Father God, please give me a burning desire to share the good news in complete accordance with your plan and your timing. I want to avoid your red card at all costs because I will not be working for the kingdom if it happens. In Jesus's name, amen.

S51:
PENALTY KICK

1 Peter 2:24, 1 John 3:4

Who Himself bore our sins in his own body on the tree, that we, having died to sins, might live for righteousness, by whose stripes you were healed.

1 Peter 2:24

When a defensive player tackles an offensive player inside the goal box or touches the ball with his hand inside the box, either is a severe infraction that warrants the stiffest penalty in soccer. Either violation results in a free penalty kick for the offensive team. The ball is placed on the penalty kick box directly in front of the goalie twelve yards away. One player is selected by his team to take the penalty kick. It's the offensive star versus the goalie. Because the offensive star is usually so accurate and there is so much territory to cover, the goalie is pretty much helpless. He must guess if the kicker will go left or right, high or low, and leap that way as soon as the ball is struck. The odds are that the offensive player will score the goal. When the goal is scored, the defense has paid the price for the penalty kick.

Do you realize that Christ paid the penalty for our sins? When we commit infractions called sin, or transgressions of the law, they can't go unnoticed by God, who cannot look on sin. God cannot ignore sin because sin separates us from him. But there came One who paid the penalty for all the sin that has been or ever will be committed. Jesus Christ bore all of those sins in his own body on the rugged cross because God loves us so much that he would rather have his Son die than see us eternally separated from him. Christ paid the penalty for us so that we wouldn't have to. But there is one thing we must do: turn from sin and turn toward God. If we do that and believe that Jesus died for our sin, we will be forgiven, our debt paid in full.

Prayer: Father God, thank you for loving me so much that you sent your beloved Son, who has been with you before the beginning of time, to die a painful death so that the penalty for my transgressions could be paid in full. I am so grateful that I can have a personal relationship with you and Jesus. In the holy name of Jesus Christ, amen.

S52:
THE ESSENTIALS
OF FOOTWORK

Nahum 1:15, Romans 10:15, Ephesians 6:15

How beautiful are the feet of them that preach the gospel,
and bring glad tidings of good things.

Romans 10:15

The top soccer players have some of the best footwork that you will
see in any sport. Watching the World Cup made me appreciate the
incredible skills that these great athletes possess. The strikers are so
fast, so adept at dribbling, and able to pick the ball out of the air
and literally kill it at their feet. Their skill comes from thousands of
hours of doing cone drills, balancing the ball, and moving it from
foot to foot at various speeds. The ability to control one possession
with the feet and initiate a scoring opportunity can sometimes mean
the difference in the game. Oh, let's not forget the uncanny passing
accuracy and blistering speed with which the top players can kick
the ball. They send the ball sizzling toward the goal as the helpless
goalie is overmatched, and the ball goes in the back of the net.

I saw an ESPN special on the World Cup, and several world-
class athletes attributed soccer to helping them develop their exper-
tise in their respective sports. Dwight Freeney, all-pro defensive end

for the Indianapolis Colts, was a goalie, and the twitch reflexes that he developed in soccer enable him to get off the line of scrimmage like a cat. Steve Nash, the Phoenix Suns' all-star guard, is convinced that he would never have played professional basketball without the footwork that he learned in soccer. Shane Victorino, the Philadelphia Phillies' fleet centerfielder, called soccer his favorite sport when he was growing up.

There are other kinds of footwork that are very valuable. One form of footwork is that we can get on our feet, go where the people are, and share the gospel. G-O are the first two letters in *gospel*. The only way some people are going to hear about the gospel is if we go out and share it with them. Another type of footwork is to show people the love of Christ through caring. We can use our feet to help deliver food to the poor, visit the sick, or talk to a friend who is feeling down. God promises that we will receive rewards in heaven for this footwork, and Paul encouraged us to go forth in peace.

Prayer: Father God, help me see the many ways that I can share the good news with my friends, family, neighbors, and coworkers. May I get on my feet and meet them where they are so that they will see the light of Christ shining forth. In Jesus's holy name, amen.

S53:
USING YOUR HEAD

Romans 12:2

Do not be conformed to this world, but be transformed by
the renewing of your mind, such that you may prove what
is that good and acceptable and perfect will of God.

The 2010 World Cup championship game between Spain and
Germany was one for the ages. Spain threatened to score numerous times during the first eighty minutes of the game only to see
Germany turn them back each time. With less than ten minutes
remaining in regular time, Spain tried a corner kick. The Spanish
player rifled the ball about twenty-five feet to the right of the goal
and about nine feet in the air. Seemingly out of nowhere, a Spanish
defender rose high above every other player, timed his leap perfectly,
met the ball with his forehead, and directed the ball toward the
upper right-hand corner of the goal. The German goalie stretched
fully in a valiant effort, but the ball sailed past his outstretched fin-
gertips into the goal. It was one of the greatest goals ever scored in
World Cup play, and it was a header. Spain won 1-0 on that amazing header.

Just as the Spanish player used his head to gain an advantage for
his team, we should use our heads to gain an advantage in our everyday lives. The book of Romans teaches us to control what goes into

our minds so that we will use our minds more effectively and make better decisions. When we control the intake, the output is so much more Christlike. We can align ourselves with God's perfect will for our lives. When we are aligned with God, we will score a lot of the goals for the kingdom.

Prayer: Father God, I want to be a great goal scorer for you by being obedient and following your plan for my life. If I follow your plan, I can be so much more productive for the kingdom. May you receive all the glory. In Jesus's name, amen.

S54:
DON'T BE OFFSIDE

Jeremiah 29:11

I know the plans that I have for you, says the Lord, plans for welfare and not for harm, to give you a future with hope.

Many controversial calls during the 2010 World Cup involved players who were called for being offside when they weren't and players who were offside but were not called. Offside occurs when an offensive player breaks behind the last defensive player before the ball is passed by his teammate. If a player runs even with the defense and, just as the ball is passed, outruns the defender to the ball, he can legally shoot and score. The spirit and intent of the rule is to prevent the offensive player from sneaking behind the defense and gaining an unfair advantage. In fairness to the officials, it's very difficult to determine who is offside on some plays.

Sometimes we get ahead of God because we believe that we have this incredible way to help him, but there could be two problems. First, we may not be working where God is working. Second, we may be working faster than God wants us to work. If we are operating outside God's plan for us, we're going to be quite frustrated. We wonder why God didn't bless the plan. When we race ahead of God, we actually get offside. God wants us to stay onside, which means following his plan in his timing to perform his work.

How do you know if you are in step with God's plan? First, the decision will bring about a sense of peace. Second, pray with God about the plan. Don't push it if you don't feel led. Third, check the Scriptures to see if your approach is consistent with God's teaching. Fourth, check with a fellow believer who you especially have confidence in. If you pass these checkpoints, the chances are that God will bless your efforts.

Prayer: Most gracious Lord, I want to see the kingdom grow, but I need to realize that it will grow at your pace and your direction, not mine. May I be diligent and in step with your perfect timing. In Jesus's name, amen.

S55:
DIGGING INTO
THE WORD

2 Timothy 3:14-17

All scripture is given by inspiration of God, and is profitable for doctrine, for reproof, for correction, for instruction in righteousness.

2 Timothy 3:16

I have a superficial understanding of the game of soccer, having not played competitively. I told my friend, Danny, that I had only come up with a few soccer devotions. Danny explained with a revealing statement that you must get into the heart and soul of the sport to understand the nuances. That advice really paid off as I began to think of the intricacies of the games that I had seen during the 2010 World Cup.

It's the same way with the deeper truths of the Bible. We must dig into the Word to find out what God wants us to know. Like eating soft-shell crab, it's a lot of work, but getting to the tasty morsels of meat is worth the labor. We can gloss over a chapter in the Bible and be thinking of what we need to do at work or school, or we can take a different approach. We can read the chapter a second time and a third time. We can pick apart the chapter verse by verse. We can read the commentaries to obtain a deeper understanding and search the cross-references. We can engage in discussions through small groups and Bible studies. We can meditate on the Scripture and wait for God to reveal an application for our lives. It's very difficult to do all of these things consistently, but if we can even come close, God will multiply our blessings. Like the heart of a watermelon, when we go deep, it's the sweetest.

Prayer: Father God, thank you for inspiring such a seamless collection of parables, stories, and truths that amazingly can be applied to what will confront me the next time I go out the door. In Jesus's name, amen.

S56:
THE SOCCER TRINITY

Acts 1:1-8, John 14:26, Romans 8:26

The Holy Spirit helps us with our daily problems and in our praying…

Romans 8:26

There are three important fundamental skills for a soccer player. First, the player must be a good passer and be able to put the ball on a teammate's foot with good timing. Second, a player needs to be able to dribble the ball with the inside and outside of both feet, quickly advancing the ball past the defenders. Third, the player must be a strong, accurate kicker in order to score goals. All expert players have mastered these three fundamental skills.

There was a bestseller fiction book called *The Shack* by William P. Young that depicted how the three members of the Holy Trinity complement each other perfectly. The author illustrated how the Trinity worked together to bring hope to a father named Mack, who was devastated by the tragic loss of his young daughter. Mack confronts the hypothetical Trinity when he stumbles upon a shack in the woods. An African American woman played God. The second character, a man of Middle Eastern descent, played Jesus. The third person, an Asian woman, played the role of the Holy Spirit. When

Mack asked the three of them which one was God, they answered simultaneously, "I am."

God is the heavenly Father, Jesus is the Son of God who came from heaven to earth to save us, and the Holy Spirit lives within us as a person. The Trinity is in us, with us, for us, goes ahead of us, and stays behind us to protect us. It's difficult to imagine, but the more you study the Bible, the more sense it makes. The members of the Trinity are perfect, and their teamwork is perfect and seamless.

Each member of the Holy Trinity loves you more than you can possibly realize. Always remember that with the Trinity by your side and living within you, all things are possible.

Prayer: Father God, what a blessing it is to have your unconditional love. Thank you for sending your son, Jesus, to die for me. I am grateful that the Holy Spirit lives in me to help me with my daily problems and to pray. In Jesus's name, amen.

S57:
BE A VALUABLE SUB!

Hebrews 12:1, Luke 12:40

Throw off everything that so easily entangles us ...

Hebrews 12:1

Many times, when the outcome of a soccer game hangs in the balance, the decisive play is not made by the team's leading goal scorer, or the goalie, or the best midfielder. Sometimes the substitute off the bench will give his team a needed spark. In soccer, there are eighteen to twenty players on a team, but only eleven can play at any given time. It is very important that the non-starters pay close attention, study the game, and be ready at all times. You might suddenly be rushed into the game if a player turns an ankle. You might only have a brief opportunity to help the team, and you want to make the most of that chance. If you aren't ready, you won't make the play that your team needs.

As a Christian, sometimes you feel as if you are not in the game for God. Either you've not studied his Word or haven't been in prayer with him lately. Perhaps there is a secret sin that has derailed you temporarily. When the opportunity comes to listen to a friend who needs to vent, or to share Christ when someone opens a door, you miss it like a wide-open penalty kick. The biggest detriment is our self-centered attitude, which is sinful and can separate us from

God. Just like a player rips off his warm-up to enter the game, you must be prepared to "throw off everything [sin] that easily entangles [you]," and "run with perseverance the race set before [you]."

If you focus on loving God, appreciate every blessing he gives you, and thank him for the sacrifice that Christ made on the cross for you, then you will want to return his love and be obedient. If you are obedient, you will stay ready and see where God is working. That is where the kingdom opportunities are. Your kindness and generosity could make the difference for a friend or family member for eternity. Remember, God chose to operate with twelve regular guys who changed the world after they received the Holy Spirit. After you have received the Holy Spirit, you are no different from those disciples and Paul. God can and will do great and mighty works through you, even when you feel like a substitute, if you will only believe.

Prayer: Dear Lord, help me stay true to you so that I'm ready to leap off the bench to make a play for the kingdom of God. In Jesus's name, amen.

S58:
MASTER THE
FUNDAMENTALS

Exodus 20:1-17, Joshua 1:8, Galatians 3:24

Wherefore the Law was our schoolmaster to bring us
to Christ…

Galatians 3:24

The great Pele from Brazil was arguably the most spectacular goal
scorer in the history of soccer. Pele had a repertoire of kicks and headers that few have been able to master. Perhaps Pele's most famous
move was the scissors kick, when he would leap high into the air
with his back parallel to the ground. Pele would contort his legs to
generate power and whip the ball over his head toward the opponent's goal. It was an amazing move that few people had ever seen.

Pele learned those amazing moves by building up to them. When
he was a kid, he learned the fundamentals of shooting, heading,
dribbling, and passing. Pele learned to kick the ball straight before
he learned to curve it left or right. He first learned a series of basic
kicks. Later, he would improvise with the scissors kick. Once Pele
mastered the basics, he moved onto the advanced skills.

In the same way, a person needs to master the fundamentals of
the Ten Commandments, which are the basic rules that God gave

us to live by. When you commit a sin and know that you broke one or more of God's rules, you will know that you need to repent, which is to say you are truly sorry, and ask for God's forgiveness. Too many people want to perform a scissors kick before they learn the basics. Too many people want the saving grace of the gospel without the repentance.

Mastering these fundamentals will help you identify personal sin such as holding too tightly to possessions. You've got to give up some things to get the best that God has to offer. If your fists are stubbornly clenched, holding on to what you think are the good things in life, you cannot open your hands so that God can give you the very best, which aren't really things. What cannot be seen, riches such as love, peace, joy, and contentment, are the things that last.

If you hold stubbornly onto your sinful habits, God cannot give you righteous habits to replace them. When you unclench your fists and admit that you have sinned against him, God will give you the best blessings that he has always planned for you to have. The biggest blessing is eternal life with him through the blood of Jesus Christ shed for you.

Prayer: Father God, give me the courage and the trust to let go of the things that are holding me back from the riches that you want to give me. Help me see that the true riches in life are a relationship with you and helping others. In the name of Jesus, who shed his blood at Calvary to cover my sins, amen.

S59:
SEE THE PITCH

1 John 1:1

That which was from the beginning, ... which we have seen with our eyes, which we have looked upon, ...

1 John 1:1

One of the most exciting plays in soccer is when teammates collaborate on a series of quick passes to set up a goal. The offense moves the ball quickly down the field before the defense can interrupt the passing flow. A well-timed series of passes will often result in a goal or a corner kick at a minimum. A successful sequence of passes energizes the crowd and fills the team with confidence and energy.

When the offensive player controls the ball, he should have his head up to see all of his passing and shooting options. It is fantastic to have a player with excellent peripheral vision who can see players with his 180-degree vision. It's important for young players to learn to dribble with their heads up so that they can see the pitch or field. Players must be confident with the ball to see the pitch while they are dribbling. When your head is down, you can't see where you are going, and you won't see the players who are open on the wings or breaking toward the goal.

It's important to look to God each day for guidance in living as a Christian. By keeping our heads up spiritually and being confident in the promises of the Lord, we can be ready to make the right plays as we live each day for him. When we allow the evil one to make us drop our heads in sadness, despair, worry, anger, or frustration, we miss the chances that God gives us to shine our light as Christians, and we miss the blessings that God places in our paths. We need the power of God to keep our heads up and eyes alert for chances to serve him.

Prayer: Father God, help me keep my head up when tough times happen so that I can still see the plays that you would have me make for your kingdom. In Jesus's name, amen.

S60:
THE HEALING POWER OF
RECONCILIATION

Psalm 34:14; Matthew 6:20-24, 26:39

… First go and be reconciled with your brother…"

Matthew 6:24

I have many fond memories of the late Steven Christopher Early, my dear friend and brother in Christ, who lost his life on July 31, 2010, after a twelve-day battle following his automobile accident. Chris, who was twenty-five, played basketball, coached, and refereed at Mount Zion UMC. Our coaches and kids loved it when Chris refereed their games, because he was very consistent and communicated very well. He thoroughly enjoyed officiating, and it showed in his enthusiastic demeanor.

Chris was passionate about sports. He was a huge fan of all Atlanta teams. His favorite Atlanta Brave was manager Bobby Cox. His dad, Steve, called him the biggest Georgia Tech fan that he ever knew, and Steve graduated from Tech! "Chris in Marietta" frequently called Atlanta sports talk shows.

Most importantly to me, Chris directed our basketball program in the summer of 2005 when our Mount Zion church league became the Christ-centered Hoops2Heaven ministry. That summer program was truly the turning point for our basketball ministry to glorify God. Chris recruited four of his buddies and did a super job as our summer director, especially considering he was a teenager. But at the end he and I fell out with each other over a small issue, and we parted on uneven terms. That fall Chris began college, and a new director took over the Hoops2Heaven ministry.

For three years I occasionally recalled our awkward departure and did nothing. But one Christmas I read an Andy Stanley book that challenged the reader to reconcile with friends and family members. I was convinced that I had to take action. I wrote Chris and apologized for the way things ended, and said I wanted to put any differences behind us. Much to my delight, Chris wrote a nice letter back, and we mended our fences! But we still had not gotten together.

In the summer of 2009 God spoke to Chris through the faith of a friend. During a long day of frolicking in the Atlantic surf and talking as best friends, Andrew told Chris how important his personal relationship with Jesus Christ was. Sharing this story at the wake, Andrew recalled looking at Chris and noticing how at peace Chris was. His story brought to my mind what Forrest Gump said as he watched Lieutenant Dan swimming, "I believe Lieutenant Dan has made peace with God."

That same summer Chris spent precious time with Susie, his birth mother, in Orlando. They spent several mornings in prayer at Good Shepherd with the priest who not only arranged the adoption but would perform Chris's funeral Mass. From those meetings the priest hoped Chris would also become a priest. But a career devoted to coaching basketball was clearly Chris's calling.

Chris called me seemingly out of the blue in November 2009 and asked if he could come back and referee. Upon hearing the stories at the wake, I mentally put the pieces of the puzzle together, and his timing made perfect sense. It was great having him back in the gym! He refereed the first full Saturday for us, but four days later he blew out his knee playing racquetball. Chris had surgery followed by extensive rehab. He struggled to salvage his sports management classes at Kennesaw State. I offered encouragement through prayer, texts, and phone calls.

In the winter and spring of 2010, Chris coached the Georgia Kings, a U-13 AAU basketball team. Through coaching this team he found his true love and passion. The coaching passion was always there (see his favorite Brave, Bobby Cox). Andrew recalled how Chris once described an inbounds play from his AAU game in excruciating detail.

He got through rehab and actually refereed some games for us in our summer league. At one of our summer devotions, Chris asked us to pray for his birth mother, who had been diagnosed with breast cancer.

Later that summer came the stunning news of his accident. As Chris lay unresponsive in the hospital due to his massive injuries, his doctor suggested playing music to stimulate his senses. His best friend, Andrew, explained how that wouldn't work because Chris never listened to music. Turn on sports talk radio if you want "Chris in Marietta" to respond, Andrew advised.

Late one night his mother, Linda, sensed his brokenness and changed her prayer, "God, if Chris is so broken that he can't be fixed, you can take him." Her prayer was in the spirit of " ... nevertheless not as I will, but as you will" (Matthew 26:39). Thirty minutes later, God called Chris home.

Chris's immediate family, his father, Steve, his mother, Linda, and sister, Meghan, loved him so incredibly. For his wake and funeral Mass, Chris was dressed in a sport coat and polo shirt, because "that's how coaches are supposed to dress." The Georgia Kings came to the funeral home as a team, dressed in their uniforms. At the funeral Mass Steve gave a touching eulogy, and the priest shared Linda's prayer for God's will to be done. Chris's love for basketball was punctuated at the funeral Mass when the priest sprinkled holy water over his basketball and one of his referee shirts.

During the first few weeks after his passing, I was grateful so many times that Chris and I reconciled. How would I feel if I had continued to ignore the Holy Spirit? I believe that I would be miserable if I had not acted. Someday you could be miserable if you fail to reconcile with your friends, family members, and especially Jesus Christ. When you are moved by the Holy Spirit like I was, I encourage you to pray and find a way to make it happen. Jesus taught that reconciliation is so important that it should happen even before you place your gift on the altar. Be reconciled to your brothers and sisters today, and to Jesus Christ, and future regrets will never materialize.

A striped shirt and Chris's *Marietta Daily Journal* article now hang on the wall of our youth sports ministry office in his memory.

Prayer: Father God, I am overwhelmed by the power of your mercy and grace and by your ability to bear fruit in the midst of an apparent disaster. Help me practice forgiveness as you did, and may I have no reconciliation regrets on the day that I see you face to face. In Jesus's holy name, amen.

S61:
ARE YOU WILLING TO BE A
SETTER FOR THE KINGDOM?

John 10:38-41

Jesus answered her, "Martha, Martha, you are worried and upset about many things ... "

John 10:41

The setter receives less credit than the other major volleyball positions that kill, block, and dig. The setter simply sets. Typically, the setter is less physically imposing than the other players, yet must play his or her position extremely well. The setter is usually the second person from the team who makes contact with the ball. After the first player blocks the ball high into the air, the setter's main goal is to deftly place the ball so that it can be driven into the opponent's court. The setter also coordinates the offensive movements of a team and ultimately decides which player will actually attack the ball.

Despite the fact that the setter is a "middle man," the middle person to touch the ball in a three-touch set, the setter's role is very important. The setter must place the ball at the apex for the jumper and position the ball in exactly the correct spot on the court. The setter "sets the table" for a perfect attempt at the spike.

Martha, who was the chief cook, bottle washer, and table setter, would have been the equivalent of the setter when Jesus came to her house for dinner. She was busy behind the scenes making the big meal and taking care of the details. Martha fretted when she saw Mary in the spotlight with Jesus. Paraphrasing, Jesus tells Martha. "Martha, why are you worried about your sister spending time with me? You do your thing, and Mary can do hers. It's fine that she spends time with me."

Are you willing to be a setter for God and occupy one of the least noticeable positions in the church while others receive the credit? Helping out at VBS or basketball camp, cleaning up after Wednesday night dinner, and putting up tables are small tasks that will not receive much attention. Are you willing to be in the background and allow others to have the jobs in the spotlight? Just remember there is plenty of glory to go around when we all do our jobs well for the kingdom. To God be the glory.

Prayer: Father God, may I follow your will and discover what I need to be doing for you and not worry about others getting the credit. I might be perfectly suited for behind the scenes work that nobody will ever see. Help me joyously support those believers who are in the spotlight so that the kingdom benefits and you receive the glory. In Jesus's name, amen.

S62:
GRAPPLING IN
THE GOAL BOX

Matthew 28:20, Hebrews 13:5,
John 15:5, Philippians 4:13

Apart from Me you can do nothing.

John 15:5

Watching the World Cup, I noticed that much of the attention went to the flashy goal scorers, such as David Villa from Spain. The highlights each evening prominently featured the goal scorers.

But it's the battles in the goal box that are the most hectic plays. When a corner kick occurs, it is flat-out rough in front of the goal. There will be bodies flying, elbows being thrown, players getting kicked, holding, clawing, and scratching. Players contort their bodies as they leap high into the air for headers. Defenders will often do anything possible, including violating the rules, to keep the opponent from getting a shot on goal. It could include stepping on top of another player's foot with his cleats. Ouch!

Satan fights us with the fervor of those goal box skirmishes. Satan uses any tactic that he can to dissuade us from obeying God. It's doing battle with Satan through daily prayer and Bible reading that gets us ready when tough times come. If we wait until the tough times to cry out to God without having the relationship, then we won't be in the position that we need to be.

By putting substantial roots down through daily communion with God, we won't be blown away when the storms come. There will be no wavering. We will know that God didn't cause the problems, and he, along with the Holy Spirit, will be there to see us through them. God promised that he will never leave nor forsake us (Hebrews 13:5) and that he will be with us until the end of the age (Matthew 28:20).

We need to memorize Scripture that will help pull us through tough times. Anyone can go into bunker mentality mode and get through stress. But it's the believer with a strong foundation that can get through stress and strain like a saint, according to Oswald Chambers, author of *My Utmost for His Highest*.

Prayer: Dear Lord, help me have the daily discipline to pray with you and study your Word. Thank you for your strength and protection that enable me to withstand the attacks of the enemy. In Jesus's name, amen.

S63:
PRACTICE LEADS
TO PERFECTION

Philippians 1:6

Being confident of this very thing, that He who has
begun a new work in you will complete it until the day of
Jesus Christ.

If you play on a soccer travel team or an elite team, you can expect
to practice several hours per day. You and your teammates will go
through special conditioning and ball control drills. Corner kicks
will be practiced over and over. Possession drills using dribble cones
will be repeated each day. The goalies will perform an exhaustive
series of drills to enhance their abilities to keep balls out of the net.
Players will work on intricate pass relays to sharpen their timing. The
coaches will review offensive and defensive strategy with your team.

If your team simply showed up at your games without this intense
practice, your team would surely be outplayed by the other team who
is putting in the repetitions. If we expect to grow as Christians, we
can't just come to church every other Sunday and expect to grow in
our love for God and other people. Daily spiritual practices such
as prayer, meditation, Bible reading, devotions, and hanging with
other brothers and sisters in Christ will help us grow effectively as

Christians. With steady diligence, our obedience and love for God will grow. We will still make mistakes called sin, but the wrongdoings should become fewer and farther between. Eventually, when we meet Christ one glorious day, he will make us perfect.

Prayer: Father God, may I use the lessons learned from my experiences to become a more ardent follower. I need to practice daily through reading the Word, meditation, and prayer. In Jesus's name, amen.

S64:
CREATING A
WINNING TEAM

Romans 12:5-8

Having then gifts differing according to the grace that is given to us …

Romans 12:6

It takes many talents meshing well together to make a successful soccer team. There are the strikers, whose job it is to put the ball into the opponent's net. The midfielders must be able to control the ball in the midfield and prevent the opponents from attacking the goal. The defenders must be conscious of offensive players sneaking behind them, and they must be able to clear the ball quickly when the ball is in the goal box. The goalie must possess catlike reflexes and be able to spring at a moment's notice to block a well-struck kick or a well-aimed header. As you can see, it takes a lot of players on the soccer team doing different jobs well to win the game.

Not all of the jobs are exciting, but they are necessary. Sometimes a player's greatest challenge is coming to grips with his or her role on the team. Mia Hamm talked about the importance of meshing individuals into a cohesive team. She was quoted as saying, "I am a member of a team, and I rely on the team, I defer to it and sacrifice for it because the team, not the individual, is the ultimate champion."

People are blessed with different spiritual talents. Some are us are quite adept at meeting new people and making them feel welcome. Others have a gift for carpentry which can be used for Habitat for Humanity. Some are gifted musicians and dancers. There are people who are really good at telling stories from the Bible, and others who excel at coaching and playing sports. Still others are very good at working with young kids at vacation Bible school. But it is up to each of us to use the specific talents that God has blessed us with to reach people for Christ. It is also up to us to sacrifice for the common good of the church, the body of Christ. If we give of ourselves selflessly and become a team focused on Jesus Christ, our church will become a champion in our community.

Prayer: Dear Lord, help me see the special gifts in my fellow believers. May I appreciate that their spiritual gifts may be much different from mine because you gave us different passions. Thank you for your wonderful love, even though I will never fully comprehend its depth and breadth. In the name of our precious Savior, amen.

VERSES BY BOOK

1 Corinthians

6:18-20	Golf51
9:22	FB39, Golf30
9:24-27	BK53
15:33	BK35

1 John

1:1	S59
1:9	BB40, BK52, BK62, S41, S50, S62
3:4	BK37, S51

1 Peter

2:2	BB50
2:24	BB34, BB40, BK52, BK58, BK59, BK60, S41, S51, S52
5:4	S49
5:7	BB47, BK51, Golf38

1 Thessalonians

4:14-18	BK57, S42
5:17	BK41

1 Timothy

1:15-16	BB46
4:12	BK68

2 Chronicles

34:1-3	BK68

2 Corinthians

4:18	FB57
5:21	BK60
9:9	BK56
11:23-28	FB42
12:6	FB49
12:10	S37

2 Timothy

3:14-17	S55
3:16	Golf29, Golf50
4:2	BB41, BB53, BK53, FB62, Golf33, Golf34
4:8	S49

Acts

1:1-8	S56
1:8	BK53, Golf32, Golf37, Golf41
2:4	BK59
9:1-19	BB32
20:24	Golf30

Colossians

1:27	BB54
3:17	BB41, BB53, BK47
3:23	S44

Daniel

3:12-25	FB63
4:3	S39
9:24-27	FB44

Ecclesiastes

2:11	BK43

Ephesians

2:8	BB40, BB41, BK52, S41
2:8-9	BK59, Golf37
2:9	BK47, S38
4:29	BK38, BK63
4:30	BB38, BB41, BB52, FB36, Golf32
6:10	Golf32
6:10-18	BK45, S61
6:10-20	S37, S40
6:15	S52

Exodus

17:11-14	FB54
20:1-17	S58
20:3	BK62, BK66, S50, S62
20:7	Golf49
20:18	BB36

Ezekiel

37:1-14	S45

Galatians

3:24	S58
4:6	BB41
5:22-23	FB56, Golf56
6:9	S48

Hebrews

11:6	S49
12:1	FB55, S47, S57
12:2	BB30
13:5	BB44, BK51, FB52, S35, S62

Isaiah

40:22	Golf53
40:25-26	Golf53
42:8	FB37
44:6	FB37
44:8	FB37
45:5	FB37
45:22	FB37
53:4	Golf39
55:9	S38

James

1:2-4	FB42
2:17	FB49
4:7	Golf51
4:14	S38

Jeremiah

12:1	S38
17:5-8	FB60
29:11	BB40, BK52, FB60, S41, S54

Job

1:13-2:10	FB38
11:23	BB41
21:7-11	S38

John

3:16	BB31, BB40, BK52, FB42, S41
3:16-17	FB50, FB59, Golf48
3:17	BB35, FB59
3:30	FB39, Golf53
4:7-26	BK55
5:1-9	BK55
8:1-12	BK55
8:7	Golf36
9:1-14	BK55
10:38-41	S61
11:35	BB44
14:2-4	FB46
14:6	BK64, Golf43, Golf45
14:12	BK68
14:16	BB39
14:16-26	BK49
14:26	BK39, BK41, BK49, S56
15:5	S35, S62
16:33	FB51, S49
18:3-11	FB58
20:25-29	FB61
21:3-8	BK67
21:19	FB60

Joshua

1:8	Golf47, S58

Lamentations

3:22-23	BB41, BB45, BK61

Luke

2:10-16	FB45
2:40-52	BK68
3:21-22	FB36
7:44-50	BK36
9:62	Golf30
12:40	S57
15:11-24	BB37
17:3-4	Golf36
24:1-12	BB43

Mark

1:15	S55
5:37	Golf44
11:1-9	S66
11:15-19	BB34
11:42	BB44
14:33	Golf44
16:1-14	BB42, BB43

Matthew

2:1-12	BK36
5:14	BK44
5:14-16	S36
5:27-32	Golf54
6:20-24	S60
6:23	BK54
6:25-33	BK47
6:33	FB41

7:7	BB48, Golf31
7:13	FB33
10:32-33	BK48, Golf45
11:28	BB49, FB40
12:34	BK63
13:36-50	Golf55
16:26	S38
17:1-2	Golf44
18:22	Golf36
25:45	BK56
26:34-49	Golf46
26:36-52	BB35
26:39	S60
26:58-75	BB42
27:32	FB41
27:38:43	FB44
28:19-20	BB41, BK53, S46
28:20	S35, S62

Nahum

1:15	S52

Philippians

1:6	FB53, S63
1:20-21	FB42
2:8-11	FB35
2:17	FB48, FB64
3:8	FB42
3:13-14	S43
4:12	FB48, FB64
4:13	S35, S49, S62

Proverbs

3:5-6	Golf52
3:6	BB40, BK52, S41
9:10	BK65
13:20	BK39
16:7	S39
21:9	BK40
26:17	BK40

Psalms

18:29	FB51
21:11-13	BK45, S61
23	BB54
34:14	S60
46:1	FB63
46:10	S45
73	BB28, S38
118:24	BK47
119:100-105	BK63, FB52
119:100-109	Golf29
119:105	BK41, FB52
139:1-14	FB47

Revelation

1:7	S42
2:10	S49
2:12:17	BK50
20:11-21:5	FB43
20:12	S38
21:1-5	BK57

Romans

5:3	S38
5:8	BB40, BK52, BK59, Golf42, S41
7:7-9	BB51, Golf40
7:18-19	Golf54
8:3	S40
8:18	BK42, FB34, S38, S49
8:26	BB38, BB44, BK38, Golf32, Golf41, S56
8:28	BK62, S50, S62
10:13	Golf35
10:15	S52
12:2	S53
12:5-8	BB29, S64

Zechariah

9:12	BB46

Zephaniah

3:17	FB39

INDEX

A

B

Freeney, Dwight	FB50, S52
fruit of the Spirit	FB56
Furyk, Jim	Golf52

G

Galarraga, Armando	BB44, BB45, BB46
Giglio, Louie	Golf53
Gilbert, Garrett	FB40
giving	BK44, BK56, BK59
God, child of	BB40
God, follow His direction	S53, S59
God, following his plan	FB60, Golf38, S54
God, gives the increase	Golf53
God, grace of	BB40, BK46, BK52, BK59, FB46, S41
God, including	Golf41
God, love of	BB30, BB40, BB42, BK42, BK49, BK52, BK56, BK59, BK60, FB42, FB47, FB48, FB58, FB61, Golf30, Golf32, Golf42, S41, S47, S51, S56
God, omnipotent	BB47
God, Omnipresence of	BK51
God, presence of	FB63
God's power	BK45, FB54, Golf32, S37
grace	BB40, BB45, BB46, BK52, BK58, Golf43, S41
Guy, Ray	FB41

H

Hamilton, Milo	BB32
Hamm, Mia	S64
Harmon, Claude	Golf34
Hartsfield, Robert	BK50
Hayward, Jason	BB50
heart, demonstrating	FB57
Heaven, assurance of	BK56
Heaven, entrance criteria	Golf45
Heaven, rewards in	BK50
Hell, avoiding	Golf55
Hill, Drew	FB51
Hogan, Ben	Golf34, Golf48
Holy Spirit	BB38, BB49, BB52, FB36, Golf32
Holy Spirit, leading of	BK38
Holy Trinity	BB49, BK49, S56
humility, learning	Golf54

I

idol worship	FB37
integrity	Golf52, Golf56
Isner, John	S47, S48

J

Jackson, Carl	Golf32
Jesus Christ, being true to	BK48
Jesus Christ, courage of	BB42
Jesus Christ, disciples of	Golf37, Golf44
Jesus Christ, focus on	BB30
Jesus Christ, hope in	BK35, BK55
Jesus Christ, feels your pain	Golf39

K

L

M

Mahut, Nicolas	S47
Manning, Archie	FB49
Manning, Cooper	FB49
Manning, Eli	FB49
Manning, Peyton	FB48, FB49
Maravich, Pete	BK35, BK36, BK40, BK43, BK46, BK48, BK50, BK63, BK66, BK68, FB45, S37
Maravich, Press	BK50, BK63, BK68
Marr, Dave	Golf33
Martinez, Pedro	BB34
McAulay, Terry	BK65
McCollister, Tom	Golf48
McCoy, Colt	FB38, FB40
McIlroy, Rory	Golf29
McQueen, Dr. Michael	BK35
mercy	BB45, BB46, BK37, BK55, BK59
messianic prophecy	FB43, S62
Mickelson, Phil	Golf45, Golf53, Golf55
Monroe, Earl	BK37
Moore, Beth	S61
Morris, Dr. George	FB39
Most, Johnny	S44

N

Nakajima, Tommy	Golf55
Namath, Joe	FB61
Nash, Steve	S52
Neal, Bert	BK57
Nichols, Henry	BK65

Rose, Derrick	BK60
Ruettiger, Rudy	FB48
Rupp, Adolph	BK50
Russell, Bill	S44

S

sacrifice	BB33, BK57, BK59, FB49, FB63, S57
Salters, Lisa	FB38
salvation	BB31, BB40, BK46, BK52, FB33, Golf42, S41
selfishness	BK45, BK62, BK66, FB60, S61
servanthood	BK63, S57, S61
sharing Jesus Christ with others	BB41
sharing the gospel	BB53, FB62, Golf34, S46, S52
Shea, Don	BK65
simplicity	BB39
sin, control of	BK37
sin, cursing	Golf49
sin, entanglement of	FB55
sin, peer pressure	BK39
sin, sexual	Golf51
Sorenstam, Annika	S39
spiritual warfare	S37, S61
Spurgeon, Charles	BK35
Stanley, Andy	S60
Stanley, Dr. Charles	BK59
Steinbrenner, George	BB41
Strasburg, Stephen	BB50
Strobel, Lee	FB43
suffering	BK42
surrender	BK61, FB42

T

V

W

Y

REFERENCES

BB41 *Yankee All-Stars Reflect on the Boss*, northjersey.com, staff report, July 13, 2010

BB46 *Joyce tops survey; players nix replay*, http://www.espn.com, June 13, 2010

BB50 *The Superfractor Seen Round The World*, Brett J. Lewis, May 25, 2010

BK35 *Amazing*, Pete Maravich video by Wayne Federman, *Amazing* by Aerosmith, 1989

BK35 *Mornings and Evenings with Spurgeon*, Charles H. Spurgeon

BK37 *Wall Must Complete Community Service*, http://espn. go.com, May 29, 2009

BK37 Mark Hall, "Slow Fade," http://castingcrowns.com, 2007

BK42 *Leader of the Pack*, http://sharingthevictory.com, 2007

BK43 *Beyond the Brass Ring*, http://powertochangeie/changed/ pmaravich.html

BK44 *Eads Home Ministries, http://www.eadshomcom/David Robinson.htm*, July 17, 2006

BK46 Copy of a handwritten note owned by Dan Farr, entitled "From the desk of....Pete Maravich"

BK47   *Calipari Not Looking Ahead to Louisville Yet*, http://vaughtsviews.com/?p=2378 Larry Vaught, December 28, 2009

BK48   *Pete Maravich Testimony*, Shreveport, Louisiana 1986

BK50   *Maravich*, Wayne Federman and Marshall Terrill in collaboration with Jackie Maravich-McLachlan, p. 377

BK53   *My Utmost for His Highest*, Oswald Chambers, 1992, February 15 *BK58 "Miracle", 2004, Movie, directed by Gavin O'Connor*, written by Eric Guggenheim

BK58   InTouch Ministries, http://www.intouch.org/resources/sermon-outlines/content/topic/our_god_of_grace_sermon_outline, Dr. Charles Stanley

BK58   *Coach Wooden One-on-One*, p. 137, Jay Carty and John Wooden

BK59   *Muhlenberg County Information Source*, Article by: Mike Fields, Lexington Herald-Leader

BK63   *Coach Wooden: One on One*, Day 55, Jay Carty and John Wooden,

BK63   *How to Be Like Coach Wooden: Life Lessons from Basketball's Greatest Leader*,pp. 11-12, 2006, written by Pat Williams, David Wimbish, Bill Walton

BK66   *Maravich*, Wayne Federman and Marshall Terrill in collaboration with Jackie Maravich-McLachlan, p.122-124

BK67   *McDonald's "The Showdown"* (1993): Michael Jordan and Larry Bird, http://www.youtube.com/watch?v=_oACRt-Qp-s

BK68   *Maravich*, Wayne Federman and Marshall Terrill in collaboration with Jackie Maravich-McLachlan, p.105

FB36   *How Did the Tradition of Pouring Gatorade on the Winning Coach Get Started?*, http://ajc.com, January 3, 2010

FB36   *Can a Gatorade Bath Result in You Taking a Bath in Court?*, http://collegesportsbusinessnews.com/june-2011/article/can-a-gatorade-bath-result-in-you-taking-a-bath-in-court, Joshua D. Winneker, April 25, 2011

FB38   Colt McCoy Interview with Lisa Walters of ABC-TV, http://youtube.com/watch?v=rVsSvx3UQOY, January 7, 2010

FB39   *The Mystery and Meaning of Christian Conversion.* Dr. George Morris, p. 167

FB41   *Who Am I*, Casting Crowns, 2003

FB49   *Manning*, John Underwood, p. 363

FB49   *True Saint* by Jill Ewert, Sharing the Victory Magazine, Jan/Feb 2010

FB49   *The Choice Is Clear*, February 2, 2010 by Rick Reilly, ESPN The Magazine

FB53   Terry Bradshaw, http://wikipedia.com

FB60   *This Day with the Master*, Dennis Kinlaw, p. 180

BB35   *Take Me Out to the Ball Game*, Jack Norworth and Albert Von Tilzer, 1908

Golf33   http://findarticles.com/p/articles/mi_m0HFI/is_4_54/ai_100839553/

Golf34   Brent's Golf Blog, by Brent Kelley, Did Ben Hogan Really Fail to Notice an Ace?, October 26, 2011 http://golf.about.com/b/2010/10/26/did-ben-hogan-really-fail-to-notice-an-ace.htm

Golf34   April 13, 1986 CBS Masters Telecast

Golf37   *"Crenshaw is a firm believer in fate"*, September 10, 2008, Dave Lagarde, http://www.pgatour.com/2008/tournaments/r060/09/10/award_2/index.html

Golf43   Time Magazine, *Sport: Lee Trevino: Cantinflas of the Country Clubs,* Monday, Jul. 19, 1971, http://www.time.com/time/magazine/article/0,9171,905380-2,00.html

Golf45   Augusta National Information–Masters Tournament Info http://www.mastersgolftickets.com/augusta_national.html

Golf46   Golf Digest, *Let Us Now Praise Amen Corner*, Herbert Warren Wind, April 1984

Golf48   *Good-bye to one of golf's best friends,* http://si.cnn.com, Jim Huber, March 2, 1999

Golf48   *1960 US Open at Cherry Hills*, http://www.arnoldpalmer.com/experience/exhibits/1960_usopen_cherryhills.aspx

Golf56   *When Losing a Golf Tournament Really Makes You a Winner*, http://yahoo.com, Shane Bacon, May 7, 2010

S37   *"Hit Me With Your Best Shot,"* 1980, Roger Capps and Pat Benatar

S49   *Mornings and Evenings with Spurgeon, Charles H. Spurgeon*

S56   *The Shack*, William P. Young, 2007, pp. 86-87

S62   *My Utmost for His Highest*, Oswald Chambers, October 21

S64   *http://thinkexist.com/quotation/i-am-a-member-of-the-team-and-i-rely-on-the-team-i/347179.htm*